Y0-IUZ-269
8.50
C1-6

Housing Policy for the 1980s

Housing Policy for the 1980s

Edited by
Roger Montgomery
University of California, Berkeley
Dale Rogers Marshall
University of California, Davis

LexingtonBooks
D.C. Heath and Company
Lexington, Massachusetts
Toronto

Library of Congress Cataloging in Publication Data

Main entry under title:
Housing policy for the 1980s.

1. Housing policy—United States—Addresses, essays, lectures.
I. Montgomery, Roger. II. Marshall, Dale Rogers.
HD7293.H75 363.5'0973 79-3278
ISBN 0-669-03443-6

Copyright © 1980 by D.C. Heath and Company

All rights reserved. No part of this publication may be reproduced or transmitted in any form or by any means, electronic or mechanical, including photocopy, recording, or any information storage or retrieval system, without permission in writing from the publisher.

Published simultaneously in Canada.

Printed in the United States of America.

International Standard Book Number: 0-669-03443-6

Library of Congress Catalog Card Number: 79-3278

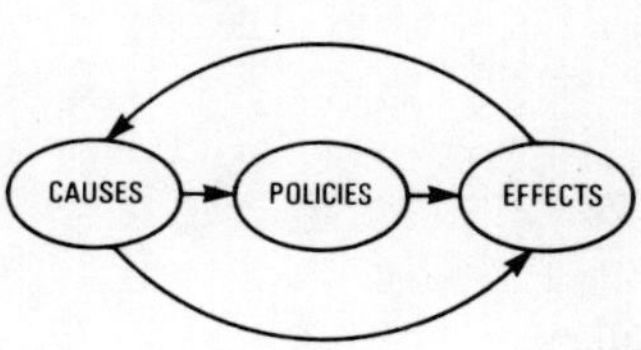

Policy Studies Organization Series

General Approaches to Policy Studies

Policy Studies in America and Elsewhere
edited by Stuart S. Nagel
Policy Studies and the Social Sciences
edited by Stuart S. Nagel
Methodology for Analyzing Public Policies
edited by Frank P. Scioli, Jr., and Thomas J. Cook
Urban Problems and Public Policy
edited by Robert L. Lineberry and Louis H. Masotti
Problems of Theory in Policy Analysis
edited by Philip M. Gregg
Using Social Research for Public Policy-Making
edited by Carol H. Weiss
Public Administration and Public Policy
edited by H. George Frederickson and Charles Wise
Policy Analysis and Deductive Reasoning
edited by Gordon Tullock and Richard Wagner
Legislative Reform
edited by Leroy N. Rieselbach
Teaching Policy Studies
edited by William D. Coplin
Paths to Political Reform
edited by William J. Crotty
Determinants of Public Policy
edited by Thomas Dye and Virginia Gray
Effective Policy Implementation
edited by Daniel Mazmanian and Paul Sabatier
Taxes and Spending Policy
edited by Warren J. Samuels and Larry L. Wade
Causes and Effects of Inequality in Urban Services
edited by Richard C. Rich
Analyzing Inequality in Urban Services
edited by Richard C. Rich
The Analysis of Policy Impact
edited by John Grumm and Stephen Wasby

Specific Policy Problems

Analyzing Poverty Policy
edited by Dorothy Buckton James
Crime and Criminal Justice
edited by John A. Gardiner and Michael Mulkey
Civil Liberties
edited by Stephen L. Wasby
Foreign Policy Analysis
edited by Richard L. Merritt
Economic Regulatory Policies
edited by James E. Anderson
Political Science and School Politics
edited by Samuel K. Gove and Frederick M. Wirt
Science and Technology Policy
edited by Joseph Haberer
Population Policy Analysis
edited by Michael E. Kraft and Mark Schneider
The New Politics of Food
edited by Don F. Hadwiger and William P. Browne
New Dimensions to Energy Policy
edited by Robert Lawrence
Race, Sex, and Policy Problems
edited by Marian Lief Palley and Michael Preston
American Security Policy and Policy-Making
edited by Robert Harkavy and Edward Kolodziej
Current Issues in Transportation Policy
edited by Alan Altshuler
Security Policies of Developing Countries
edited by Edward Kolodziej and Robert Harkavy
Determinants of Law-Enforcement Policies
edited by Fred A. Meyer, Jr., and Ralph Baker
Evaluating Alternative Law-Enforcement Policies
edited by Ralph Baker and Fred A. Meyer, Jr.
International Energy Policy
edited by Robert M. Lawrence and Martin O. Heisler
Employment and Labor-Relations Policy
edited by Charles Bulmer and John L. Carmichael, Jr.
Housing Policy for the 1980s
edited by Roger Montgomery and Dale Rogers Marshall
Environmental Policy Formation
edited by Dean E. Mann
Environmental Policy Implementation
edited by Dean E. Mann

Contents

Foreword

Scholars, who are supposed to operate without bias, almost always have at least one. In my case it is the belief that my colleagues within the academic community approach problems in the best possible way—from a multidisciplinary perspective. As a result, the Housing and Urban Development Department's Office of Policy Development and Research not only has brought visiting scholars to Washington to engage in day-to-day research but also is providing subsidies to scholarly journals to prepare special supplements on subjects that are crucially important to policymakers in the fields of housing and urban development.

This book, an expanded version of an earlier *Policy Studies Journal* symposium issue, concerns housing policy in the 1980s. Recent changes in housing supply and demand mean that in the years ahead the nation will face issues sharply different from those in the past. The effect of inflation on the housing market is the primary concern here, and the implications of demographic change, open-housing policy, environmental controls, and housing-subsidy policies are examined in that light.

The chapters are exceptionally interesting, and I am delighted to demonstrate to a wider audience the value of governmental support for independent research and debate on issues of national importance.

Donna E. Shalala
Assistant Secretary for Policy
Development and Research
U.S. Department of
Housing and Urban
Development

Foreword

Acknowledgments

The Policy Studies Organization gratefully thanks the Department of Housing and Urban Development for its financial aid to the symposium on which this book is based. Thanks are particularly owed to Donna Shalala, Assistant Secretary for Policy Development and Research, and to Helen English, a program analyst in the Office of Policy Development and Research. However, no one other than the individual authors is responsible for the ideas advocated here. In addition, the editors wish to acknowledge the fine work done by Mindy Leiterman in organizing the symposium.

Introduction

As the 1980s begin, continuing inflation afflicts housing in the United States. Despite a sharp induced recession in home building, inflation constitutes the central housing problem of the early 1980s. The broad outlines of the situation are well known. Statistics such as the inflation of median house prices from $27,000 in 1972 to $60,000 in 1979 have been front-page news for several years. This collection of original interdisciplinary papers addresses the public-policy issues that stem from this severe and ongoing inflation.[1]

The general nature of the forces behind current house-price escalation are familiar: the baby-boom generation coming of household-forming age; a secular trend to smaller households, thus increasing overall consumption; a new consumer propensity and capacity to spend on homeownership as a prime investment good, tax shelter, and inflation hedge; increasing differential locational preferences, such as the snowbelt-sunbelt shift; the ascendency of high-prestige, high-accessibility inner areas versus low-prestige, low-accessibility outer suburbs that puts intense pressure on dwellings in certain locations; sharp increases in land and money costs and equally steep increases in the whole spectrum of operating costs; a trend toward more costly units as suppliers respond rationally to heightened effective demand and higher production costs; successful insulation of housing finance from countercyclical monetary policy; and the conclusion of a long struggle to make housing credit instruments into readily marketable securities. Combined as they are in present-day America, these forces seem irresistable.[2]

Intractability of Today's Inflation

As housing-policy analysts are well aware, the cumulative effects of these forces have been to drive up housing prices faster than the general price index has increased and faster than incomes have risen. The disparity between these rates results in two critical, closely related problems. First, the standards of housing consumption must decline, or alternatively, consumers must spend relatively more to stay even or increase consumption. This affects everyone, perhaps most importantly the middle-income, mass-market consumer—and voter. Second, in a dramatic shift, housing deprivation based on high cost relative to income has replaced the classic problem of slums in the lives of poor people.[3] Boiled down to essentials, these two housing problems can be restated in terms of broad policy goals for the early 1980s. First, good policy should help maintain effective demand among the middle class, that is, maintain the effective capacity to own or rent dwellings of appropriate equality in desired locations. Second, equitable policy must help ameliorate the impact of house-price-based deprivation among the poor. The current recession in construction can only exacerbate such deprivation.

The chapters in this book address these two broad policy objectives rather than focusing directly on housing costs as such. Why such an indirect approach to the inflation problems? Why not directly attack the question of house-price inflation itself? The answer lies in the intractable nature of so many of the forces powering the price rises. To begin with, the baby boom cannot be undone, although it is pertinent to note that the housing-demand effects of the boom have peaked, or will shortly, and by the late 1980s will substantially diminish. However, that will happen over too long a run to be germane to the policy discussion here. Perhaps the lifestyle changes that have led to smaller households can be modified, although public policy grinds slowly in terms of such effects. This problem rephrased as overconsumption receives attention in the first two chapters of this book. The policy proposals they make highlight the problem of intractability because they call for fundamental changes in the direction of tax and land-use policy. Similarly, the increasing tendency of consumers to devote larger shares of discretionary income to housing may also be tied to lifestyle changes as much as market rationality and thus be equally immune from feasible public action. So too it is with the locational-preference issue, although in the long run the political saliency of eastern decline versus western growth may generate counteractive public policies with substantial housing repercussions. To summarize, important public-policy impacts that will directly modify the structure of demand within the time span to which these chapters are addressed seem remote indeed.

On the supply side, the situation is much the same because of the general tendency to transform increased demand into higher prices rather than an enlarged supply. Land-cost inflation, for instance, illustrates this phenomenon. Added demand for residential space in preferred locations does not generate additional house sites. Rather, it raises the prices of those already well located. The inability to create new locations via public policy typifies the obstinacy of location-based inflation on the supply side of the market. Only to the extent that nonmarket factors, such as environmental policy, affect land prices may some abatement be possible.

With respect to money costs, government action has powered inflation rather than dampened it. A reversal is unlikely owing to competing priorities and contradictory federal policies. On one hand, high interest rates reflect central government efforts to slow inflation across the whole economy. On the other hand, where heretofore antiinflation monetary policy could count on turning off housing credit by pricing it above demand and by diverting funds to other money markets, in the present period the successful campaign for policies designed to improve the liquidity of mortgages and the competitive position of housing's claims on capital has blunted such antiinflationary policy. Coupled with the supply-policy inconsistencies are the rising demand pressures from the consumers' increasing propensity to spend on housing and their view of housing as a preferred investment. Perversely, the high rates, given the ample supply of loan funds and the insatiable character of housing demand, simply power inflation rather than dampen it. Money costs tie into the broad features of national economic policy and therefore lie well beyond the purview of this book.

Only the draconian credit rationing and unprecedented interest rates toward the end of 1979 had any powerful impact on the housing economy. By early 1980 new-house starts had pitched down to half the 1978 rate. House prices, however, continued to inflate, albeit at a lesser rate than they had through the mid- and late-1970s. The resulting and potentially catastrophic recession in the home-building industry gave little indication of significantly moderating prices. Pent-up demand coupled with severe supply restrictions constitute the perfect formula for maintaining the upward pressure. While it is true that rescinding some of the anti-disintermediation policies removed one factor behind house-price inflation, these policies were more facilitating than fundamentally determinative. The structural causes remain. It seems safe to predict a repetition of the mid-1970s experience, when a sharp recession seemed almost to power the following inflation in housing.

An equally potent, though more limited, contradiction obtains with respect to the behavior of suppliers who rationally target the production of new homes to the highest possible income strata, or alternatively in the case of homeowners who invest in upgrading the existing stock of dwellings, thus gentrifying neighborhoods and further escalating prices. Policies that could be directed against such rational behavior do not seem worth the costs. In the second case, improvement and rehabilitation of older houses has for so long been a high-priority target both nationally and locally that to stop it seems perverse. With respect to the rational market manners of the homebuilders, the social disadvantages of cheapening the product are no less hidden. A generation of American self-flagellation over ticky-tacky developments, coupled with the real objectives of the environmental movement, suggests to the contrary that new houses may not be expensive enough, especially in terms of improved site environment and neighborhood design.

This quick review of the policy prospects for direct action aimed at reducing house-price inflation suggests why this book turns instead to coping with some of its effects. Among the most important of these are gaining a better understanding of the forces at work, acting in ways that will maintain mass-market demand, and instituting measures to ameliorate the prices poor people must pay for housing. Such coping policies are necessitated by the absence of any opportunity to significantly change underlying forces. This perspective has colored both the call for chapters and their final selection for this book, and it helps explain their diversity.

Overview of the Chapters

Chapters 1 and 2 deal with perhaps the most basic of the book's several themes in directly discussing demand for owner-occupied housing. In chapter 1, Nonna Noto analyzes the demographics underlying demand forces responsible for so much of the current price inflation, which will likely cause a reciprocal deflation by the end of the century. She examines the role of federal tax and financial policy in compounding inflation by encouraging overconsumption and overinvestment in housing. Her chapter concludes with a broad summary of macro-policy options to promote efficiency in consumption and reduce the overinvestment tendency. Noto's wide-ranging treatment of demographic factors and her audacious questioning of the historic American support of homeownership through federal policy provide a fitting keynote for the chapters that follow.

In a chapter that parallels the opening chapter, urban planner-political scientist William Baer starts at much the same point. He focuses on the same inefficiencies associated with overconsumption but turns to local policy, and in particular land-use control, as a locus of remedial policy. Baer suggests that such local laws as those defining the groups that may legally occupy a single-family dwelling are implicated in the overconsumption, which he estimates at some 15.7 million units in total. Taken together, chapter 2, which looks to local government action, and chapter 1, which focuses on federal policy, emphasize the complex intergovernmental policy environment of the eighties, a recurrent theme in this book.

The arguments presented in these first two chapters suggest the contradictory nature of housing policy with respect to price inflation. Such anomalies are not limited to tax and local land-use measures. Such effects characterize practically all government action designed to stimulate homeownership, especially those policies designed to ensure a dependable flow of credit. In chapter 3, housing economist Alden Shiers reviews one of the most recent of such policies—the short-term certificate deposits popularly called money-market certificates. He shows that they have achieved their objective of evening credit flows. The observer, however, must conclude that, ironically, in so doing they have effectively insulated the market from antiinflation policies.

Understanding the new dimensions of demand must play a central role in housing policy for the 1980s, and this book has sought a range of explorations in this area. In chapter 4, economists Elizabeth Roistacher and Janet Young direct their attention to the effect of the growing labor-force participation of women on housing demand. They argue that two-earner families have not yet had their full impact on increasing housing demand because the incomes of wives are discounted either by households or by lenders. However, they conclude by observing, "Today's two-earner family may well be tomorrow's divorced couple,'' and this implies a major change in demand. The newly divorced parent and other single parents form the subject for sociologist Robert Weiss's study in chapter 5. He draws on unstructured conversational interview data to fill in detail about the ''restructuring of demand'' that Roistacher and Young discuss as a macrosocial phenomena.

Nearly all students of housing-demand changes agree that an increased demand for rental housing accompanies the demographic and economic changes discussed by Roistacher, Young, and Weiss. Yet clear signals now suggest the rental supply is diminishing, not increasing, relative to demand. Urbanologists George Sternlieb and James Hughes address this snowballing crisis in their chapter on the future of rental housing. The composite picture they present is gloomy indeed. They explain what may turn out to be one of the most politically volatile housing issues in the eighties, the cost and availability of private rental housing.

Despite the enormous pressures on the rental sector of the market, it is in owner-occupied housing that inflation has proved most severe. In a very interesting chapter, economists Barton Smith and Robert Ohsfeldt analyze the various elements of the single-family house-price inflation between 1970 and 1976 in Houston, Texas. Their analysis of marginal-price changes for various attributes of the housing bundle leads them to conclude that price inflation chiefly reflects ''the shortage of affordably priced housing in locations where people want to live. . . . Rather than a housing shortage, there exists a quality-neighborhood shortage.'' Shortages of neighborhood quality, and locational attributes that are closely tied to them, appear particlarly resistant to short-run market-based remedies.

Location and land, which figure so importantly in housing inflation, are the subject of planner-economist David Dowall's review of the price impacts of environmental controls in chapter 8. Often seen as a villain responsible for substantial inflation, such controls have heretofore received less than systematic attention to unsnarling their price impacts. Dowall's chapter begins to redress this lack, arguing that the controls which are most inflationary are least amenable to reform.

Closely related to the environmental-control issue is the matter of suburban exclusion. In chapter 9, political scientist Sharon Krefetz addresses perhaps the most potent local policy initiative designed to counter exclusion, the Massachusetts antisnob zoning law. She finds indications of limited success but suggests that the implementation of open-housing laws will require additional public expenditures to help local communities meet the spillover costs of subsidized housing. In so doing, Krefetz reiterates the complex intergovernmental context of housing policy.

The policy questions around antisnob zoning serve to point up a series of broader economic questions that relate segregation to costs. Barton Smith, in chapter 10, looks at some of these questions. His findings from

Houston confirm previous work that indicates lower rates of housing consumption and homeownership among blacks. Perhaps more pertinent to the theme of this book, in the ongoing debate over whether blacks or whites tend to pay more for their dwellings (quality constant) he adds weight to the conclusion that whites pay a premium for their prejudices. The differential extends to inflation rates as well, and prices increased between 1970 and 1977 at twice the rate in upper-middle-class white areas as in black ones. Thus an inflationary environment proves to have a regressive effect by continuously worsening the wealth position for black households.

The remaining chapters treat aspects of present American policy for low- and moderate-income housing. In chapter 11, John Quigley, a policy analyst and economist concerned with housing, reviews the subsidy systems and evaluates the remarkable large-scale, federally funded social experiment on housing allowances begun in 1974. He concludes with the point nearly universally avoided in discussion—the mutually exclusive nature of the two goals of our subsidy system, improving the housing stock or increasing consumption, in Quigley's terminology, and easing the high-rent burden. Although a major social experiment may provide some data useful to program design, it cannot make the necessarily normative tradeoff between these conflicting goals. In chapter 12, Mahlon Straszheim, another housing-policy-oriented economist, evaluates the Section 8 program, the most innovative feature of the 1974 public-housing legislation. The existing-housing component of this program provides needy households with voucherlike certificates to cover a part of their rent expenses in an approximation of a housing-allowance system. Straszheim finds the program highly effective in the sense of transferring resources to those most in need but far from adequate in terms of horizontal equity because it aids but a small fraction of those eligible by income standards. His discussion of the prospects for improvement emphasizes the effects of modifications in technical requirements, such as rent-level and income limits, and thereby suggests the damage inflation does to such programs.

The 1974 public-housing legislation had other major impacts. Perhaps most critical among these, it legislated a new approach to planning where subsidized housing would be located and in what amounts. In so doing, because of the broad entitlement features that replaced the grant-in-aid application game, it had influence far beyond the inner-city boundaries that had traditionally limited local-government initiative in subsidized housing. In chapter 13, planner-policy analysts Karen Christensen and Michael Teitz report on their studies of the Housing Assistance Plan (HAP) as a mechanism for linking federal housing goals with diverse local preferences. While institutional pressures on the Department of Housing and Urban Development (HUD), including an emphasis on high production at least cost, prevented the realization of HAP's full promise, Christensen and

Teitz argue that important changes in the direction of more rational and comprehensive delivery of subsidized housing have nevertheless occurred. Suburban acceptance of housing responsibility has resulted in the dispersion of subsidized housing into suburbs, in their view, but problems of equity for low-income minority households and specialized fragmentation remain.

In yet another spin-off from the 1974 housing legislation, many more local jurisdictions have instituted technical assistance programs for homeowners, tenants, and neighborhood groups than had heretofore been the case. In chapter 14, John Hutcheson, a political scientist, argues that inflated housing costs will increase the need to provide such assistance on housing issues. His study of neighborhood planning groups in Atlanta suggests that housing issues are the most salient in older, minority, and lower-socioeconomic-status neighborhoods. Therefore, local governments should, in Hutcheson's view, concentrate resources for housing information and assistance in those communities, even though rapidly escalating housing costs also will increase the salience of housing issues in the higher-socioeconomic-status areas. Presented in the context of the studies of primarily federal programs, chapters 13 and 14 remind us again of the intergovernmental dimension of housing policy.

The final chapter, a comparative study of housing policy by political scientist Susan Fainstein, provides a needed cross-national perspective on U.S. housing policy. In a context set by Western European policy, Fainstein argues that political factors result in a smaller, less consistent American program for housing low- and moderate-income families. She points at the two-class division that has emerged around housing in Western Europe that puts a private-homeowner class on one side and a broad spectrum of public-housing tenants that must include much of the stable working and lower-middle classes on the other side.

Changes in the Politics of Housing Policy

How policy in the 1980s will actually address the problems analyzed in these chapters depends significantly on political changes that began in the 1970s. Three of the most important of these are the increased priority being given to budget cutting in Washington, the growth of congressional influence on the policy process, and the decline of the external constituency for low- and moderate-income housing that existed in the late 1960s.[4]

Cutting governmental expenditures has become a pervasive theme in Washington—in Congress, the White House, and the departments.[5] Apparent increases in public support for fiscal constraint and concern about inflation have changed the political climate. Government officials respond by attempting to control spiraling costs and reduce the size of public expenditures. At the same time, Watergate-related reforms designed to strengthen Congress have served to augment the tools available for legislative cost-cutting. For example, the Senate Budget Committee created by the Congressional Budget and Impoundment Control Act of 1974 has started to insist that all appropriations be reconciled with Budget Committee ceilings. The requirement that the total costs of a program throughout its life be specified makes the construction of low- and moderate-income housing look extremely costly, adding to its unpopularity in Congress. And the recently created Congressional Budget Office has given Congress an additional resource with which to influence public policy. In addition to the new political mood and institutions, the broad coalition for housing assembled during the Johnson administration has disintegrated owing to shifting alignments and splits within the component groups. As a result of these changes and the loss of housing stalwarts like Senators Sparkman and Brooke, it takes much more effort to enact low- and moderate-income housing legislation than it did in the late 1960s. Advocates report that they have to bend to the wind, cut back, and make concessions to keep enough legislators in line.

This changed political climate also transforms the likely outcomes of debates over the two main housing problems, maintaining mass-market demand and ameliorating the impact of inflation on the poor. Given the widely held assumption that total federal allocations for housing will not increase in the near future, attention focuses on tradeoffs and on modest new twists in old programs rather than on major innovations.

Concern with costs has influenced the debate about the importance of new production versus conservation of existing housing, decreasing the popularity of Section 8 new construction. Inflation has made the costs of constructing new low-rent housing so high that the program is dying of its own weight; allocations that bought 400,000 units a few years ago can cover only 265,000 units in 1980. Programs that result in more units per dollar, including rehabilitation of existing units and of public housing, are gaining in favor. So are proposed programs for the construction of new rental housing for moderate-income groups using a modification of the old Section 236 approach providing shallower subsidies for financing indexed to rising costs. Because of lower unit costs in this program, a given total allocation would reach more voters, but the greater coverage would be at the expense of the poor, who would receive less assistance.

Another side of the present economy's political impact, the much heralded recession, deserves attention. In the past, one of the responses to economic slowdowns has been an increase in new housing construction as an antirecession tool to stimulate employment. Yet few seem to expect the current slowdown and decrease in housing starts to be met with such a dramatic change in the direction of federal policy. Some suggest that the president himself would have to be out of work before officials would believe that the situation was serious enough to require such a stimulus. Others think that the circumstances could become dire enough and that housing will be used again as one of the conventional stimuli in spite of problems with lags in impact on the economy.

The assumption of budget ceilings changes not only the debate about new construction versus conservation but also the priority given to the dispersion or deconcentration of housing for the poor. The goal of deconcentration requires federal expenditures, which are increasingly unpopular. New construction of housing for the poor has proven to be very expensive, side payments to resistant local governments, as suggested by Krefetz, are more difficult, and the flexible fair-market rents discussed by Straszheim either increase the costs of the program or decrease the number of beneficiaries. Meanwhile, market forces and subsidized rehabilitation are contributing to a revitalization of central cities, which results in rising housing costs that displace the poor.

The three political changes identified here have been associated with a growing interest in off-budget mechanisms for influencing housing. As one HUD official commented, "Most housing policy is made in the Department of Treasury," and much of it has been oriented toward maintaining mass demand. As many authors point out in this book, homeowners receive very special, strongly regressive tax treatment in the United States. The tax expenditures involved amount to more than the total housing budget, but modifications are so potentially destabilizing to the macroeconomy and so politically unpopular that they do not appear to be on the agendas of the main participants in the housing-policy arena. Priority is given to meeting middle-class demands rather than restructuring them. Cost-cutting is done in programs for low-income groups rather than for upper-income groups. The same holds true for other off-budget mechanisms, such as special tax treatment for developers, and the regulation of financial mechanisms, such as alternative mortgage instruments—care is taken to respond to the interests of the mass market, the bulk of the voters.

The impact of the changes in the politics of housing policy depends heavily on the results of national elections. In Washington, attention always focuses on the next election—who will win the presidency and which party will control the Senate and the House? Since the parties typically advocate somewhat different housing strategies, the policies fluctuate as the parties alternate control.[6] However, in an era of inflation and changing electoral coalitions, the positions of the parties are still evolving, so the implications for housing policy of Republican or Democratic victories are even less clear than usual.

Uncertainty about the direction of housing policy in the 1980s is increased further by the complex intergovernmental policy environment emphasized in this book. Whereas aspects of housing typically were the responsibility of either the national government or the private market, in the seventies many state and local governments gradually accepted increased responsibility for housing-finance programs, for instance, partly owing to pressure from their own constituents and from federal programs. At the same time, increasing federal involvement in areas such as land-use control have brought it further into traditional local arenas. Having policy initiated, implemented, and evaluated at multiple governmental levels increases the number of contradictory goals and the difficulty of knowing what actions are causing what results and of making adjustments for problems following from earlier policy adjustments.

We can only speculate about whether the costs of governmental cost-cutting—costs for the poor and the renters, for the environment, and for the quality of collective life—will create their own backlash. Political dynamite lies in the present set of contradictions in American housing. The rapid price inflation has reached a level where it tends to harden class divisions between those with an unprecedented paper wealth stemming from homeownership and those without such wealth. Only by the most dedicated labor of two-earner households can movement occur from the lower to higher housing status. Reciprocally, any instability in household or job relationships increasingly carries the additional cost of an abrupt move downward in housing class. The high-housing-status sector pushes for cost-cutting, except with regard to special treatment for property, defending their possession and the tax advantages of increasingly expensive and scarce housing. The lower-housing-status sector pushes for rent control and publicly regulated, perhaps directly subsidized or publicly owned, rental stock. The likelihood of such a dichotomous population is uncertain. A willingness by policymakers to forego heavy cost-cutting in order to maintain mass-market demand and supply a modicum of housing for the poor can blunt the trend toward heightened class divisions. An opposite course, however, can only reap increased divisiveness from the effects of continuing inflation.

Notes

1. We appreciate the assistance of housing officials and other participants in a Policy Studies Organization roundtable on housing policy who contributed to the substance of this introduction.

2. Some of the forces behind house-price inflation have received careful study, some have not. Among the more useful works are William Alonso, *The Population Factor and Urban Structure* (Working Paper No. 12, M.I.T.-Harvard Joint Center for Urban Studies, August 1977); Franklin James, *Back to the City: An Appraisal of Housing Reinvestment and Population Change* (Washington: Urban Institute, December 1977); and a

collection of papers, *The Cost of Housing, Proceedings of the Third Annual Conference* (Federal Home Loan Bank of San Francisco, December 6-7, 1977); and on changes in housing finance, Dwight M. Jafee and Kenneth R. Rosen, "Mortgage Credit Availability and Residential Construction Activity," in *Brookings Papers on Economic Activities* 3 (1979); and *New Sources of Capital for the Savings and Loan Industry, Proceedings of the Fifth Annual Conference* (Federal Home Loan Bank of San Francisco *forthcoming*).

3. Bernard J. Frieden and Arthur P. Solomon, *The Nation's Housing, 1975 to 1985* (Cambridge, Mass.: M.I.T.-Harvard Joint Center for Urban Studies, 1977), develops the expanded, new view of housing deprivation.

4. For earlier treatments of housing policy, see Harold Wolman, *Politics of Federal Housing* (New York: Dodd-Mead, 1971); and Carolie Bryant, "The Politics of Housing and Housing Policy Research," *Policy Studies Journal* 3 (June 1975):397-400. See also Kenneth R. Tremblay, Jr., "The Targets of American Housing Policy: A Bibliography," *Policy Studies Journal* 3 (Autumn 1979):161-165.

5. A wide variety of governmental documents provide evidence of this concern in the housing field. For example, Congressional Budget Office, "The Long Term Costs of Lower-Income Housing Assistance Programs," March 1979; General Accounting Office, "Why Are New House Prices So High, How Are They Influenced By Government Regulations, and Can Prices Be Reduced?" May 11, 1978; HUD Task Force on Housing Costs, "Final Report of the Task Force on Housing Costs," May 1978; "HUD Conference on Reducing the Development Costs of Housing" (see bibliography prepared by Larry Keating of the Georgia Institute of Technology); U.S. Congress, House, 1979 Hearings and Report of House Subcommittee, "Housing and Community Development Amendments of 1979"; U.S. Congress, Senate, Committee on the Budget, Hearings before the Committee on the Budget, Congressional Budget Office, "Homeownership: The Changing Relationships of Costs and Incomes and Possible Federal Roles," 95th Congress, 1st Session, 1977, pp. 111-178.

6. Roger Montgomery and Martin Gellen, "Emerging Issues in American Housing Policy," in Donald Phares (ed.), *A Decent Home and Environment: Housing Urban America* (Cambridge, Mass.: Ballinger, 1977).

Part I
Policies for Restructuring Demand: Owner-Occupied Housing

1 Tax and Financial Policies for Owner-Occupied Housing in the 1980s

Nonna A. Noto

Analysis of federal tax and financial subsidies to homeownership frequently focus on the short-run economic-equity concern of which income groups benefit relative to others. This chapter takes a longer-run, intergenerational perspective and adddresses the implications of the imbalance in the age distribution of U.S. households for the housing market over the next 40 years. Possible unintended consequences of federal policies that encourage investment in owner-occupied houses are considered in the context of this demographic imbalance.

Spurred by their observations of the rapid rate of increase in housing prices during the 1970s, many families and individuals began buying houses for investment purposes in addition to shelter requirements. However, demographically based projections of housing demand presented in the first section of this chapter suggest that while the rate of increase in the price of owner-occupied housing is likely to remain high during the 1980s and 1990s, it is likely to fall off after 2000, when the absolute increase in the number of young house-buying households is expected to ease off. This forecast suggests that households that will be making their housing-purchase decision during the 1980s based on the belief that the current rate of increase in the real price of houses will persist until their retirement years are likely to find their expectations disappointed in the future. As discussed in the second section of this chapter, federal policies that subsidize investment in housing relative to other assets may encourage investment choices that prove to be inefficient in the longer run.

Understanding that the rate of increase in demand for owner-occupied housing is likely to drop off after 2000 suggests that a resource-efficient national housing strategy would seek to accommodate the heavy demand for owner-occupied housing anticipated over the next two decades without over-building for the subsequent two. The third section of this chapter considers

---

The views expressed in this chapter are solely those of the author and do not express the position of the Congressional Research Service or the Library of Congress.

The author would like to thank Beth Innis and Ben Steffen for their assistance in the preparation of the statistical materials. A number of people made valuable suggestions on an earlier version of the chapter: Andrew Reschovsky, Dennis Zimmerman, Barbara Miles, Grace Milgram, Bernard Gelb, Jane Gravelle, Alan Talley, Morton Schussheim, Ken Malpass, and James Robinson.

alternative tax and financial policies that could help ease upward pressures on prices for owner-occupied housing during the 1980s.

The Age Distribution of U.S. Households and the Demand for Owner-Occupied Housing

There is a substantial imbalance in the age structure of the U.S. population. Figure 1-1, from the Census Bureau, illustrates how the large cohort of the baby-boom generation, born between 1946 and 1964, hence aged 14 to 32 in 1978, stands out in sharp contrast to the smaller cohorts born during periods of low fertility rates in the 1930s and 1970s.[1]

The baby-boom generation is expected to dominate the age composition of net household formation over the next several decades. Figure 1-2 depicts the annual change (averaged over 5-year periods) in the number of U.S. households according to four categories for age of household head. The chart is based on census data adapted by Thomas Marcin, with estimates for 1950 to 1975 and projections from 1980 to 2020 based on the assumption of a replacement-level fertility rate of 2.1 children per woman.[2]

The baby-boom generation creates a peak as it moves through each of the age brackets. From the late 1960s to the late 1970s, baby-boom-generation households were under 30 years of age, as marked by the first peak of the dotted line. From the late 1970s until the early 1990s, the number of households under age 30 declines, but the baby-boom generation swells the number of households in the 30-to-44 age bracket. From the 1990s until the 2010s, this large group appears in the 45-to-64 age bracket and emerges after 2015 as the over-64 group.

This unevenness in the age distribution of U.S. households holds important consequences for the housing market because households traditionally have exhibited differing housing preferences over their life cycle. Drawing from data collected by the 1977 Annual Housing Survey, tables 1-1 and 1-2 present some of these differences according to six age brackets for age of household head: under 25, 25 to 34, 35 to 44, 45 to 54, 55 to 64, and over 64.[3]

According to rows 2 and 3 of table 1-1, the youngest households, under age 25, are the most likely to rent rather than own and to live in multiunit structures or mobile homes rather than single-unit structures. Households in the 25- to 34-year-old group show the greatest tendency to shift from rental to owner-occupied housing and from multiunit to single-unit structures. Another large fraction of households makes this transition to ownership status and single units in the 35- to 44-year-old group. The transition to owner-occupancy and single-unit structures slows down for households over age 44.

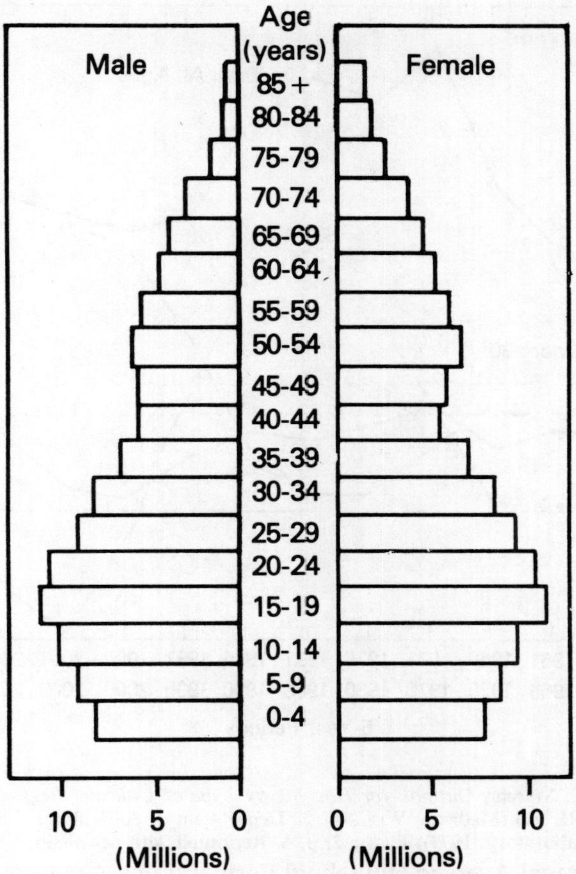

Source: U.S. Bureau of the Census, *Current Population Reports*, Series P-20, No. 336, "Population Characteristics" (Washington: U.S. Government Printing Office, 1979), cover.

Figure 1-1. Distribution of the U.S. Population by Age and Sex, 1978

The middle-bracket years, 35 to 44 and 45 to 54, embrace the period of peak household size (row 4) and peak family income (row 5). They are also the years of peak house value, as measured by the percentage of owners with houses valued at $50,000 or over (row 6).

Finally, the households approaching and in retirement years, aged 55 to 64 and 65 and over, with decreased family size and lower incomes, show a slight tendency to move away from single-unit structures toward multiunit structures and mobile homes and lower-value owner-occupied units or rentals. The fraction of owners declines from 81 percent for households aged

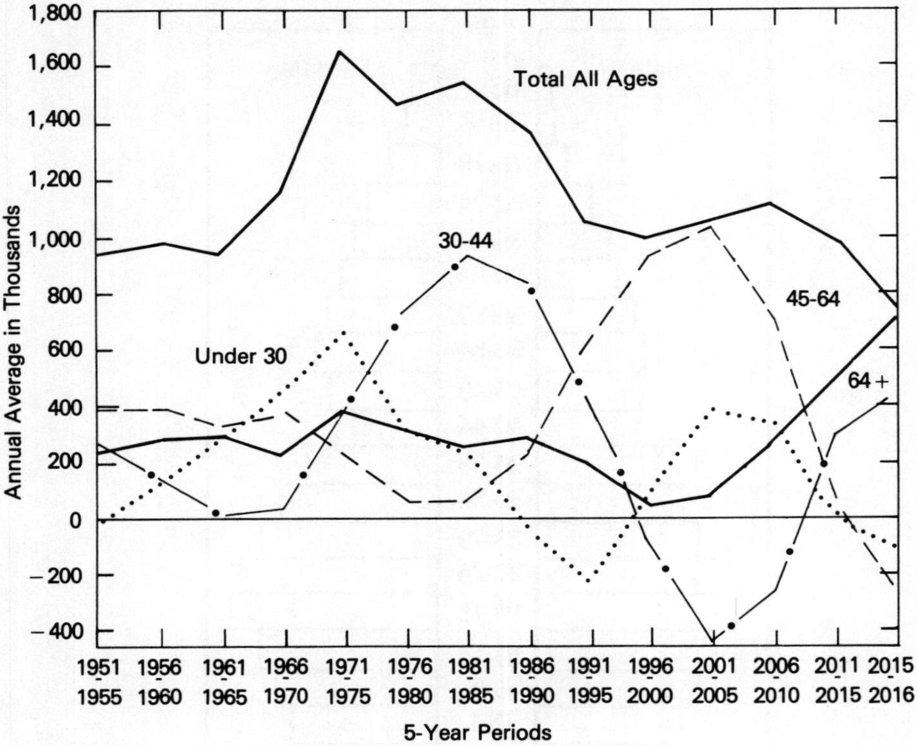

Source: Thomas C. Marcin, *Outlook for Housing by Type of Unit and Region: 1978-2020,* Research Paper FPL 304 (Madison, Wisc.: U. S. Department of Agriculture, Forest Service, Forest Products Laboratory, 1977), Figure 2, p. 6. Reprinted with permission.

Figure 1-2. Annual Average Household Formation by Age Groups, 1950-1975, with Projections to 2020

55 to 64 to 76 percent for households 65 and over. Similarly, the percentage of households in single-unit structures declines from 78 to 71 percent between these two age brackets.

Young and old households show systematic differences in their housing-purchase activities. Older households are much less mobile than younger households. Data from the 1977 Annual Housing Survey presented in table 1-2 reveal the considerable disparity that lies behind the commonly cited nationwide figure that one out of every five U.S. households moves each year. The mobility rate ranges from 63 percent among households under age 25 down to only 6 percent among households over 64 (row 1).

Table 1-1
Housing Characteristics by Age of Household Head, 1977

	Age of Household Head						
	Under 25	*25-34*	*35-44*	*45-54*	*55-64*	*Over 64*	*All Households*
1. Number of households in sample universe (000s)	4,267	11,838	9,280	9,066	8,527	10,954	53,932
2. Owners (%)	25	56	75	81	81	76	69
3. Type of structure:							
a. Single unit (%)	37	63	79	81	78	71	71
b. Multiunit (%)	50	29	17	15	17	24	23
c. Mobile home (%)	13	7	5	4	5	5	6
4. Average household size (number of persons)	2.29	3.09	4.03	3.36	2.38	1.74	2.85
5. Median family income ($)	8,590	14,451	17,395	18,203	13,189	6,047	12,594
6. House value: percentage of owners with houses valued at $50,000 or over (%)	9	26	34	32	26	16	27

Source: U.S. Bureau of the Census, 1977 Annual Housing Survey, National Public Use File, unpublished tabulation.

Table 1-2
Housing-Purchase Activity by Age of Household Head, 1977

	Age of Household Head						
	Under 25	*25-34*	*35-44*	*45-54*	*55-64*	*Over 64*	*All Households*
Of all households:							
1. Recent movers—moved within last year (%)	63	33	18	12	8	6	20
2. Recent purchasers—moved to owned unit within last year (%)	11	13	9	6	4	2	7
Of recent purchasers:							
3. First-time buyers (%)	87	51	25	18	15	12	40
4. Repurchasers (%)	13	49	75	82	85	88	60
House value—percentage with houses valued at $50,000 or over:							
5. First-time buyers, value of present house (%)	11	24	22	20	13	7	21
6. Repurchasers, value of previous house (%)	4	22	38	34	32	18	30
7. Repurchasers, value of present house (%)	4	48	53	49	38	15	43
Of recent movers:							
8. Percentage of previous owners that became renters (%)	58	31	29	23	28	37	31
9. Percentage of previous renters that became owners (%)	18	31	33	31	22	13	27

Source: U.S. Bureau of the Census, 1977 Annual Housing Survey, National Public Use File, unpublished tabulation.

Because mobility rates are higher among renters than owners, a more precise measure of activity in the ownership market is the percentage of households in each age bracket that purchased within the last year (row 2). This measure reaches its highest value among households aged 25 to 34, with 13 percent of those households purchasing. Only 2 percent of households over age 64 purchased during the year prior to the survey.

Among purchasers, the highest incidence of first-time buyers is among the youngest households. Eighty-seven percent of recent purchasers under age 25 were first-time buyers; only 12 percent of households over 64 were (row 3). Already by the 25- to 34-year bracket, half the house buyers are repurchasers (row 4).

Drawing on equity gains on their previous residences, repurchasers generally are able to afford higher-value houses than first-time buyers (compare rows 5 and 7), and repurchasers are likely to buy houses higher in value than their previous residences (compare rows 6 and 7).

Among first-time buyers, households in the three age groups from 25 to 54 are the most likely to purchase high-value houses. Among repurchasers, slightly older households, in the three age groups from 35 to 64, are the ones likely to have had the greatest fractions of their previous residences in the high-value range. However, like first-time buyers, it is the younger-repurchaser households, from ages 25 to 54, who are the most likely to buy in the high-value range.

There is some evidence of a tendency for the oldest households to trade down in the housing market, in contrast to the trading up observed among younger households. Among repurchaser households over 64, the fraction whose present house is valued at over $50,000 is lower than the percentage with previous houses in that range. Households over 64 also exhibit the highest tendency to trade down from ownership to rental (row 8) and the lowest tendency to trade up from rental to ownership status (row 9).

These differences in housing behavior among the age brackets suggest that, depending on the age distribution of the households, a projected increase in the overall number of households could have different implications for demand pressures in the homeownership versus rental market. Although, according to figure 1-2, the early 1970s marked a time of peak net household formation, it was not a period of peak demand for owner-occupied housing or single-family units. In large part, as a consequence of the preponderance of new households under age 30 during the 1970s, the decade experienced a large increase in demand for apartments, mobile homes, and low-priced single-family units. If, as it ages, the baby-boom generation follows the patterns of housing behavior exhibited by previous generations, certain changes in emphasis in the pattern of housing demand can be anticipated over the next two decades.

During the 1980s, the baby-boom generation, by then entering the 35- to 44-year age group, can be expected to continue to increase its rate of homeownership and to upgrade its housing—either through trading up or home improvements. Strong demand can be expected for single-family units, generally of larger size and with more amenities than the housing this generation purchased when it was younger, during the 1970s. Demand for owner-occupied and single-family units is likely to remain strong throughout the 1990s, when the members of this large population cohort, by then entering the 45- to 54-year range, can be expected to continue to upgrade their residences.[4]

What is likely to happen to the demand for owner-occupied housing over the subsequent two decades, 2000 to 2020? This is the period in which the baby-boom generation will be entering its retirement years and may want to cash in on its housing investment.

Figure 1-3 presents a simple index of demand pressure in the market for owner-occupied housing. It is the difference between the number of households in the 25- to 34-year bracket and the number of households aged 65 and over. This approximates the gap between the potential additional demand for owner-occupied housing from the generation ready to buy its first house and the potential supply of owner-occupied housing from the existing stock by households reaching the stage of life when they eventually will vacate their owner-occupied units.[5]

According to this simple measure, the market pressure for existing owned houses is likely to shift from one of considerable excess demand during the 1980s and 1990s to one of potential excess supply after the turn of the century. During the 1980s and 1990s, there are expected to be over 2 million more households in the younger age cohort than in the older one. Between 2000 and 2015, the situation is likely to be reversed, with approximately 2 million more older households than younger ones. By 2020 there may be almost 7 million more households in the 65-and-over bracket than in the 25-to-34 bracket.

The housing market in the aggregate, including both the rental and ownership components, depends on new construction to meet the demand for housing units by net additional households. Figure 1-4 compares net household formation with new construction of net additional housing units—using actual data for 1960 to 1979 and projections for 1980 through 2020.

The graph of net household formation duplicates the pattern for total households across all age brackets presented in figure 1-2. Annual average net household formation for the 1960-2020 period is likely to have peaked already during the 1971-1975 period at above the 1.6 million level. It is expected to remain high—above the 1.4 million level—from 1981 to 1990 and then drop back to around the 1 million level characteristic of the 1960s from 1991 to 2015. For the 2016-2020 period, the increase is projected at only 0.8 million per year, just half the peak rate of 1971 to 1975.

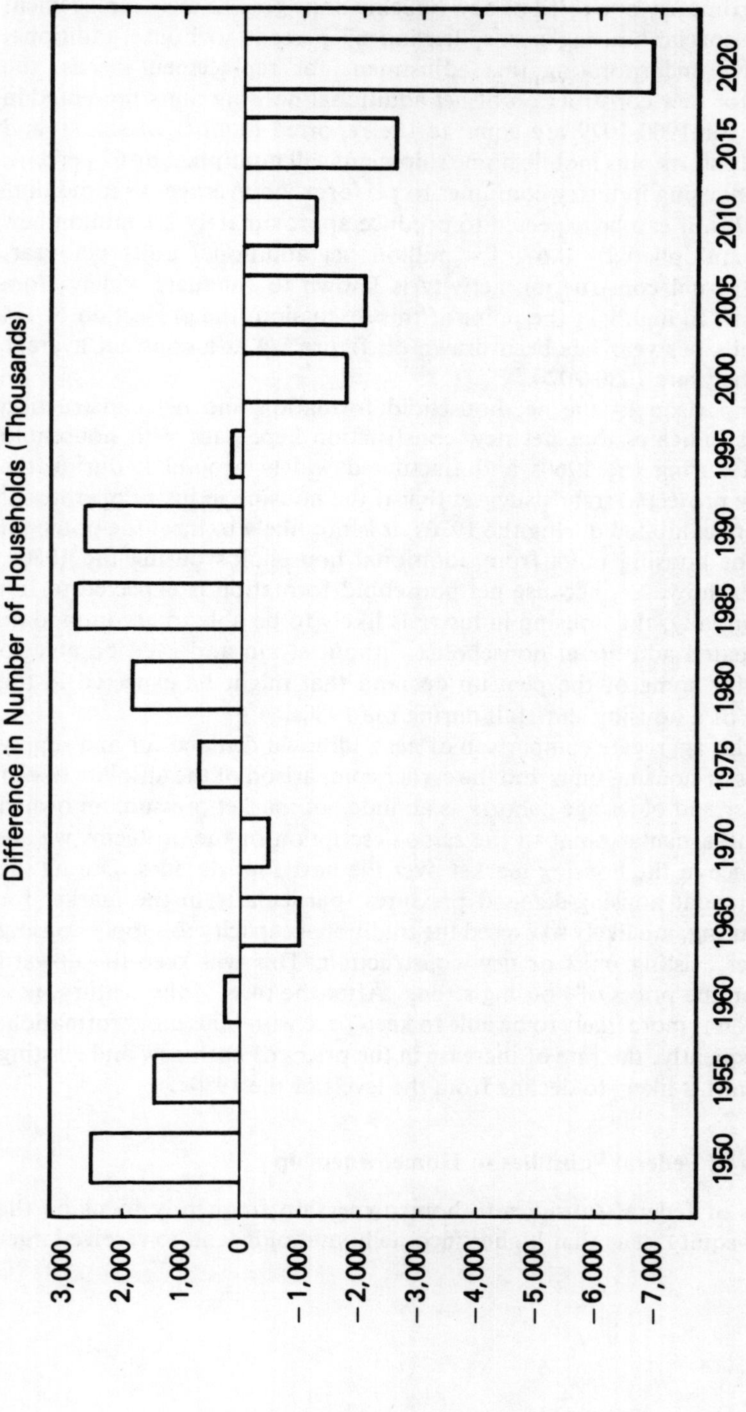

Source: See appendix 1A for data.

Figure 1-3. An Index of Demand Pressure on Owner-Occupied Housing: The Number of Households Aged 25 to 34 Minus the Number Aged 65 and Over, 1950-2020

Approximately one-third of new housing units goes to meet replacement and other special-housing needs, leaving 67 percent to house additional households.[6] Incorporating this adjustment for replacement needs, the estimates for new construction of net additional housing units presented in figure 1-4 for 1960-1979 are equal to the reported number of single- and multifamily starts plus mobile home shipments, all multiplied by 67 percent.

If the housing industry continues to perform, on average, as it did during the 1970s, it can be expected to produce approximately 2.1 million new units or, multiplied by 0.67, 1.4 million net additional units per year. Although actual construction activity is known to fluctuate widely from year to year, to highlight the point of this discussion, the projection of 1.4 million units per year has been drawn on figure 1-4 at a constant average level for the years 1980-2020.[7]

A comparison of the net household formation and net construction trend lines indicates that net new construction kept pace with household formation during the 1960s and fluctuated widely around it during the 1970s. The projected trends suggest that if the housing industry operates at the capacity exhibited during the 1970s, it is not likely to meet the potential demand for housing units from additional households during the 1980s. After 1990, however, because net household formation is expected to fall off substantially, the housing industry is likely to be able to accommodate the anticipated additional households without strain and even be able to make up for some of the pent-up demand that might be expected in the aftermath of a housing shortfall during the 1980s.

Both this aggregate comparison of net additional demand for and supply of all types of housing units and the earlier comparison of the absolute size of the younger and older age cohorts as an index of market pressure on owned housing in particular point to the same description of the problems we are likely to face in the housing market over the next four decades. During the 1980s, potential housing-demand pressures, particularly in the market for owned housing, are likely to exceed the traditional capacity to supply housing from either existing units or new construction. This will keep the upward pressure on the prices of housing strong. After the turn of the century, new construction is more likely to be able to keep pace with household formation, and consequently, the rate of increase in the prices of both new and existing housing units is likely to decline from the levels of the 1980s.

Criticisms of Federal Subsidies to Homeownership

Criticisms of federal subsidies to homeownership frequently focus on the economic-equity issue that higher-income households tend to receive larger

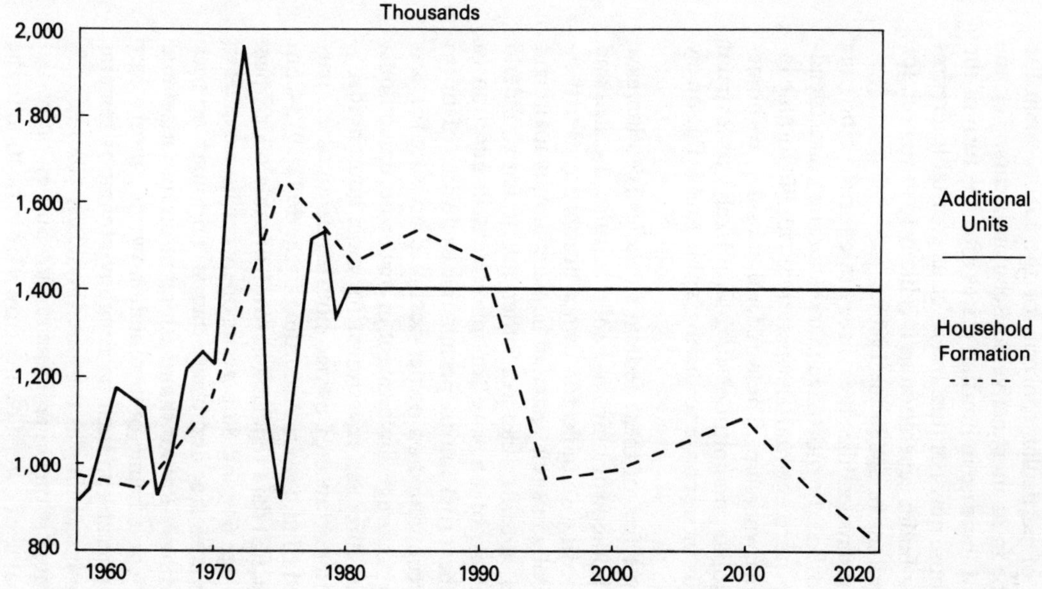

Sources: Household formation data from Thomas C. Marcin, *Outlook for Housing by Type of Unit and Region: 1978-2020,* Research Paper FPL 304 (Madison, Wisc : U.S. Department of Agriculture, Forest Service, Forest Products Laboratory, 1977). Reprinted with permission. Data point entered every 5 years (1960, 1965, and so on) represents an annual average over the previous 5 years. Actual data for 1960-1975, projected data for 1980-2020. See appendix 1A for data. Housing construction data includes privately owned single- and multiunit starts and mobile home shipments multiplied by 0.67. Housing data for 1960-1963 from U.S. Department of Commerce, Social and Economic Statistics Administration, Bureau of the Census, *Construction Reports, Housing Starts, 1959 to 1971*, C-20 Supplement (Washington: U.S. Government Printing Office, 1972), p. 38. Data for 1964-1978 from U.S. Department of Commerce, Bureau of the Census, *Construction Reports*, C20-79-1, "Housing Starts, January 1979" (Washington: U.S. Government Printing Office, 1979), p. 10. Data for 1979 from unpublished estimates. Construction projections for 1980-2020 explained in text.

Figure 1-4. Comparison of Net Household Formation with New Construction of Net Additional Housing Units, 1960-2020

subsidies than lower-income ones.[8] This chapter is concerned instead with the economic-efficiency issue of using federal policy to subsidize households to invest in housing relative to other assets. This federal policy influence on investment decisionmaking is of particular concern for the 1980s, when the baby-boom generation will be in its most active housebuying years. The anticipated decline in the rate of increase in housing prices after the turn of the century is a warning that a house may not turn out to be as profitable a retirement investment for the baby-boom generation as it is likely to have been for households that will reach retirement age in the 1980s.

Federal assistance to homeownership takes three basic forms: mortgage interest rate subsidies, support of the mortgage market through direct lending programs and secondary mortgage-market operations, and favorable income tax treatment of homeownership. These federal subsidies to homeownership are large in dollar magnitude[9] and are likely to expand significantly during the 1980s in response to demographic and inflationary pressures.[10]

The economic-efficiency effect of these federal subsidies is to increase the aggregate demand for homeownership and thus to raise the demand pressure on the price of housing suitable for owner-occupancy. Furthermore, by tax sheltering capital gains reinvested in housing and by making it easier to borrow funds for housing than for other investments, federal policy encourages the purchase of housing for investment in addition to shelter purposes. Finally, the provision to permit the exclusion of up to $100,000 in capital gains accumulated on owner-occupied housing for taxpayers 55 and over further encourages investment in owner-occupied housing as an essentially tax-free retirement investment for most households.

Survey data reveal the importance of owned housing as an asset, particularly for households aged 65 and over. According to the 1972-1973 Consumer Expenditure Survey (CES) data reported in row 3 of table 1-3, 57 percent of all households over age 64 (and 86 percent of owner households in this age group) own their homes free and clear; that is, no longer do they have any mortgage outstanding.[11] Rather than cashing in on that asset and trading down to a smaller owned unit or a rental, however, most older households tend to enjoy the return on their housing investment by remaining in their mortgage-free home as long as they are physically able.

Other data from this latest Consumer Expenditure Survey point out how important the market value of owned homes (row 4) is in relation to the market value of other financial assets (row 5). It is not until the over-64 age bracket, when mortgage debts have essentially been paid off, that the average market value of financial assets per household exceeds the average estimated market value of owned homes.

The CES also presents an estimate of the annual rental value of owned homes (row 6). This number represents the income equivalent of the gross

Table 1-3
Importance of Owned Housing as an Asset by Age of Household Head, 1972-1973

	Age of Household Head						
	Under 25	*25-34*	*35-44*	*45-54*	*55-64*	*Over 64*	*All Households*
1. Number of households in sample universe (1000s)	6,238	14,160	12,024	12,977	11,481	14,250	71,220
2. Owners (%)	9	40	68	73	74	66	59
3. Without mortgage—own home free and clear (%)	2	4	11	24	43	57	25
4. Estimated market value of owned home ($)[a]	2,062	11,249	18,740	19,428	17,050	12,050	14,283
5. Market value of financial assets ($)	901	2,615	4,092	6,690	11,668	13,511	7,094
6. Estimated annual rental value of owned home ($)[a]	227	1,075	1,565	1,629	1,318	974	1,202
7. Imputed net rental income from owned home ($)[a, b]	33	74	−33	126	342	461	182
8. Investment income ($)[c]	45	128	255	485	903	1,134	533
9. Imputed net rental income in relation to investment income [(7) ÷ (8)] (%)	73	58	−13	26	38	41	34
10. Family money income after taxes ($)	5,773	9,969	12,114	13,069	10,277	5,764	9,731
11. Imputed net rental income in relation to money income after taxes [(7) ÷ (10)] (%)[d]	1	1	0	1	3	8	2

Source: U.S. Department of Labor, Bureau of Labor Statistics, *Consumer Expenditure Survey: Integrated Diary and Interview Survey Data, 1972-1973*, Bulletin 1992 (Washington:, U.S. Government Printing Office, 1978), Table 3, pp. 42-47.

[a]House value and annual or imputed rental figures are averages over all households, including both owners and renters. To approximate values for owner households only, divide by percentage of households that are owners (row 2).

[b]Imputed net rental value is equal to estimated annual rental value (row 6) minus annual expenses including mortgage principal payments in addition to expenditures on owned dwellings for mortgage interest, property taxes, property insurance, ground rent (mobile homes), and repairs.

[c]Investment income includes income from estates, trusts, interest, dividends, rental income, royalties, and roomers and boarders.

[d]The comparison is with money income after taxes because imputed rental income to homeowners is not taxed.

annual return on investment in owned housing received in the form of income in kind from housing services. To get an estimate of the imputed net rental income from owned homes (row 7), the major expenses associated with financing, operating, and maintaining that housing investment have been subtracted from annual rental value.[12]

Imputed net rental income is low among the four age brackets under 55, which face high mortgage payments. It even reaches a negative value for households in the 35-to-44 age bracket. For households 55 to 64 and 65 and over, whose mortgages are nearly paid off, the margin of rental value over expenses increases substantially.

How does this income in kind from owned housing compare with income from other investments (row 8) and total family money income after taxes (row 10) for older households? Row 9 expresses imputed net rental income as a percentage of investment income. Looking at both owner and nonowner households in an age bracket as a group, the estimated value of the income in kind received from owner-occupied housing, net of expenses, can be thought of as supplementing investment income for households over age 55 by approximately 40 percent.

Viewed as a supplement to money income after taxes (row 11), imputed net rental income rises from 1 percent for younger households, to 3 percent for households 55 to 64, to 8 percent for those 65 and over. At this stage of life, average money income per household falls, while the equity value of the house increases.

Thus the value of the owned home—whether expressed in terms of estimated market value or imputed net rental income—appears to hold an important role for households 55 and over. It serves both as an asset that can be cashed in and as an investment that generates income in kind in the form of housing services as a supplement to money income.

The Social Security Administration's 1968 Survey of the aged found that among elderly households (aged 65 and over), owners in general were likely to be better off than renters. In addition to the equity in their homes, with median equity value of $11,000, owners were more likely to have financial assets and higher median incomes than nonowners. Only 24 percent of owners had no financial assets, compared with 46 percent of nonowners. The median amount of financial assets among owners was estimated at $1,800, less than 20 percent of the median equity of their homes, but far in excess of the $100 estimated for nonowners. Finally, median income among owners was $2,404, compared with $1,480 among nonowners.[13]

It appears from these two surveys that a house is likely to be the first major asset acquired by households that can afford to invest. As households grow older, their incomes increase, and their mortgages are paid off, they accumulate other investments, such as financial assets. The value of owned housing remains a substantial portion of assets for the average household, though, even for the oldest groups.

It is precisely because investment in housing appears to be such an important asset for older households—whether they choose to cash in on it or to consume the income in kind from it—that the prospect of changing rates of return on investment in owner-occupied housing over the next four decades holds such serious consequences for the large number of households that will be making their major housing-purchase decision in the 1980s. Federal policies that bias households' investment decisions in favor of housing as a retirement asset may lead to costly disappointment for these households later if their major asset, their house, fails to appreciate at the rate they have anticipated by the time they retire.

Taking a macroeconomic perspective, federal policies that divert the flow of investable funds toward housing and away from other assets may be especially costly at this time in terms of slowing the rate of growth in labor productivity over the next 40 years. Two anticipated labor-market phenomena suggest that it will be important to increase the investment in capital per worker in U.S. industry after 1985. A relative shortage of young workers is expected in the 1985-2000 period, reflecting the decrease in births in the late 1960s and the 1970s compared with the preceding 1946-1964 period. After 2000, as the baby-boom generation reaches retirement age, the dependency ratio (the ratio of the nonworking to working population) can be expected to rise further.

Both these labor-market projections emphasize the importance of higher productivity per worker after 1985. This is likely to require larger capital investment per worker by industry and a higher savings rate for the nation as a whole. Thus concerns for both the asset position of individual households in their retirement years and the strength of the economy as a whole motivate the search for alternative tax and financial policies that will stimulate savings and investment without biasing the selection of assets toward housing versus other productive investments.

Alternative Tax and Financial Policies

The prognosis for the housing market in the 1980s is that the number of households desiring to purchase a housing unit for owner-occupancy will continue to increase at a rate in excess of the rate of net new construction of units for the owner-occupancy market. This will sustain the upward pressure on housing prices observed during the late 1970s, thus fostering further speculative investment in housing.

Current federal tax and financial policies favoring homeownership further encourage expenditure on owner-occupied housing both by subsidizing the consumption of housing as shelter and by raising the after-tax rate of return on housing versus other investments, particularly as a retirement investment. Continuing the present homeowner preference system in the

1980s is likely to exacerbate the demographically induced demand pressures on house prices, as well as result in a very large increase in the size of these tax and financial subsidies.

National housing-policy efforts, working on both the demand and supply sides of the market, can help ease the upward pressure on housing prices during the anticipated period of exceptionally heavy demand during the 1980s. In an effort to cool these demand pressures, there is a case for neutralizing the financial market and tax bias toward owner-occupied housing as both a consumption and an investment item. On the supply side, policies that would augment the supply of housing suitable for owner-occupancy from the existing housing stock would help the United States through this bottleneck period when potential net additional demand is likely to outpace net additional supply in the market for owner-occupied housing.

Cooling the Demand for Owner-Occupied Housing

Consideration of the distorting effect of the special tax treatment of owner-occupied housing on both current consumption and longer-run investment decisions suggests two possible areas for change in the tax laws. One area involves itemized deductions; the other involves capital gains and investment income.

One possible change in the tax deductions for housing expenditures would be to replace the current deductions—now restricted to interest and property-tax payments—with a general housing deduction, proportional to family size. Housing expenses eligible for this deduction would include both principal and interest on mortgage payments, rent, depreciation of a mobile home, or housing maintenance and rehabilitation expenditures. This change would substitute a tax subsidy for housing expenditures in general that would not be biased in favor of owning versus renting, toward new construction versus rehabilitation, or toward debt financing versus cash purchase. In addition, if this tax subsidy for housing consumption took the form of a dollar-for-dollar tax credit rather than a deduction, the dollar size of the subsidy would not be biased in favor of high-income households versus low-income ones. Another approach to reducing the tax-incentive value of the itemized deductions for owner-occupied housing would be to place a dollar limit on the amount of housing-related interest and property taxes that could be deducted.

A possible change in the area of capital gains taxes is to extend the favorable tax treatment now given to housing to other types of investments. For example, capital gains on other types of investments such as corporate stock could be reinvested with taxation deferred or levied at a very low rate.

In addition, a certain dollar amount of capital gains over a lifetime on these investments could be excluded from taxation if these assets were liquidated only after a person reached retirement age.

Other possible changes in tax and financial policies relate to savings plans. A recently established financial market vehicle that offers tax incentives for private saving for retirement is the Individual Retirement Account (IRA). This plan defers until retirement the taxation of both the current income placed into the savings account and the interest earned on the savings. Increasing the acceptabiliy of IRAs as collateral with which to leverage other borrowing would enhance their attractiveness as an investment during preretirement years.

Under provisions for Registered Home Ownership Savings Plans (RHOSPs), Canadian households can set aside before tax $1,000 per year, up to $10,000, in order to save for a down payment.[14] Similar plans, referred to as *Individual Housing Accounts*, have been proposed in the United States. These would provide for either a tax deduction or tax credit for amounts contributed to a savings account established for the purpose of purchasing a home.[15] The U.S. League of Savings Association has proposed that in addition to a tax credit, the interest earnings on such accounts should be tax free.[16]

The Independent Housing Account, like the Canadian RHOSP, would subsidize savings only for the purpose of purchasing a house. A more general way to encourage savings and investment would be to allow a deduction, covering interest as well as other investment income, equivalent, perhaps, to the average return expected on a $10,000 investment per household.[17] Extending the favorable tax treatment now applied to housing to other forms of investment income could help redress the imbalance between homeowners and renters.

The common objective of any of these proposed changes in the tax laws is to encourage aggregate savings and investment without biasing the choice of investment vehicle toward housing. The strategy is to make the tax treatment of the capital gains and income generated by other types of investment comparable to that for owner-occupied housing for the small investor.

Increasing the Supply of Existing Housing Units Suitable for Ownership

Acting on the supply side of the market, finding alternatives to new construction may provide a key to designing an efficient housing policy that would accommodate the anticipated heavy demand for homeownership by young households in the 1980s, yet would not overbuild for the future. Using tax and financial policies to encourage the transfer of the housing stock among generations, the upgrading of existing units, the improvement of neighborhoods, and the condominium-style conversions from rental to ownership status may be important options on the supply side of the market to help ease the upward pressure on housing prices during the 1980s. These alternative strategies would be particularly important for slow-growth regions such as the Northeast or central cities that have most of their land area developed and have a large fraction of their housing stock in rentals, multiunit structures, run-down units, or deteriorated neighborhoods.

In older metropolitan areas, including both the central city and suburban portions, a large fraction of the supply of existing owner-occupied units currently is occupied by older middle-aged households that continue to live in large units purchased during their child-rearing years and by retired households that continue to live in housing purchased at locations convenient to employment centers.[18] Policies that would encourage older households to trade down to smaller housing units would help increase the supply of existing larger, higher-quality housing units available for owner-occupancy at locations accessible to employment centers. Intergenerational filtering would help ease pressure on prices for these larger, higher-priced housing units. Increasing the rate of turnover would be particularly advantageous during the 1980s in the face of heavy demand for these units by the large generation entering its young middle-age house-buying years.

Recent public-policy moves at the state and local levels have worked counter to encouraging housing turnover among older households. Property tax relief has been offered to senior-citizen households directly in the form of circuit breakers and homestead exemptions. It has been offered indirectly, under Proposition 13 in California, via a lid on the rate of increase in assessment for properties that are not resold—a provision that favors low-mobility households, such as the elderly, and discourages housing turnover.

These proposals are all based on the sympathetic premise that households should not be forced to move because they no longer can afford the costs of maintaining their houses, particularly when those higher costs are related to the inflation in housing values that is beyond the control of the individual household. Nonetheless, it is important to recognize the consequences for the overall housing market of subsidizing older households to remain in units that are in heavy demand by younger households.

Particularly after 1985, housing-market forces should make it increasingly attractive for older households to trade down. With peak demand for owner-occupied housing of higher quality by a large generation in the 35- to 44-year age bracket, the housing assets of older households should be reaching peak values and should have served their purpose as a vehicle for retirement savings. At the same time, the decreased number of new households under age 30 should lower the relative prices on smaller units for owner-occupancy, on rentals, and on mobile homes.

Housing turnover by older households may be encouraged by the income tax provision, enacted in 1978, that permits an exclusion of up to $100,000 in accumulated capital gains on owner-occupied housing for taxpayers aged 55 and over. This provision has the potential to ease pressures on prices of owner-occupied housing in the 1980s by increasing the number of existing larger, high-priced, single-family units put up for sale by older households that now have a tax-free financial incentive to trade down in the housing market.

Another way to encourage this housing turnover is to work on the supply side to create attractive housing alternatives for senior citizens—both in retirement areas and in their home areas. The construction of retirement communities in the less densely developed, lower-priced areas of the country helps ease the pressure on housing prices and facilitates the intergenerational housing-transfer process. But many senior citizens are not interested in moving away from the region or community in which they have lived. To stimulate the turnover of the housing stock by this group, planners at the local level need to encourage housing options for senior citizens in central cities, suburbs, and nonmetropolitan communities.[19]

Particularly for local housing markets in slow-growth areas that are anticipating a small net increase in total households, policies that encourage and facilitate improvements to existing homes may serve quite an important role in supplying the higher-quality housing desired by middle-aged households. Especially in older central cities, joint public-private efforts at neighborhood improvement may contribute importantly to returning structurally sound units to the stock of acceptable housing in neighborhoods that had become unacceptable.[20]

In the short run, the trend toward condominium conversion is causing displacement problems for many urban households. In the longer run, however, particlarly for built-up cities with a large multifamily rental stock, the condominium-style conversion of multiunit structures from rental to ownership status may prove to be quite an efficient way to accommodate the demand by the middle-aged generation for owner-occupancy in multiunit structures rather than requiring households to switch to single-family units in order to own. Condominium conversion also can serve as a holding action for multiunit structures during the period of the late 1980s and 1990s, when demographic determinants of housing demand will favor owner-occupancy over renting. After the year 2000, when the demand for rentals is expected to rebound in response to an anticipated large population group in their twenties, multifamily condominium structures could be converted back to rental status on a large scale more easily than single-family units.

Substantial changes may be required in the traditional mechanisms for housing finance in order to accommodate the increased activity in the market for existing homes, housing rehabilitation, and condominium or cooperative conversion. Mortgage lending would not be biased toward new versus existing housing. Neither loan terms nor the availability of loan guarantees or secondary mortgage-market support from federal programs would favor new versus existing housing using other than strict financial criteria. Mortgage credit might be made as available for condominium and cooperative units as it is for single-family units. Financing could be available for rehabilitation and home improvements on terms comparable with those for building new structures or purchasing a higher-priced existing unit. Risk-pooling arrangements among financial institutions, perhaps with public support, may be needed to increase the private sector's willingness to service the credit needs of inner-city neighborhoods.

During the 1980s, the pattern of housing demand by the baby-boom generation is likely to continue to shift from rental to owner-occupancy status and, accompanying that in most cases, from multiunit to single-units structures. The upgrading of existing single-family units, the condominium conversion of multifamily units, and neighborhood improvement all can help satisfy this changing pattern of housing demand by means other than the new construction of single-family dwellings.

With the prospect of declining rates of increase in housing values in the future, it is particularly important for the 1980s to be efficient in the use of housing resources so as not to overbuild for the future in response to an immediate period of peak demand for owner-occupied housing. Changes in tax and financial policies toward housing can help ease upward pressures on the price of owner-occupied housing during the 1980s. On the demand side, policies can reduce the subsidies to ownership of single-family units versus other forms of housing accommodation and versus other types of investments. On the supply side, policies can encourage the adaptation of the existing housing stock, in addition to new construction, to meet the changing patterns of housing demand.

Notes

1. U.S. Bureau of the Census, "Population Characteristics," *Current Population Reports*, Series P-20, No. 336, Washington, U.S. Government Printing Office, 1979.

2. Thomas C. Marcin, *Outlook for Housing by Type of Unit and Region: 1978-2020*, Research Paper FPL 304, Madison, Wisconsin, U.S. Department of Agriculture, Forest Service, Forest Products Laboratory, 1977. These household projections are based on series II population projections, which assume a fertility rate of 2.1 children per woman, from the U.S. Bureau of the Census, "Projections of the Population of the United States: 1975-2020," *Current Population Reports*, Series P-25, No. 601, Washington, U.S. Government Printing Office, 1975.

3. Data in tables 1-1 and 1-2 are from a special unpublished tabulation of the U.S. Bureau of the Census, 1977 Annual Housing Survey, National Public Use File. Individual calculations are based on different subsamples of the sample universe.

4. For a discussion of the relationship between demographics and housing demand, see Thomas C. Marcin, *The Effects of Declining Population Growth on the Demand for Housing*, General Technical Report NC-11, St. Paul, Minnesota, U.S. Department of Agriculture, Forest Service, North Central Forest Experiment Station, 1974.

5. This is a simple attempt to measure the capacity of the existing housing stock to house the changing population if it were turned over among generations. Some young households, of course, may purchase newly constructed units. A 1977 survey of conventional mortgage borrowers found that only 18.3 percent of first-time buyers bought newly constructed houses compared with 29.4 percent of repeat buyers. See Dennis J. Jacobe and Thomas J. Parliment, *Homeownership: Affording the Single Family Home* (Chicago: United States League of Savings Associations, 1978), p. 46.

6. Frieden and Solomon report that the ratio of new construction to household formation for the 1950-1970 period was 1.5 to 1. A ratio of 1.5 to 1 means that for every three housing units built, two are to accommodate additional households and one is to cover other aspects of housing demand such as replacing units lost through accidents or public demolitions, replacing physically obsolete mobile homes, accommodating demand for second homes, maintaining normal vacancy rates, and providing for upgraded housing and living environments. They forecast that the ratio of new construction to household formation for the 1975-1985 period would be in the range of 1.66 or 1.7 to 1. The more conservative past figure of 1.5 to 1 is used for the projections here. See Bernard J. Frieden and Arthur P. Solomon, *The Nation's Housing: 1975 to 1985* (Cambridge, Mass.: M.I.T.-Harvard Joint Center for Urban Studies, 1977), pp. 47 and 62.

7. During the 1970s, the total number of privately owned multifamily and single-family starts and mobile home shipments ranged from a high of 2.93 million in 1972 to a low of 1.36 million in 1975. Housing-construction data for 1970 through 1978 from U.S. Department of Commerce, Bureau of the Census, "Housing Starts, January 1979," *Construction Reports*, C20-79-1, Washington, U.S. Government Printing Office, 1979, p. 10. Data for 1979 from unpublished estimates.

8. For an overview and analysis of federal mortgage programs and tax provisions for homeownership, see Henry J. Aaron, *Shelter and Subsidies: Who Benefits from Federal Housing Policies?* (Washington: Brookings Institution, 1972).

9. Federal programs offering direct interest rate subsidies include the Department of Housing and Urban Development's (HUD) Section 235

homeownership assistance program; the Government National Mortgage Association's (GNMA) secondary market operation, the Tandem Plan; and the Farmers Home Administrations (FmHA) rural housing insurance fund. Other federal programs subsidize interest rates indirectly and expand the total supply of credit to the mortgage market by providing loan guarantees (or loan insurance) or through direct-lending operations. Examples are the loan and loan-guarantee programs of the Federal Housing Administration (FHA) and the Veterans Administration (VA).

Federal direct expenditure outlays for the HUD Section 235, GNMA, FmHA rural housing, FHA, and VA programs were estimated at approximately $1 billion in fiscal year 1978. In addition, these five lending programs supported gross annual credit activity estimated at $26 billion for the year. (*Gross annual credit activity* represents all loans obligated under direct-loan programs and the value of all commercial loans insured under mortgage-guarantee programs.)

Federal direct expenditure and gross credit activity estimates from U.S. Congress, Senate, Committee on the Budget, "Homeownership," in *Tax Expenditures: Relationships to Spending Programs and Background Material on Individual Provisions*, Committee Print, 95th Congress, 2d session, Washington, U.S. Government Printing Office, 1978, p. 248.

Federal income tax provisions favoring homeownership include the deductibility of mortgage interest and property taxes, the nontaxation of the income in kind (imputed net rental value) received from owner-occupied housing, the deferral of taxes on capital gains reinvested in housing, and the one-time elective exclusion of up to $100,000 in capital gains accumulated on owner-occupied housing over a lifetime for taxpayers 55 years of age and over.

For fiscal year 1978, the tax expenditures or foregone tax revenues associated with the favorable individual income tax treatment of homeownership were estimated at $14 billion.

Federal tax expenditure estimates from U.S. office of Management and Budget, "Tax Expenditures," Special Analysis G, in *Special Analyses, Budget of the United States Government, Fiscal year 1980*, Washington, U.S. Government Printing Office, 1979, p. 208.

10. If the current tax provisions and lending programs remain intact, the dollar level of direct expenditures and tax-revenue losses associated with owner-occupied housing is likely to increase at a rate in excess of the rate of growth in the number of households during the 1980s. This projection of a disproportionate increase in these federal subsidies to homeownership is based on the expectation of a larger fraction of U.S. households being in those age brackets traditionally associated with high rates of homeownership and large outstanding mortgages.

The average annual rate of increase in the number of U.S. households during the 1980s is expected to be approximately 1.8 percent. But the revenue cost of the mortgage-interest deduction, for example, can be expected to increase at approximately 2.4 percent per year, solely in response to changes in the number and age composition of U.S. households—not even allowing for inflationary effects. See Nonna A. Noto, "The Impact of Demographic Changes on the Revenue cost of the Mortgage Interest Deduction," Report No. 79-204 E, Washington, Congressional Research Service, Library of Congress, 1979, p. 36.

The increase in the dollar size of tax and direct expenditure subsidies would be aggravated further by continuation of high interest rates and inflation in housing prices, which are likely to lead to greater mortgage borrowing, larger interest-rate subsidies or tax deductions, larger property tax deductions, and larger capital gains deferrals and exclusions.

11. U.S. Department of Labor, Bureau of Labor Statistics, *Consumer Expenditure Survey: Integrated Diary and Interview Survey Data, 1972-73*, Bulletin 1992, Washington, U.S. Government Printing Office, 1978, Table 3, pp. 42-47.

12. The expenses subtracted here include the mortgage principal payment in addition to payments for mortgage interest, property taxes, ground rent (for mobile homes), and repairs. This differs slightly from the commonly accepted definition of imputed net rent, which does not subtract the mortgage principal payent but does subtract depreciation. The mortgage payment has been subtracted here to come closer to a measure of the return to financial equity in the housing investment. In a period of rapidly inflating house prices, for many owners there may be no depreciation in the sense of declining dollar resale value of the asset over time. In fact, currently, an important part of the anticipated return on investment in a house is the capital gain on the appreciated resale value of the house. For a standard definition of imputed net rent, see Richard Goode, *The Individual Income Tax* (Washington: Brookings Institution, 1976), p. 118.

13. Janet Murray, "Homeownership and Financial Assets: Findings from the 1968 Survey of the Aged," *Social Security Bulletin* 35, 8 (August 1972):3-23. Financial assets were found to be considerably understated and underreported in comparison with home equity in both the 1963 and 1968 Surveys of the Aged; see note 2, p. 4. Still, the overall conclusions would hold even with a substantial increase in the estimated median values for financal assets.

14. Information from Pierre Cossais, Canada's Department of Finance, Ottawa, as reported in "Moving Can Leap Big Cost Barriers," *Chicago Tribune*, January 30, 1979, p. 1. For a list of references on RHOSPs, see Eric L. Swanick, "Registered Home Ownership Savings Plans (RHOSPs): An Introductory Bibliography," Public Administration Series Bibliography P-211 (Vance Bibliographies, P.O. Box 229, Monticello, IL 61856, 1979).

15. For a synopsis of legislative proposals on Independent Housing Accounts introduced in the 96th Congress, 1st Session, see United States League

of Savings Associations, "Memorandum for the Washington Press," Washington, July 5, 1979.

16. Jacobe and Parliment, *Homeownership*, pp. 77-78.

17. For a synopsis of legislation introduced in the 96th Congress, 1st Session, that would offer tax incentives for savings, mainly through exclusion from gross income of a certain amount of interest on savings accounts, see the U.S. League of Savings Associations, "Memorandum."

18. For a discussion of two other planning issues related to the low mobility of senior citizens, see Dowell Myers, "A New Perspective on Planning for More Balanced Metropolitan Growth," *Growth and Change* 9 (January 1978):8-13; and Henry Thomassen, "Circuit Breaking and Life Cycle Lock-In," *National Tax Journal* 31, 1 (March 1978):59-65.

19. For a detailed discussion of housing for the elderly, see U.S. Department of Housing and Urban Development, Office of Policy Development and Research, *Occasional Papers in Housing and Community Affairs*, Vols. 1 and 3. Volume 1 is a symposium, Robert Paul Boynton (ed.), *The Housing of Independent Elderly*, HUD-497-PDR (Washington: U.S. Government Printing Office, 1978). Volume 3 is by Irving Welfeld and Raymond J. Struyk, *Housing Options for the Elderly*, HUD-497-3-PDR (Washington: U.S. Government Printing Office, 1979).

20. For an attempt to measure the extent of dissatisfaction with housing associated with neighborhood inadequacy, see Frieden and Solomon, *The Nation's Housing*, pp. 91-98.

Appendix 1A

Table 1A-1
Total U.S. Households by Age Class, 1950-2020
(In 1000's)

Year	Age of Household Head							
	18-24	*25-29*	*30-34*	*35-44*	*45-54*	*55-64*	*Over 64*	*Total*
1950	2,109	4,104	5,032	9,909	8,587	6,992	6,526	43,259
1955	2,130	4,074	5,238	11,014	9,595	7,936	7,954	47,941
1960	2,550	4,289	5,366	11,605	10,896	8,609	9,469	52,784
1965	3,446	4,816	5,087	11,949	11,536	9,623	10,990	57,447
1970	4,335	6,150	5,591	11,661	12,256	10,825	12,407	63,225
1975	5,848	7,918	7,213	11,862	12,905	11,351	14,372	71,479
1980	6,202	9,143	8,861	13,881	12,302	12,316	16,071	78,776
1985	6,147	10,335	10,136	17,201	12,276	12,657	17,687	86,439
1990	5,863	10,857	11,208	20,324	13,966	12,146	19,393	93,757
1995	5,795	9,397	11,144	22,538	17,145	12,088	20,448	98,555
2000	6,753	8,940	9,895	23,345	20,130	13,701	20,727	103,491
2005	7,779	9,781	9,323	21,790	22,266	16,719	21,090	108,748
2010	8,045	11,213	10,108	19,766	23,058	19,469	22,585	114,244
2015	7,874	11,444	11,496	19,585	21,551	21,396	25,557	118,903
2020	7,825	10,983	11,445	21,981	19,607	22,006	29,095	122,942

Sources: Figures for 1980 to 2020 based on Census Series II projections, assuming 2.1 children per woman, as presented in Thomas C. Marcin, *Outlook for Housing by Type of Unit and Region: 1978-2020*, Research Paper FPL 304 (Madison, Wisc.: U.S. Department of Agriculture, Forest Service, Forest Products Laboratory, 1977), Table A15, p. 27. Figures for 1950 to 1975 are adjusted Census estimates, obtained from Thomas Marcin.

2 Empty Housing Space: An Overlooked Resource

William C. Baer

Years ago the housing problem was defined in terms of inadequacy—too little housing to begin with, and much of it substandard. Today we are approaching the opposite problem. There is a great deal of housing, it is frequently built to excessive standards, and it is generally considered too expensive. Despite this change in the housing problem, the package of policy solutions has resolutely resisted major modification. This chapter casts the housing scene in a nontraditional light. It suggests an extremely cost-effective approach to easing part of the problem of providing rental units, as described by Sternlieb and Hughes in chapter 6, as well as ameliorating the extent of an impending problem described by Noto in chapter 1.

In 1937, President Roosevelt saw "a third of a nation ill-housed." In 1949, Congress declared as its goal "a decent home and a suitable environment for every American family." Following 20 years of experience and study, in 1968, Congress reaffirmed that goal and declared that "it can be substantially achieved within the next decade by the construction or rehabilitation of 26 million housing units, 6 million of these for low and moderate income families."[1]

In all this there has been emphasis on the physical inadequacy of the existing stock and on the need to build new units. With sufficient number of new units we could scrap the inadequate old ones (the way we do automobiles) and upgrade the stock. In fact, this is what happened. From 1959 to 1968, the nation completed 14,510,500 units; from 1969 to 1978 (the decade referred to in Congress's goal), the nation completed 17,573,100 units, an increase of 20 percent. During this last decade, we also have experienced a substantial scrappage of the stock in the form of housing abandonment. Moreover, the quality of the housing stock has improved dramatically. In 1950, 34 percent of the nation's housing units lacked some or all plumbing facilities, while only 2.6 percent were in that condition in 1976. In 1950, 6.2 percent of the households lived in overcrowded units; by 1976, only 1.5 percent were overcrowded.

One might conclude from these figures that the housing problem is over. Of course it is not. The problem has merely changed from one of

---

The author is grateful for the research assistance provided by Deborah Chankin, on whose unpublished directed research paper, "Housing Shortage and Empty Space: Underutilized Housing in Urban America," parts of this article are based.

physical and numerical inadequacy to one of high costs. Our housing stock is adequate—indeed, more than adequate—by any of the traditional measures, and there is plenty of it. But there is still a housing problem, and it appears serious. Owner-occupied housing today is readily available, but it is extraordinarily expensive. Rental housing is comparatively cheaper, but it is in scarce supply.

In the decade since Congress reaffirmed its national housing goal and stressed the need to build 26 million units, the Consumer Price Index (CPI) has risen about 100 percent. Owner-occupied housing has increased still more to about 150 percent. Nationally, *new* homes sell on average for $78,100, along with a 12.38 percent first-mortgage rate, up from $68,300 and 10.32 percent a year earlier. In a housing market hot spot like Los Angeles County, the average price for *existing* dwellings rose from $33,000 in 1969 to $115,000 in 1980, with current mortgage rates of around 15 percent.

Rental costs have not increased as fast as the CPI or even income. They stand at about 70 percent. This comparatively low rent increase has tended to discourage the construction of new rental units. Rental vacancy rates are at their lowest (5 percent) in 30 years. The chance for a better gain from the owner-occupied market has induced many owners of apartment complexes to convert to condominiums, thereby further reducing the supply of rental units.

How do households cope with the problem of rising costs? For those already owning homes, rising house prices are a double-edged sword. While prices and mortgage payments rise, the equity in their existing unit allows them to make a down payment on a more expensive unit. The comparatively recent requirement that the incomes of wives must be counted toward meeting monthly housing costs has kept a number of households eligible for more expensive loans. Furthermore, homeowners are devoting a higher proportion of their incomes to housing. The old rule that housing costs should not exceed 2½ times annual income has given way to multiples of up to 5 times. No doubt this change in income-to-house value ratio is partially explained by considering ownership as a major financial investment over and above mere shelter costs.

Renters also are devoting a higher percentage of their incomes to housing. In 1960, 35 percent of all renters paid 25 percent or more of their incomes on housing. By 1976, 47 percent endured this rent-income ratio. Moreover, renters are now particularly active in lobbying for rent-control measures at the local level, which regulate and limit rent increases.

The preceding is a familiar litany. The numbers change over the years, but the lamentations have remained the same. And so has the governmental response. To ease the housing problem, the federal government has manipulated the supply and cost of money through tight and easy money policies and through establishment of FHA and VA loans. It also has attempted to reduce the cost of the components of the housing package by land writedowns and public-facilities loans and grants. It has lowered the cost of owning the housing stock through accelerated depreciation allowances and interest and property tax deductions from adjusted gross income. Finally, government has augmented the income of households to increase housing consumption through payment of interest subsidies, rent supplements, and housing allowances. However, government has never consciously designed programs to better adjust the allocation of the existing stock to meet social needs.

Underutilization of the Nation's Space

Despite the high cost of owner-occupied housing, and despite the relative scarcity of rental units, there is a substantial amount of housing space in this country—about 1.75 rooms for every man, woman, and child. The problems are its uneven distribution and frequently inefficient utilization. In our preoccupation with looking at the upper end of the scale, that is, crowding and overcrowding, we have failed to examine the other end, that is, undercrowding or underutilization, and we have failed to develop standards for measuring this aspect of housing-space utilization.

Traditional standards for crowding in housing have ranged from 2 or more persons per room (PPR) down to 1.01 PPR, with only minimal agreement as to the correct standard.[2] A reasonable synthesis of these views would claim that 1.01 to 1.50 PPR is crowding, while 1.5 or more PPR is *overcrowding*, thereby denoting the appropriate degrees of room crowding. However, rarely has there been any general discussion of undercrowding, save for a limited literature on the elderly and their difficulties in maintaining a large house.

Let us posit, therefore, a lower limit to the PPR measure as a standard for determining underutilization. For convenience sake, that is, to accord with available census data, we will say that 0.50 PPR or less represents, in general, underutilized space—space that might be put to more intensive use without undue hardship imposed on existing users or the new users. This standard would permit doubling the occupancy without transgressing the PPR ratio for crowding.

In 1970, 50 percent of the nation's housing units were underutilized by this 0.50-PPR measure, and by 1976, 57 percent of the units were underutilized, despite the seeming increase in housing costs. At the same time, crowding had been reduced from 6 to 4 percent of the units, while overcrowding had been reduced from 2 to 1 percent.

However, a simple measure such as this should be modified to reflect the complexities and subtleties of family and household existence and the varied use of the housing stock. Let us assume some minimal configuration of rooms where our criteria of underutilization would not apply. People probably need or should require some minimal set of rooms (kitchen, living room, and bedroom) that uses more space per capita than a larger housing unit with more people. This notion squares with a set of standards promulgated by the American Public Health Association that suggest a declining minimum square feet of area per person in households from one to six persons as follows: 380, 383, 330, 290, 284, and 256.[3] Therefore, let us assume that no unit with five or more occupants is considered underutilized, since much more information is required about age, sex, and relationship of the occupants, as well as the number and use of the rooms, before such a judgment could be made.

Here we must resort to older data to reveal the impact of applying these criteria. A special 1970 Census report provides this information for standard metropolitan statistical areas (SMSAs) and shows that a total of 15.7 million units were underutilized by this criteria in 1970, 78 percent of which were owner-occupied (see table 2-1).

As a measure of severely underutilized space, we might consider only those units of seven or more rooms, with only one or two occupants, that is, those units which at a minimum have five more rooms than people, or a PPR ratio at a maximum of 0.29. Even with this conservative measure and underutilization, there were 1,772,976 such units in the United States in 1970—91 percent of which were owner-occupied.

In many cases, this extra space could be more efficiently utilized by the present occupant taking in a roomer or boarder. In other cases, some alteration or remodeling would be required to provide an outside entrance and a separate bathroom and kitchen for use as an apartment.

Table 2-1
Underutilized Units: SMSAs, 1970

Number of Occupants and Unit Size	*Owner*		*Renter*		*Total Units (000s)*
	Units (000s)	*Percent*	*Units (000s)*	*Percent*	
1 Occupant 4 Rooms	682.0	04	1,020.0	06	1,702.0
1-2 Occupants 5 Rooms	3,256.0	21	1,277.3	08	4,533.3
1-3 Occupants 6 Rooms	3,981.0	25	720.8	05	4,701.8
1-4 Occupants 7 Rooms	2,507.4	16	263.8	02	2,771.3
1-4 Occupants 8+ Rooms	1,850.9	12	156.4	01	2,002.2
Total	12,277.3	78	3,438.3	22	15,710.6

Source: U.S. Bureau of The Census, *Census of Housing: 1970,* Final Report HC(7)-3, "Space Utilization of the Housing Inventory," Washington, 1972, Table B-3.

Assuming that 20 percent of these units could be seriously considered as containing usable space for additional occupants (that is, the unit and the present occupants are amenable to more intensive space use) and that of the remaining 13,937,622 less severely underutilized units, 10 percent would be suitable to house additional occupants, almost 1,750,000 units (roughly equivalent to a year's production of new units) might be seen as an additional housing resource. The precise number is not important—even half this estimate is a large number of housing units. The point is that hundreds of thousands of units could be more intensively utilized at relatively low cost. The problem is how to reallocate them for more efficient use. *Mandatory* redistribution is one approach, but it would be frequently arbitrary, ultimately inefficient, and probably illegal. *Voluntary* sharing of space would seem eminently more feasible, and indeed it is already being done, particularly among the elderly. From a policy perspective then, we should examine policies that encourage or discourage excessive consumption of space and eliminate or modify policies that impede or thwart voluntary reallocation.

Government Policies and Housing Space

What accounts for the increasing consumption of space per capita by American households? One reason, of course, is the growing prosperity of the nation and national expectations about higher standards of living. Another aspect is the trend toward smaller households—young people leaving the home earlier to set up separate households; older people remaining in separate households even at the expense of a certain physical inconvenience; and the growing trend toward divorce with separate households.

However, there are also government policies that work to encourage or thwart the consumption of extra space. One of the major policies is the federal income tax deductions for mortgage interest and property tax for homeowners. As incomes rise owing to increased national prosperity and inflation, taxpayers move to higher tax brackets that permit higher-percentage deductions, ameliorating the seemingly high costs for homeownership and encouraging overconsumption. Moreover, there is another provision in the income tax law that encourages the elderly or near elderly to sell homes that may have become too big for them. As of July 26, 1978, a homeowner 55 or older may sell his or her home and receive any capital gains up to $100,000 tax free. This $100,000 exclusion can be used only once in a lifetime, and there are certain restrictions to prevent short-term speculation to realize this tax-free gain, but it does provide encouragement to the elderly to switch from owning or renting a large unit to owning or renting a smaller unit without paying a capital gains tax. Since the elderly constitute a disproportionately large percentage of all occupants who underutilize housing space (about 30 percent of all underutilized housing units and about 50 percent of all severely underutilized housing units) and most of them are owner-occupants, this new legislation may have removed a significant tax barrier to the elderly in their housing decisions.

More important barriers, however, that cut across all age groups are local zoning ordinances governing single-family housing. In an effort to preserve the residential character of an area; protect property values; promote family and youth values; and control density, traffic congestion, and the impact on schools and other public facilities, local government have resorted to strict zoning controls in single-family areas. As a part of the zoning ordinance there is typically a definition of who (what family groups and unrelated individuals) are allowed to reside in such an area. Table 2-2 provides some examples from California.

These examples suggest the range of restrictions found in local zoning ordinances. On the one hand, there is a lenient interpretation of what is appropriate for a residential area, as exemplified by San Jose's definition of a family as a household and allows roomers, to a strict interpretation, as found in Pasadena's ordinance, which permits no more than two unrelated persons and no roomers or boarders in its largest and most underutilized houses. In the latter case, the concept of renting even a room in a single-family

Table 2-2
Illustrative Zoning Requirements for Single-Family Residential Areas

City	*Definition of Family*	*Borders or Roomers*
Los Angeles	Not more than five unrelated persons plus four foster children	R1: None allowed R2: Allowed if no cooking in room
Long Beach	Same as Los Angeles	Same as Los Angeles
Pasadena	Not more than two unrelated persons	None in areas zoned for 12,000 sq. ft. minimum lots; up to three rooms rented in areas zoned for 7,500 sq. ft. or less
San Jose	One or more persons living as a single housekeeping unit; excludes fraternities, clubs, and so on	Up to three roomers "clearly secondary to use of the dwelling as a family residence"
San Francisco	Not more than five unrelated persons, unless legal guardian	None in R1 or R2

Source: Deborah R. Chankin, "Housing Shortage and Empty Space: Underutilizing Housing in Urban America," unpublished directed research paper, School of Urban and Regional Planning, University of Southern California, June 5, 1978, pp. 18-19. Reprinted with permission.

area is seen as inimical to the purpose of a single-family residential area. Nevertheless, such an orientation inhibits flexibility and creativity toward more intensive use of the housing stock.

Two recent Supreme Court decisions in this area show both promise and disappointment in achieving a greater flexibility. In the first hearing of a case on the substance of zoning decision since the famous *Euclid* v. *Ambler Realty Co.*, 272 U.S. 365 (1926), the Supreme Court in *Village of Belle Terre* v. *Boraas*, 416 U.S. 1 (1974) upheld a local zoning ordinance that permitted no more than two unrelated individuals to reside in a house in an area zoned for single-family units and thus made illegal the inhabitation of a house by six college students. In a more recent case, *Moore* v. *the City of East Cleveland*, 431 U.S. 494 (1977), however, the court stretched the definition of a family to include the extended family, thereby allowing a grandson to live with his grandmother after his mother had died, which had been deemed an illegal occupancy under the East Cleveland zoning ordinance. There were a number of concurring and dissenting opinions in this latter case, so the court's direction in this area is not clearly demarcated. However, there appears to be general agreement that if a city wishes to control population density and its side effects, a superior way is by limiting the number of people that can live in a unit, not by employing a restrictive definition of family or limiting the number of unrelated people living in the same unit.[4]

Conclusion

It has been estimated that there are over 15 million housing units with surplus space, and that as a reasonable estimate, 850,000 to 1,750,000 of these units could be thought of as feasibly providing additional housing space. Homeowners might well wish to increase their incomes by renting out several rooms; those who rent these units might well wish to defray their housing costs by acquiring roommates. Local zoning ordinances, however, typically prevent this more efficient allocation of housing stock when the units are located in areas zoned for single-family units.

At the moment, there appears to be little prospect that communities will change their zoning ordinances to permit this more effective utilization of housing stock. However, if housing prices continue to increase and developers are discouraged from rapidly increasing the supply of rental units because of lagging rents and rent control or its prospect, this underutilization orientation to viewing the supply of housing may become more acceptable. Certainly the supply of underutilized housing offers a cost-effective approach to the immediate problems of high rents, scarce supply, and increasingly low-income renters and the longer-term prospect of overbuilding.

Notes

1. Housing and Urban Development Act of 1968, Public Law 448, 90th Congress.
2. William C. Baer, "The Evolution of Housing Indicators and Housing Standards: Some Lessons for the Future," *Public Policy* (Summer 1976):361-393.
3. American Public Health Association, *Planning the Home for Occupancy*, Chicago: Public Administration Service, 1950.
4. A very recent case by the New Jersey Supreme Court emphasizes some of these points; see *New Jersey* v. *Baker*, 81 N.J. 99 (1979).

3 Six-Month Money-Market Certificates and Housing

Alden F. Shiers

One important aspect of housing policy is the financing of housing. A very large percentage of residential construction is financed by the lending activities of commercial banks, savings and loan associations, and mutual savings banks. Combined, these three financial institutions hold over 60 percent of the total mortgage debt outstanding in the United States. The financial institutions will have to attract an adequate flow of deposits in order to finance the construction of housing at desirable rates during the 1980s. In the past, however, episodes have occurred where deposit flows have not been adequate to serve the financial needs of the housing industry. The term *disintermediation* is used to designate periods during which there is a sharp slowdown in the flow of deposits to financial institutions. The result of disintermediation is a steep decline in the number of new housing units started. The elimination of disintermediation would thus create a more stable supply of housing. This chapter examines one recent attempt—the introduction of 6-month money-market certificates—to remedy the problem of disintermediation. Before analyzing the role of money-market certificates, some necessary background information on interest-rate ceilings and disintermediation is first provided.

Interest-Rate Ceilings and Disintermediation

One of the causes of disintermediation is the imposition of maximum interest rates that commeral banks, savings and loan associations, and mutual savings banks are allowed to pay on their time and savings deposits. (Credit unions are also subject to interest-rate ceilings on deposits. They are not considered here because they are not an important source of credit for housing.) When market interest rates rise above the legal ceiling rates on time and savings deposits, this provides an incentive for savers to purchase securities that offer a rate of return higher than that offered on deposits. As a consequence, the flow of deposits is reduced, the supply of mortgage credit is curtailed, and the number of housing units started is cut back.

The United States experienced this sequence of events in 1966, in 1969-1970, and again in 1973-1974. In the summer of 1977, market interest rates started increasing once more. By the end of that year, yields on U.S.

Treasury securities had risen above ceiling interest rates on both savings accounts and time deposits with longer maturities. It was feared that disintermediation would occur and disrupt the housing market as it had done previously under similar circumstances. In an effort to prevent that from happening, federal regulators of depository institutions authorized a new kind of 6-month savings certificate called a *money-market certificate* (MMC). Commerical banks, savings and loans, and mutual savings banks were permitted to offer MMCs after June 1, 1978.

The ceiling interest rate on new MMCs was allowed to float with the interest rate on 6-month Treasury bills established in the weekly Treasury bill auctions. The ceiling rate on MMCs at commercial banks was established as equal to the current discount yield on 6-month Treasury bills. (Treasury bills are sold at a discount from their face value, hence the term *discount yield*. The difference between the discount yield on Treasury bills and yields on MMCs is explored in Kasriel [4].) Savings and loan associations and mutual savings banks were allowed a ceiling rate on MMCs that was 0.25 percent higher than the commercial banks. However, on March 15, 1978, the extra 0.25 percent was eliminated if the interest rate was 9 percent or higher. The minimum denomination for MMCs was set at $10,000, the same as for Treasury bills. Thus the MMCs were specifically introduced so that depository institutions could compete more effectively for loanable funds when market interest rates rise above ceiling interest rates on time and savings deposits. (The elimination of ceiling interest rates on deposits has often been recommended; see, for example, [7, 8]).

Since their introduction in June of 1978, MMCs have proven to be very popular. Their growth at federally insured savings and loan associations can be seen in table 3-1. At the end of April 1978, MMCs outstanding at insured savings and loans amounted to about $74.6 billion and comprised about 17 percent of savings capital. Gilbert and Lovati report that commerical banks had $23 billion of MMCs outstanding in December of 1978, representing about 4.5 percent of their net time and savings deposits [1]. (Net time and savings deposits of commercial banks exclude negotiable certificates of deposit of $100,000 and above.) They also report mutual savings banks had about $12.8 billion of MMCs outstanding at the end of 1978, and MMCs comprised about 7.7 percent of mutual savings bank deposits at the end of November 1978. The significance of the MMCs has been stated as follows by the chairman of the Federal Home Loan Bank Board, Robert McKinney: "Of all the actons taken by the Bank Board in 1978, none had a more immediate and positive effect than authorizing the money market certificate. The MMC was responsible for the fact that, despite high interest rates, we witnessed neither disintermediation nor the steep decline in housing starts many expected. In addition to giving savers a better return on their money, the MMC permitted savings and loan associatons to continue to supply mortgage loans to borrowers" [4, p. 6].

Table 3-1
Six-Month Money-Market Certificates (MMCs) at FSLIC-Insured Savings and Loan Associations

Month	*MMC Balances Outstanding at End of Month (Millions of Dollars)*	*MMCs as Percent of Total Savings Balances*
1978		
June	5,400	1.35%
July	11,790	2.92
Aug.	15,080	3.72
Sept.	19,338	4.70
Oct.	26,660	6.43
Nov.	34,630	8.31
Dec.	40,790	9.66
1979		
Jan.	54,950	12.88
Feb.	60,850	14.17
Mar.	68,760	15.71
Apr.	74,590	17.07

Source: *Federal Home Loan Bank Board News,* May 25, 1979.

A more comprehensive discussion of interest-rate ceilings and disintermediation can be found in McKelvey [5]. The next sections analyze the role of MMCs in preventing disintermediation in 1978 by comparing past periods of disintermediation with 1978.

Disintermediation in 1969-1970

Table 3-2 shows the disintermediation that took place in 1969 and the beginning of 1970. During most of the months of 1969, deposit growth rates were quite low, and in many cases they were negative. Because of the deposit outflows that occurred in 1969, interest-rate ceilings on deposits were raised on January 21, 1970. The difference between market rates and ceiling rates was thereby substantially reduced in February of 1970. Market interest rates also reached their peak in January of 1970, and so the growth rate of deposits during the remainder of 1970 tended to be higher than during 1969. The deposit figures for commercial banks include negotiable certificates of deposit of $100,000 or more. This is probably why the commercial banks show negative rates of deposit growth for every month in 1969 except December, and why commercial bank deposits increased at faster rates during 1970. Commercial bank holdings of large negotiable certificates of deposit fell from $23.5 billion in December of 1968 to $10.9 billion in December of 1969. They then increased to $25.3 billion in December of 1970.

Table 3-2
Market Interest Rates less Ceiling Interest Rates on Deposits at Savings and Loan Associations, and the Growth of Time and Savings Deposits

	Interest-Rate Differentials			*Annual Rates of Growth of Time and Savings Deposits at:*[a]		
Month	*Short Term*[b]	*Medium Term*[c]	*Long Term*[d]	*CB*	*SLA*	*MSB*
1969						
Jan.	1.43	0.80	0.79	−6.4%	−0.8%	4.5%
Feb.	1.41	0.94	0.91	−2.9	5.5	6.3
Mar.	1.33	0.94	1.08	−4.1	12.4	12.5
Apr.	1.40	0.78	0.90	−2.4	−4.6	−3.4
May	1.33	0.85	1.08	−2.4	5.8	5.7
June	1.75	1.61	1.39	−3.0	12.2	6.5
July	2.25	1.89	1.77	−18.5	−9.8	−2.8
Aug.	2.26	2.02	1.83	−16.4	−0.1	1.8
Sept.	2.38	2.10	2.33	−3.7	7.9	5.9
Oct.	2.29	1.97	2.22	−3.7	−3.6	−3.2
Nov.	2.45	2.13	2.32	−1.2	2.1	2.9
Dec.	2.97	2.39	2.73	3.7	9.5	10.5
1970						
Jan.	3.16	2.25	2.99	−8.0	−12.6	−1.6
Feb.	2.16	1.32	1.80	1.2	1.8	4.6
Mar.	1.71	0.77	1.20	11.2	14.8	11.2
Apr.	1.48	0.79	1.49	19.7	2.1	−0.4
May	2.04	1.37	1.97	10.9	6.6	5.9
June	1.74	1.32	1.86	11.4	15.9	9.3
July	1.47	0.88	1.58	35.6	4.7	5.5
Aug.	1.41	0.80	1.56	28.8	4.7	3.2
Sept.	1.24	0.65	1.24	29.8	15.6	10.3
Oct.	0.93	0.48	1.06	20.3	9.6	4.7
Nov.	0.29	−0.36	0.37	15.1	9.2	4.6
Dec.	−0.14	−0.88	−0.14	28.8	23.5	20.8

Sources: *Federal Reserve Bulletin* 56 and 57: A-17, A-33, A-11, A-8, A-37, *Federal Home Loan Bank Board Journal* 3 and 4: S.3.1, S.4.12.

[a]Figures for commercial banks are seasonally adjusted; figures for savings and loan associations and mutual savings banks are not seasonally adjusted.

[b]Interest rate (discount basis) on 3-month Treasury bills less ceiling rate on savings deposits.

[c]Interest rate (discount basis) on 9- to 12-month Treasury bills less ceiling rate on 1- to 2-year time deposits.

[d]Interest rate on 3- to 5-year Treasury securities less ceiling rate on 4- to 6-year time deposits.

As a result of the deposit flows to the mortgage-lending institutions in 1969, the number of new private housing units started fell by 2.7 percent during 1969 and declined by another 2.3 percent during 1970. In contrast, private housing increased by 10.9 and 16.7 percent during 1967 and 1968, respectively.

Disintermediation in 1973-1974

Table 3-3 shows the interest-rate differentials and deposit flows that existed during 1973-1974. Deposit flows for commercial banks in table 3-3 do not include large negotiable certificates of deposit, as in the previous table. The difference between market rates and ceiling rates on deposits increased during the first part of 1973, reaching a peak in August. Interest-rate differ-

Table 3-3
Market Interest Rates less Ceiling Interest Rates on Deposits at Savings and Loan Associations, and the Growth of Time and Savings Deposits

	Interest-Rate Differentials			*Annual Rates of Growth of Time and Savings Deposits at:*		
Month	*Short Term*	*Medium Term*	*Long Term*	*CB*	*SLA*	*MSB*
1973						
Jan.	0.31	−0.17	0.29	13.3%	19.0%	10.2%
Feb.	0.56	0.18	0.61	9.2	10.8	7.2
Mar.	1.05	0.78	0.85	10.0	20.9	14.8
Apr.	1.29	0.76	0.74	9.1	4.6	1.6
May	1.35	0.88	0.78	10.7	10.4	6.7
June	2.19	1.30	0.76	9.8	18.0	12.2
July	2.77	1.47	N.A.	6.7	−1.1	−4.4
Aug.	3.42	1.82	N.A.	13.4	−6.3	−6.0
Sept.	3.23	1.57	N.A.	10.4	10.0	3.8
Oct.	1.91	0.67	N.A.	14.4	5.1	−3.0
Nov.	2.62	0.90	−0.54	11.0	6.8	4.0
Dec.	2.11	0.51	−0.70	12.1	15.8	15.6
1974						
Jan.	2.52	0.51	−0.56	15.6	11.5	3.7
Feb.	1.87	0.01	−0.73	12.2	9.5	6.0
Mar.	2.71	0.84	−0.17	10.1	21.6	15.8
Apr.	3.08	1.58	0.49	9.3	−1.1	−6.4
May	2.98	1.71	0.74	5.0	2.7	−7.9
June	2.65	1.66	0.64	11.5	13.7	9.8
July	2.30	1.54	0.89	8.3	−2.4	−5.8
Aug.	3.71	2.38	1.14	8.6	−5.8	−7.9
Sept.	2.81	2.02	0.88	4.8	7.2	4.4
Oct.	2.21	1.09	0.48	12.2	2.2	−2.1
Nov.	2.22	0.79	0.15	11.8	6.2	4.1
Dec.	1.90	0.29	−0.28	2.9	16.9	13.8

Sources: *Federal Reserve Bulletin* 61 and 62: A-12, A-30, A-27, A-8, A-11, *Federal Home Loan Bank Board Journal* 7 and 8: S.4.1, S.4.2.

N.A. means not applicable because ceiling rates on time deposits of $1,000 or more with maturities of at least 4 years were suspended.

See table 3-2 for notes.

entials then declined to a low point in February of 1974 and rose to new peaks in August of 1974. The flow of deposits to commercial banks remained at a fairly high level during 1973-1974. However, savings and loan associations and mutual savings banks experienced net outflows of deposits during the months of July and August in both 1973 and 1974. It is worth noting that these outflows of deposits occurred in 1973 even though interest ceilings were suspended on long-term deposits.

It also should be noted that because 1974 was a recession year, it becomes difficult to compare the effect of deposit ceiling rates on the growth of deposits in 1974 to the growth of deposits in other years. The growth of deposits would be expected to be less in 1974 because real disposable personal income fell during that year. However, it does seem quite likely that some of the slowdown in deposit growth rates during 1974 was due to the high market rates of interest.

Overall, the growth rate of deposits at savings and loan associations during 1974 was only 6.7 percent, whereas it was 9.9 percent in 1973 and 18.7 percent in 1972. For mutual savings banks, the growth of deposits fell from a rate of 12.5 percent during 1972, to 5.3 percent during 1973, to only 2.3 percent in 1974. As noted earlier, the commercial banks did not fare so badly. Their time and savings deposit growth rates fell from 13.5 percent in 1972, to 11.4 percent in 1973, to 9.4 percent in 1974.

The slowdown in the growth rates of time and savings deposits during 1973-1974 was reflected again in declines in new private housing units started. Housing starts, which had increased by over 40 percent in 1971 and by nearly 15 percent in 1972, fell by 13.2 percent in 1973, by 34.6 percent in 1974, and by 13.3 percent in 1975.

The 1978-1979 Experience

Table 3-4 displays the same information for 1978-1979 as tables 3-2 and 3-3 showed for the prior disintermediation periods. As can readily be seen in table 3-4, interest-rate differentials have increased to levels comparable with those of 1969-1970 and 1973-1974. In fact, during 1979, both the short- and medium-term interest-rate differentials were substantially larger than in the 1969-1970 and 1973-1974 periods. Also, in 1979, the development of the money-market mutual funds began to provide the financial intermediaries with a significant new source of competition for deposits. However, with one possible exception, the deposit flows to the financial intermediaries have not declined so much as in the previous periods examined. The one exception is that growth of deposits at commercial banks has been less than it was in the 1973-1974 disintermediation period. Overall it thus appears that the MMCs have enjoyed success in preventing disintermediation.

Table 3-4
Market Interest Rates less Ceiling Rates on Deposits at Savings and Loan Associations, and the Growth of Time and Savings Deposits

	Interest Rate Differentials			*Annual Rates of Growth of Time and Savings Deposits at:*		
Month	*Short Term*	*Medium Term*	*Long Term*	*CB*	*SLA*	*MSB*
1978						
Jan.	1.20	0.30	0.21	8.2%	9.7%	6.8%
Feb.	1.21	0.36	0.26	7.6	7.1	3.8
Mar.	1.07	0.32	0.26	6.0	21.9	15.9
Apr.	1.06	0.46	0.40	5.0	1.8	−0.6
May	1.18	0.78	0.60	7.2	7.2	3.3
June	1.46	1.03	0.81	7.9	19.9	8.7
July	1.82	1.29	1.04	10.3	9.0	3.6
Aug.	1.79	1.29	0.81	11.5	6.7	1.6
Sept.	2.59	1.51	0.88	11.8	18.7	13.0
Oct.	2.88	1.95	1.11	9.1	8.0	1.8
Nov.	3.54	2.70	1.47	10.4	6.1	1.1
Dec.	3.87	2.94	1.73	2.4	16.6	12.5
1979						
Jan.	4.10	3.04	1.86	2.1	13.2	1.9
Feb.	4.02	2.89	1.66	6.3	7.9	5.5
Mar.	4.21	2.88	1.75	5.6	22.8	17.6
Apr.	4.24	2.78	1.82	11.8	−3.1	−4.6
May	4.34	2.77	1.80	8.7	5.5	−0.3

Sources: *Federal Reserve Bulletin* 65: A-14, A-29, A-27, A-10, *Federal Home Loan Bank Board Journal* 12: S.4.1, S.4.12.
See table 3-2 for notes.

It also should be noted that the deposit growth rates are probably somewhat distorted for the months of March and April in 1979. The distortion is due to a change in regulations pertaining to the MMCs. Until March 15, 1979, savings and loan associations and mutual savings banks were allowed to offer an interest yield on MMCs one-quarter of a percentage point higher than the yield on 6-month Treasury bills. Compounding of interest also was allowed on MMCs. After March 15, 1979, savings and loans and mutual savings banks were no longer allowed to offer the additional 0.25 percent point, nor were they allowed to compound interest on the MMCs. The very large growth of deposits at savings and loans and mutual savings banks during March of 1979 reflects unusually large purchases of MMCs right before the regulatory change, and the negative growth of deposits in April also reflects the impact of the regulatory change.

Housing starts did not decline in 1978, as they did during the previous periods of rising market interest rates. The number of private housing units started increased by 1.6 percent in 1978. However, private housing starts during the first 6 months of 1979 declined by about 12 percent from their level in the first half of 1978. Mortgage interest rates increased throughout the first half of 1979, so the decline in housing starts is not unexpected. Without MMCs acting to attract deposits to financial intermediaries, the decline in housing starts would undoubtedly have been much greater.

Other Effects of MMCs

In past periods of disintermediation, savings and loan associations have supplemented their deposit flows by increasing their borrowings of advances from the Federal Home Loan Bank Board (FHLBB). The savings and loans can then issue mortgage loans with the proceeds of these advances. Table 3-5 shows how both advances and advances as a percentage of savings and loan associations liabilities plus net worth have increased during the disintermediation periods and then decreased during intervening years. Of particular note here is that use of FHLBB advances increased in the second half of 1978, even after MMCs were introduced. Thus, even though the MMCs have worked to counteract disintermediation during 1978, savings and loan associations have still increased their use of FHLBB advances during this latest period of rising market interest rates.

In addition to FHLBB advances, federally sponsored credit agencies exist to make more mortgage credit available during periods of disintermediation. These agencies include the Federal National Mortgage Association (FNMA), the Government National Mortgage Association (GNMA), and the Federal Home Loan Mortgage Corporation (FHLMC). The impact of these agencies on the mortgage and housing markets has been much debated. In general, it would appear that the agencies have essentially

Table 3-5
FHLBB Advances and Advances as a Percentage of SLAs' Liabilities plus Net Worth

Date	*FHLBB Advances Outstanding (Millions of Dollars)*	*FHLBB Advances Outstanding as a Percentage of SLAs' Liabilities plus Net Worth*
Jan. 1969	$ 5,357	3.49%
Dec. 1970	10,615	6.01
Jan. 1973	7,831	3.17
Dec. 1974	21,804	7.38
Jan. 1977	15,183	3.81
Jan. 1978	21,422	4.40
June 1978	25,273	5.14
Dec. 1978	32,670	6.24

Source: *Federal Home Loan Bank Board* 2 and 12: S.2.2, S.3.1, S.3.4, S.4.1.

no effect on the housing and mortgage markets over the long run (perhaps a year), but may stabilize the intended markets over shorter time periods. (Empirical analysis on this point may be found in Hendershott and Vallani [2] and Jaffee and Rosen [3].) The activity of these agencies, as well as the change in total nonfarm residential mortgage debt outstanding, is show in table 3-6. The figures indicate that FNMA increased its mortgage holdings at a faster rate during disintermediation years, but it is not clear that the other two agencies did likewise. However, because there is a time lag between a decrease in the flow of deposits to financial intermediaries and a corresponding change in the mortgage loans they hold, the actions of GNMA and FHLMC could still be stabilizing. This is particularly true of GNMA during 1975. Because of the disintermediation in the previous year, mortgage debt outstanding rose by only 7.7 percent, yet GNMA increased its mortgage holdings by over 54 percent.

It seems too early to judge the effects of MMCs on the federally sponsored credit agencies. To the extent that the MMCs stabilize the flow of deposits during periods of rising interest rates, less reliance will be needed on these agencies to stabilize the mortgage and housing markets. However, FNMA clearly stepped up its purchases of mortgages during 1978, even though deposit flows were stabilized by the MMCs. The other two agencies did not act in the same manner as FNMA. Hence, the overall impact of MMCs on these agencies' activities remains to be seen.

MMCs and Profitability

A concern expressed regarding the impact of MMCs was their effect on the profitability of financial institutions, particularly the savings and loan associations and mutual savings banks. Since the interest rates paid on MMCs are higher than the regulated interest rates on other deposits, their use increases the cost of funds to depository institutions. If the interest earned on mortgages does not rise commensurately, then the profitability of the mortgage lenders is jeopardized. Some evidence on this issue is presented in table 3-7, which shows the spread between the interest return on mortgages and the average cost of funds for federally insured savings and loan associations. Except for the last entry in the table, the dates selected show the maximum spread between the interest return and the cost of funds since 1966. Thus the interest return on mortgages was 1.54 percentage points greater than the average cost of funds for January through June of 1966. The spread declined and then rose to a peak of 1.46 percentage points in July through December of 1969 before declining again. Other cyclical peaks were reached between January and June of 1973 and January and June of 1978.

Table 3-6
Annual Percentage Increase in Mortgage-Debt Holdings of Federally Sponsored Credit Agencies and Total Nonfarm Residential Mortgage Debt

Year	*FNMA*	*GNMA*[a]	*FHLMC*[a]	*Total Nonfarm Residential Mortgage Debt*
1969	52.8%	14.2	N.A.	6.8
1970	41.4	17.3	N.A.	6.0
1971	14.8	49.6	170.0	10.8
1972	11.2	29.1	85.6	12.7
1973	22.2	9.1	88.3	20.7
1974	22.3	39.4	58.5	7.9
1975	7.6	54.6	23.2	7.7
1976	3.4	35.5	5.4	11.8
1977	4.4	39.5	42.4	16.2
1978	26.0	19.2	33.4	14.7

Source: *Federal Reserve Bulletin* 60: A-44; 61: A-42; 65: A-41.

Note: N.A. = Not applicable because agency was created in 1970.

[a]Rates of growth based on figures that include outstanding principle balances of mortgages backing securities insured or guaranteed by the agency.

Table 3-7 indicates a decrease in the spread between interest returns and the cost of funds since MMCs were introduced in July of 1978. Yet, historically, the 1.75 percentage point spread is still high, and at this point, it does not appear that MMCs have seriously eroded the profits of savings and loan associations. Moreover, the recent authorization of nationwide variable-rate mortgages should work to protect the profitability of depository institutions during future periods of rising market interest rates.

Implications for Monetary Policy

MMCs can have a beneficial role to play with respect to monetary policy in the 1980s. Because of the problem of inflation, the Federal Reserve faced a

Table 3-7
Interest Return on Mortgages Held less Average Cost of Funds for FSLIC-Insured Savings and Loan Associations

Period	*Percentage Point Difference*
Jan.-June 1966	1.54
July-Dec. 1969	1.46
Jan.-June 1973	1.64
Jan.-June 1978	1.85
July-Dec. 1978	1.75

Source: *Federal Home Loan Bank Board* 6 and 12: S.4.8, S.4.10.

dilemma in determining monetary policy during periods of rising interest rates in the 1970s. If the Federal Reserve increased the money supply more rapidly to lower interest rates and prevent disintermediation, this would have exacerbated the inflationary problem. However, more restrictive monetary policies to combat inflation would have resulted in higher interest rates (at least in the short run), disintermediation, and a reduction in residential construction.

The MMCs can help in overcoming this dilemma because they ease the problem of disintermediation. They can thus allow the Federal Reserve to pursue a monetary policy geared to combatting inflation during the 1980s without having as much concern as before with disintermediation and its negative impact on housing. This can be a very significant and beneficial result of the introduction of MMCs.

References

[1] Alton, Gilbert R., and Jean M. Lovati. "Disintermediation—An Old Disorder with a New Remedy." *Review, Federal Reserve Bank of St. Louis* 61 (January 1979):10-15.

[2] Hendershott, Patric H., and Kevin Villani. "The Federally Sponsored Credit Agencies: Their Behavior and Impact." In Robert Buckley, John Tuccillo, and Kevin Villani (eds.), *Capital Markets and the Housing Sector*. Cambridge, Mass.: Ballinger, 1977, pp. 291-309.

[3] Jaffee, Dwight M., and Kenneth Rosen. "Estimate of the Effectiveness of Stabilization Policies for the Mortgage and Housing Markets." *Journal of Finance* 33 (June 1978):933-946.

[4] Kasriel, Paul L. "New Six-Month Money Market Certificates—Explanations and Implications." *Economic Perspectives, Federal Reserve Bank of Chicago* 2 (July-August 1978):3-7.

[5] McKelvey, Edward F. *Interest Rate Ceilings and Disintermediation*. Staff Economic Studies, Board of Governors of Federal Reserve System, Washington, 1978.

[6] McKinney, Robert H. "Statement by Chairman, FHLBB," *Federal Home Loan Bank Board Journal* 12 (April 1979):3-9.

[7] *Report of the President's Commission on Financial Structure and Regulation*. U.S. Government Printing Office, Washington, 1971.

[8] U.S. Congress, House, Committee on Banking, Currency, and Housing. *The Financial Institutions and the Nation's Economy*. U.S. Government Printing Office, Washington, 1975.

Part II
Demographic Changes and Housing Demand

4 Two-Earner Families in the Housing Market

Elizabeth A. Roistacher and
Janet Spratlin Young

During the 1970s, housing prices across the United States rose rapidly, and the incidence of two-earner families—those in which both husband and wife are working—has increased.[1] In addition to these two trends, the 1970s were also a period in which a good deal of legislation prohibiting sex and marital status discrimination in mortgage lending was enacted, the most recent law being the Equal Credit Opportunity Act (ECOA) of 1975.

It has been suggested that the passage of the ECOA may have been instrumental in creating the especially pronounced rise in house prices in the years immediately following its enactment.[2] However, the legitimization of the borrowing power of women and two-earner families in particular, by this or by any earlier law, is only one of many factors shaping the current high demand for housing. Demographic and labor-market trends, as well as the high rate of inflation in the economy as a whole, also affect the housing market, in many cases through their impact on the two-earner family.

This chapter addresses the role of the two-earner family in the complex set of forces shaping the housing market of the 1970s, examines data on the role of the two-earner family in the housing market, and speculates about the future role of the two-earner family in the housing market of the 1980s. Our basic conclusions are that two-earner families have yet to exert their full impact on the housing market and that they will remain a central component of housing demand. However, at the same time, rising divorce rates may turn many two-earner families into two single-earner households, thereby altering the structure of future housing demand.

Incomes of Wives and Housing Demand

The rising labor-force participation of married women has been a major means by which families have increased their real incomes in the postwar era. As of 1977, in 23 million families both husband and wife were earners.

The authors would like to thank Edward Dolbow for patiently carrying out our computer work and Charles M. Sivesind and Richard M. Young for their helpful advice.

This chapter represents the opinions of the authors and not necessarily those of the Federal Reserve Bank of New York or the Federal Reserve System.

This was 49 percent of all husband-wife families, up from 44 percent in 1967.[3] Historically, working wives have tended to be from lower-income families, but this is changing. Between 1960 and 1977, 60 percent of the increase in working wives occurred in families in which the husband's income was above average.[4] In addition, between 1967 and 1977, there was a 75 percent increase in the percentage of wives working in families headed by husbands earning at least $25,000 a year.[5] Nevertheless, over the last two decades, the average contribution of the wife in households where both spouses work has remained relatively constant at about 25 percent of the family's income, and consequently by 1977, the average income of families with both husband and wife working was 31 percent greater than that of families in which only the husband worked.[6]

In addition to having high incomes, two-earner families are increasingly likely to have children. As of 1978, more than 50 percent of wives with children under 18 years of age were in the labor force, and wives with children under 6 years of age are joining the labor force more rapidly than those with children of school age (6 to 18 years old).[7]

The increase in employment among women in these two categories—wives whose husbands are already in the higher-income brackets and mothers of small children—can be explained in part by a substitution effect: as employment opportunities for women improve and hourly earnings rise, women will substitute market activity for nonmarket activities such as child care, housework, or volunteer work outside the home. There also may be an income effect at work here. As a result of rising rates of inflation, coupled with the recessions of the 1970s, the recent growth in real incomes has fallen well below that experienced in the 1960s.[8] As a result, women may now be entering the labor force in an attempt to maintain desired or expected levels of consumption and, in particular, to maintain desired housing consumption.

Income and family structure are the primary determinants of housing demand, and two-earner families with their high incomes and increasing prevalence of children are both willing and able to consume more housing. Moreover, for a variety of reasons, the greatest impact of the increase in the numbers of these households is likely to be felt in the market for owned rather than rented housing. For families with high taxable incomes, the progressive nature of the tax system, coupled with the tax advantages of home ownership, lowers the price of owned housing relative to that of rented housing.[9] These tax advantages increase with inflation because the tax burden rises with nominal income. In addition, demand for ownership as a hedge against inflation is spurred if its expected rate of return exceeds that of other forms of investment. In the 1970s, not only did inflation proceed at a record pace, but the return on housing outstripped the alternatives most readily available to the average household: savings certificates, stocks, and bonds. Finally, our current stock of rental housing does not in general provide the amenities preferred by families with children. Consequently, as the two-earner families of the postwar baby boom continue to pass through their (oftentimes delayed) child-bearing years, the biggest impact will be on the suburban single-family ownership market.[10]

Discrimination in Lending

Even though two-earner families have higher incomes, their ability to achieve the housing consumption they desire may be restricted by the attitudes of financial institutions toward the earnings of women. Financial institutions have been criticized for discounting the earnings of women—be they wives or heads of households—in determining the size and terms of mortgages. [By *discounting* we mean that a dollar of income earned by a female (or wife) is treated as less important in determining the size of a mortgage than is a dollar of income earned by a male (or husband).] These criticisms have led to the enactment of legislation at both the federal and state levels making it illegal for lenders to discriminate on the basis of sex and/or marital status and, in some instances, specifically to discount the earnings of wives.

The federal government has prohibited sex discrimination under a number of statutes. The Civil Rights Act of 1968 as amended by the Housing and Community Development Act of 1974 prohibits discrimination in housing and lending on the basis of sex. The Housing and Community Development Act of 1974 also amended the National Housing Act to specify that mortgage lenders "consider without prejudice the combined income of both husband and wife." The Equal Credit Opportunity Act, passed in late 1975, prohibits discrimination on the basis of sex and marital status in all transactions for obtaining or improving housing. In addition to these federal statutes, thirty-six states and the District of Columbia have enacted laws prohibiting sex discrimination or marital-status discrimination in housing markets. The bulk of this legislative activity clusters between 1972 and 1975.[11]

Statutes by themselves, however, may have little impact without strict enforcement mechanisms. Compliance with Title VIII relied primarily on complaints of borrowers until a legal suit (*National Urban League et al.* v. *Office of the Comptroller of the Currency et al.*, CA76-0718) resulted in agreements with the Federal Deposit Insurance Corporation, the Office of the Comptroller of the Currency, and the Federal Home Loan Bank Board to strengthen their enforcement efforts.

Enforcement of the ECOA was strengthened by Regulation B, effective in 1977, which requires, among other things, that borrowers be informed of why an adverse decision was made on a loan application and that they be informed of their rights under the law. In addition, Regulation B provides for mandatory record-keeping by lenders to facilitate monitoring of lending activities by the regulatory agencies. Such a data base will permit analysis of loan applications to test for aspects of sex and marital-status discrimination.[12]

Neither Title VIII nor the ECOA specifically prohibits the discounting of wives' incomes. Therefore it is a matter of legal interpretation whether such a practice is interpreted as sex or marital-status discrimination. However, the ECOA specifies that practices that effectively result in differential treatment on the basis of sex or marital status may be interpreted as discrimination. Such an "effects test" increases enforcement powers because it makes it more difficult for lenders to argue that what appears as discrimination is really based on some other measure of risk.

Are Wives' Incomes Discounted?—What the Data Show

The argument that the rise in two-earner families coupled with sex discrimination legislation has fed the recent housing boom has induced us to examine available data on the role of wives' incomes in housing consumption. The empirical work presented here investigates the extent to which discounting may have been occurring in recent years. Our model however, does not allow us to distinguish between discounting of wives' incomes by financial institutions and discounting by the household itself. If the wife is a temporary participant in the labor force—either by choice or because of cyclical declines in the economy—then the two-earner household may be reluctant to commit itself to the long-term expense of mortgage payments on the basis of the wife's temporary earnings.[13] However, as women's job security, job opportunities, and labor-market experience continue to increase, we can expect both households and financial institutions to view these earnings as less transitory and to count wives' incomes more heavily in housing-consumption decisions.

To examine the relationship between wives' earnings and housing consumption, we have used data from both the Annual Housing Survey and the Panel Study of Income Dynamics.[14] The data show that despite their higher incomes, the average (or median) house value for two-earner families is actually slightly lower than the average value of homes for one-earner families. This pattern, evident in 1969, 1974, and 1976 (see table 4-1), suggests that wives' incomes may be discounted in the housing-consumption decision either by households or by lenders.

This does not mean that wives' incomes are unimportant in housing-consumption decisions. If two-earner families tend to have the same housing outlays but higher incomes, then the fraction of income devoted to housing will be less. Hence the benefit of a working wife may not be in helping to

Table 4-1
Mean Values for Selected Characteristics of Recent Purchasers (Husband-and-Wife Families): 1974, 1975, 1976

	All Husband-Wife Families	*Both Husband and Wife Are Earners*	*Husband Earner, Wife Not*
1976			
House value[a]	$38,358	$38,165	$38,941
Total family money income[b]	$19,036	$21,246	$16,667
House value/income	2.7	2.0	3.5
Wife's labor income	$ 3,270	$ 6,123	—
Age of husband	37	35	40
Unweighted n = 2,607			
1974			
House value	$30,833	$29,882	$31,889
Total family money income	$16,110	$17,781	$14,530
House value/income	2.7	1.9	3.5
Wife's labor income	$ 2,584	$ 5,164	—
Age of husband	37	35	40
Unweighted n = 2,279			
1969			
House value	$18,118	$17,140	$19,683
Total family money income	$11,385	$11,960	$10,465
House value/income	1.6	1.5	1.9
Wife's labor income	$ 1,570	$ 2,566	—
Age of husband	38	36	40
Unweighted n = 172			

Sources: Annual Housing Survey, 1976 and 1974; *Panel Study of Income Dynamics*, 1969.

Note: Means are based on weighted data

[a]House value is an interval variable in the Annual Housing Survey. House value is estimated as interval midpoint except for highest and lowest brackets.

[b]This includes the labor income of husbands as well as any asset income of husband and wife, transfer income of husband and wife (pensions, Social Security, welfare), and income of other family members.

to purchase a more expensive home, but in keeping the housing burden low. It is interesting to note that in all three years, the two-earner families had on average substantially lower house value-income ratios, although both family types exhibited a sharp increase in this ratio over those years.

The difficulty with looking at average income and housing expenditures is that these do not take into account other critical factors. For example, these results could reflect differing age and wealth positions of one- and two-earner families. If most two-earner families are young with few assets and most single-earner households are older and wealthier, then the higher wealth position of the single-earner family could more than compensate for its lower average income. This suggests that some measure of permanent income or wealth is a superior indicator of housing demand. Differences in the age and wealth distributions of one- and two-earner families help to explain why the ownership rate is lower for the latter group (74 percent for husband-wife families with two-earners versus 78 percent for such families in which the wife does not work).

To control for differences in these other characteristics of one- and two-earner families, we estimated multiple regression models of housing demand. We examined both the decision to purchase and the value of recently purchased homes. In the first stage, the decision to purchase is expressed as a function of family income, wife's income, demographics, and previous tenure. In the second stage, the value of a newly purchased home is expressed as a function of these same independent variables:[15]

$$Pr(P) = a_0 + a_1 Y_t + a_2 Y_w + \sum_{i=1}^{6} b_i D_i + \epsilon \qquad (4.1)$$

$$HV = c_0 + c_1 Y_t + c_2 Y_w + \sum_{i=1}^{6} d_i D_i + \mu \qquad (4.2)$$

where HV = house value
$Pr(P)$ = 1 if household purchased home in past year, 0 otherwise
Y_t = total current family income
Y_w = the wife's current labor income
D_1 = size of family
D_2 = 1 if there are three or more adults, 0 otherwise
D_3 = 1 if the household head is white, 0 otherwise
D_4 = the age of the household head
D_5 = the age squared of the household head
D_6 = 1 if the household owned is previous residence, 0 otherwise.

Demographic variables are included to represent household tastes. While the ideal income variable is permanent rather than current income, we had no way of incorporating this into our models except to the extent that age of household head and previous ownership account for this.

The coefficients that most concern us are those on the income terms. In general, both dependent variables should be positively related to household income, but it may matter who earns the income. If the important factor is total income, regardless of who earns it, the coefficient on total income in our equations would be positive and significant, while the coefficient on wife's income would be insignificantly different from zero.[16] If, however, wives' incomes are discounted either by households or lenders, the coefficient on wife's income would be negative and significant.

The ownership equation (see table 4-2) provides us with some interesting insight into the purchase decision. When we estimate the model excluding previous ownership, we find that, controlling for differences in age and income of one-and two-earner families, the two-earner family is less likely to purchase a home. However, once we take into account previous ownership, two-earner families have purchase rates that are not significantly different from those of otherwise identical one-earner families. This suggests that neither households nor lending institutions are discounting wives' incomes in the decision to purchase. But since the previous owners are much more likely to purchase than otherwise similar renters, a crucial determinant of purchase appears to be the ability to accumulate a down payment in the form of equity in a previously owned home. As the price of housing continues to escalate, the importance of previous ownership as a determinant of purchase will increase.

Our house-value equation investigates the following question: Given that a household decides to purchase a home, does a two-earner family consume a house of equivalent value to that of an otherwise identical one-earner family? The negative and significant coefficient on wife's income in our regression results (see table 4-3) indicates that her income is discounted, and in contrast to the homeownership equation, this is true even when

Table 4-2
Probability of Home Purchase as a Function of Income and Demographics for Husband-Wife Families Who Moved in Past Year, 1976

Independent Variables	*Equation 4.1 Coefficient*	*t*	*Equation 4.2 Coefficient*	*t*
Y_t = total family income	.147D-04[a]	20.67	.784D-05	12.67
Y_w = wife's labor income	−.488D-05	−3.01	.125D-05	.91
D_1 = family size	.024	4.86	.009	2.11
D_2 = 1 if other adults	−.076	−3.76	−.030	−1.79
D_3 = 1 if white	.102	4.83	.016	.88
D_4 = age of husband	.016	5.85	.006	2.71
D_5 = (age of husband) sq.	.109D-03	3.57	−.575D-04	−2.23
D_6 = 1 if previous owner	—	—	.641	51.16
Constant	−.304		.016	
Mean of dependent variable[b]	.456		.456	
Number of observations	6558		6558	
R^2 (adj.)[c]	.133		.380	

Source: Data drawn from Annual Housing Survey, 1976.

Note: Dependent variable = 1 if household purchased in past year.

[a]Scientific notation, for example, .784D-05 = .00000784.

[b]Unweighted mean.

[c]Adjusted for degrees of freedom.

Table 4-3
House Value as a Function of Income and Demographics for Husband-Wife Families Who Moved and Purchased in Past Year: 1974, 1975, 1976

Independent Variables	*1976*		*1975*		*1974*	
	Coefficient	*t*	*Coefficient*	*t*	*Coefficient*	*t*
Y_t	1.213	12.92	1.105	28.5	1.171	30.2
Y_w	−.2614	3.45	−.4452	−4.61	−.3414	−3.78
D_1 = family size	153.5	.59	−669.8	−2.12	310.9	1.34
D_2 = 1 if more than 2 adults	−2701.	−2.66	1093.	− .936	−1660.	−1.68
D_3 = 1 if white	−1190.	.93	2328.	1.56	1814.	1.42
D_4 = age of husband[a]	808.3	5.51	946.7	.97	768.0	5.25
D_5 = (age of husband) sq.	8.335	−5.08	−91.99	−1.31	−8.385	−5.03
D_6 = 1 if previous owner	5227.	7.90	4841.	6.46	2903.	4.54
Constant	−4798.		−2945.		−7853.	
Mean of dependent variable[b]	$35,675		$38,031		$29,113	
Number of observations	2,607		2,000		2,279	
R^2 (adj.)[c]	.430		.389		.384	

Note: Dependent variable = house value.

Source: Data drawn from Annual Housing Survey, 1974, 1975, 1976.

[a]1975 regression also included terms for age of wife and (age of wife) squared and number of children in unit. Only the term for age of wife was significant at the .05 level. Inclusion of age of wife renders age of husband insignificant.

[b]Unweighted mean.

[c]Adjusted for degrees of freedom.

previous ownership is taken into account. We estimate this same equation for three consecutive years and find the same result.[17]

The negative sign of wife's income may partially be explained by the fact that two-earner families incur greater expenses than one-earner families, inducing them to spend less on housing. For example, the two-earner family may incur additional expenses for transportation and meals outside the home as well as for child care and housekeeping services. Alternatively, two-earner families may choose to consume less housing in order to reduce housework, since both husband and wife spend less time at home.

Nevertheless, our results indicate that wives' current incomes are discounted either by households or by lenders, suggesting that two-earner families have not exercised their full potential in housing markets. Moreover, if housing prices continue to rise, many one-earner families, who tend to bear relatively high housing/income burdens, may be induced to become two-earner families.[18]

Why the Current High Demand for Housing?

Despite the wide variety of state and federal statutes passed prohibiting discrimination, wives' incomes are discounted either by mortgage lenders or by households themselves. While our data are too early to ascertain the full impact of the ECOA, it is hard to believe that with a stroke of a pen, financial institutions have so radically altered their treatment of wives' earnings that this law has been a major contributor to the rapid rise in house prices since 1976.[19]

Rather than blaming the current escalation in housing prices on the recent antidiscrimination legislation, a far more reasonable culprit would appear to be the high rate of inflation in the economy as a whole, which has increased household demand for housing as an investment good.

In addition, demographic factors also have bolstered demand. Children of the postwar baby boom have reached the age at which households typically buy their first homes. Even with no change in the labor-force participation of women, such a bulge in this age group would have a dramatic impact on housing demand. But because the rising numbers of two-earner families are concentrated among these younger households (Census data show that nearly half the two-earner families are in the less-than-35 age bracket), the incomes of this cohort are higher than they have been traditionally, and as a consequence, the tax advantages of home ownership are greater.[20] This, combined with the general rise in nominal earnings and increased demand for housing as an investment good, has motivated households in the baby boom cohort to purchase their first home at an earlier age than has been typical in the past.[21]

In addition to these demand factors, changes in housing finance—many of which are discussed elsewhere in this book—are also helping to facilitate the current housing boom. While housing markets have long been subject to cyclical shortages of mortgage funds as these funds leave the housing market in search of higher returns elsewhere in the economy, recent innovations in the mortgage market, in particular, the introduction of money-market certificates, have significantly reduced the cyclical sensitivity of the supply of mortgage funds. In addition, GNMA passthrough securities have opened up capital markets to mortgage originators and usury ceilings in many areas have been lifted. We currently have record interest rates, but we are not observing the kind of disintermediation experienced in the past—especially in 1974. The increased usage of variable-rate mortgages may further insulate housing from cyclical financial constraints.[22] However, the introduction of graduated-payment mortgages may increase the demand for funds. This new instrument may be of particular interest to two-earner families, who have the expectation of two growing incomes to meet future higher mortgage payments.

As for the 1980s?

As the baby-boom cohort ages, demographic pressures on housing markets should ease, although this will probably not occur until the end of the 1980s. At the same time, however, as women's earnings become more permanent contributions to family incomes, we can expect the higher incomes of the two-earner family to be increasingly translated into higher housing demand.

Much depends on the continued high incidence of the two-earner family, which is itself a function of economic conditions. Over the long run, there is little reason to expect the labor-force participation of wives to fall. Indeed, the shortage of young (entry-level) workers that is anticipated for the mid-1980s can be expected to improve labor-market opportunities for women wishing to enter or return to the work force.

The numbers of two-earner families depends not only on the labor-force participation of wives, but also on changes in family structure—in particular, on rising divorce rates. Between 1960 and 1978, the divorce rate rose steadily from 2.2 per 1,000 total population to 5.1 per 1,000 population, and it has been estimated that if the current level of divorce continues on a lifetime basis, the proportion of marriages ending in divorce may approach 40 percent.[23]

Women's labor-force participation and the nation's rising divorce rate are clearly interrelated. Not only does divorce force many women to enter the labor market to support themselves and their families, but the economic independence that accompanies employment enables other women to leave bad marriages.[24] Today's two-earner family may well be tomorrow's divorced couple.

If the 1980s bring both higher labor-force participation rates for women and higher divorce rates, the structure of housing demand will vary from what would result from increased labor-force participation rates alone.[25] There would be more households, so more units would be required, but the average expenditure per unit would be less. Reduced space and increased mobility requirements of divorced individuals will increase the demand for rental housing, although the tax advantages of ownership may bolster the market for cooperative and condominium units. Our own tabulations of the 1976 Annual Housing Survey indicate that divorced males and females who own are more than twice as likely as owners in general to select condominiums or cooperatives. Of course, tax advantages of homeownership will be reduced because of the lower household incomes when one family becomes two households—and it will usually be the wife who suffers the greatest decline in economic well-being.

However, just as the increasing labor-force experience of married women can be expected to motivate households and lending institutions to apply more of wives' incomes to housing, the rising employment opportunities for single and divorced women should similarly increase their incomes and their housing options.

So as we look to the 1980s, we can expect an increasing importance of two-earner families in the housing market, with some restructuring of demand as the divorce rate remains high. How lenders respond to the earnings of wives, as well as of divorced and single women, will depend not only on their changing employment and income status, but also on the existence of legislation prohibiting discrimination. Perhaps the greatest impact of antidiscrimination laws in general is not so much through their direct enforcement, but through reducing the acceptability of discriminatory attitudes and behavior and accelerating the legitimization of new attitudes.

Notes

1. Between 1970 and 1978, the median price of an existing single-family home rose by 112 percent; over the same period, the Consumer Price Index (CPI) increased by only 68 percent. While the Median price of an existing home has risen more rapidly than the CPI in all but two years during the 1970s, existing house prices have risen most rapidly relative to the CPI in the most recent few years: between 1976 and 1978, the annual increases in the median price of an existing home were 7.9, 12.6, and 13.5 percent, as compared with increases in the CPI of 5.8, 6.5, and 7.6 percent. (The series

for existing single-family homes is published by the National Association of Realtors.).

2. For instance, Robert J. Mylod, president of the Advance Mortgage Corporation, has written that "at a stroke [the ECOA] increased the mortgaging power of millions of two-income families 40 to 60 percent . . . . It may be no more than coincidence, but the Act became effective in late 1975 and the current single-family housing boom and the escalation in home prices began in 1976" (*U.S. Housing Markets*, subscribers' special release, April 28, 1978).

3. These data were provided by the Bureau of Labor Statistics, U.S. Department of Labor. Earners' data are based on a question that asks whether either husband or wife had any earnings in the past year. 1967 is the first year for which these data are available. Earners' data should not be confused with labor-force participation rate data, which deals with people either working or looking for work during a particular week.

4. Paul Ryscavage, "More Wives in the Labor Force Have Husbands with 'Above-Average' Incomes," *Monthly Labor Review* 102 (June 1979):40. Also see David Ignatius, "Women at Work: The Rich Get Richer as Well-to-Do Wives Enter the Labor Force," *Wall Street Journal*, September 8, 1978, p. 1. This article notes that in the past there has been a strong negative correlation between a wife's decision to work and the economic status of the family. For instance, 1951 data indicated that women whose husbands earned less than $3,000 annually were 3 times as likely to work as those whose husbands earned more then $7,000.

5. "Wifely Recompense," *Journal of Commerce*, September 4, 1979.

6. Beverly Johnson, "Changes in Marital and Family Characteristics of Workers, 1970-78," *Monthly Labor Review* 102 (April 1979):49.

7. Ibid. The proportion of wives in the labor force with children under 6 years of age rose from 31 to 42 percent in the 1970s (a gain of 35 percent); for mothers with children between the ages of six and seventeen years of age, the rate rose from 49 to 57 percent (a gain of only 16).

8. Constant (1977) a dollar median family income rose at an annual rate of 2.96 percent between 1960 and 1970. Between 1970 and 1975, however, virtually all growth in the median family income was attributable to inflation. In constant dollar terms, it expanded at only 0.06 percent per year. Since 1975, growth rates have increased, but they have not yet reached the values of the 1960s. Between 1975 and 1977, median family income rose at an annual rate of 1.80 percent.

9. In addition to the deductibility of mortgage interest and property taxes, homeowners also benefit from tax-free income in the form of imputed rent.

10. Delayed child bearing has probably induced some two-earner families to select city rather than suburban locations and has helped foster

the "gentrification" of cities. For a discussion of how two-earner families are helping to alter the structure of cities, see Elizabeth A. Roistacher and Janet Spratling Young, "Working Women and City Structure: Implications of the Subtle Revolution," *Signs (forthcoming)*.

11. Ketron, Inc., *An Examination of State Laws Prohibiting Sex and Marital Status Discrimination in Housing and Home Finance*, March 1978, pp. 8-10.

12. Some studies of sex discrimination in mortgage lending have already been undertaken. Currently, Robert Schafer of Harvard University is doing an analysis of California and New York mortgage data to test for discrimination on the basis of sex and marital status. See also Harold Black, Robert L. Schweitzer, and Lewis Mandell, "Discrimination in Mortgage Lending," *American Economic Review* 68 (May 1978):186-189. this study has found negative and insignificant coefficients for females, marital status (not married), and blacks with respect to acceptance of mortgages. The coefficients on sex and marital status were not statistically significant, but this may be a function of the scarcity of observations on women. These results, however, are based on a voluntary survey of banks lending decisions undertaken jointly by the Office of the Comptroller of the Currency and the Federal Deposit Insurance Corporation.

13. Because women have lower seniority and less work experience, one would expect them to be more vulnerable to layoffs than men of the same age. In addition, employers may discriminate against women when cuts are made. In fact, the aggregate data do not indicate that the layoff rates of women are significantly higher than those for men. But women tend to be employed in industries and occupations where employment fluctuates little over the business cycle, and these aggregate data do not standardize for industrial-occupational mix.

Even though aggregate layoff rates are not higher for women, female unemployment rates are higher than those for men. This appears to be related primarily to the higher turnover rates of women. Women move in and out of the labor force more frequently, and each time they re-enter, they typically go through a period of unemployemnt. Barry R. Chiswick and June A. O'Neill, *Human Resources and Income Distribution, Issues and Policies* (New York: Norton, 1977).

14. The Annual Housing Survey is available for the years 1973 to 1976, although we utilized only the last 3 years. The Michigan Panel Study of Income Dynamics is available every year since 1968. Unfortunately, when we cut the sample down to married couples who purchased in a given year, the Panel Study was left with only 150 to 300 cases in a given year, and regression results were generally insignificant for wife's income. Hence we base most of our analysis on the Annual Housing Survey, for which we have more than 2,000 cases of married couples who moved and purchased in each year.

15. Both equations are estimated using ordinary least squares (OLS). Ideally, the ownership model should be estimated by a nonlinear technique such as logit analysis. Past research on home ownership, however, had indicated that while estimates of coefficients vary between O.L.S. and logit, the direction and significance of coefficients remains unaltered. See Elizabeth A. Roistacher and John L. Goodman, Jr., "Race and Home Ownership: Is Discrimination Disappearing?" *Economic Inquiry* 14 (March 1976):59-76.

16. Alternatively, our model could have been specified using such independent variables as wife's income and all other family income (most of which would be husband's income). The interpretation of the coefficients would be somewhat more straightforward, since in this alternative specification of the house-value (house purchase) equation, the marginal propensity to consume (purchase) out of wife's income is equal to the coefficient on wife's income.

In our specification, the marginal propensity to consume (purchase) out of wife's income is obtained by summing the two income coefficients:

$$HV = aY_t + bY_w = a(Y_0 + Y_w) + bY_w = aY_0 + (a + b)Y_w$$

where HV is house value, Y_t is total income, Y_w is wife's labor income, and Y_0 is income other than wife's labor income. The advantage of our specification is that the test for significance of the wife's income is simpler; it involves testing whether one coefficient is statistically different from zero rather than whether one coefficient is statistically different from another coefficient. Interestingly, the coefficients on total income in our specifications are exactly identical to the coefficients that would occur on other income in the alternative specifications.

17. In addition to our analysis of Annual Housing Survey data, we also estimated our house-value model using the Panel Study of Income Dynamics for the years 1969 through 1976. These results indicate that the coefficient on wife's income has been getting less negative over time and indeed actually becomes positive in recent years. In most years, however, the coefficients are not statistically significant, probably because there are only 150 to 300 observations of new purchases in any given year of the Panel Study.

18. This suggests a simultaneous-equation model of housing demand rather than the single-equation model presented in this chapter. In the more complex model, both wives' labor-force participation and the demand for housing are jointly determined.

19. We were told one interesting anecdote that presents a different view on the impact of the legislation. A woman active in a political organization concerned with sex discrimination in lending is said to have complained that no cases have been raised under the ECOA because as soon as a lender

learns that a woman is planning to bring suit, the organization will offer her the requested loan.

20. "The Big Clout of Two Incomes," *Dunn's Review* 113 (April 1979):43.

21. Data from the 1970 Census and the 1976 Annual Housing Survey indicate that husband-wife families are purchasing homes at earlier ages: in 1970, 49 percentof husband-wife families in which the husband was less than 35 years of age were homeowners, and by 1976, the figure for that age group had increased to 58 percent.

22. The possibility that Regulation Q might be lifted remains one more factor that could further reduce the cyclical shortage of mortgage funds.

23. Bureau of the Census, "Divorce, Child Custody, and Child Support," *Current Population Reports*, Special Studies Series P-23, No. 84, U.S. Department of Commerce, June 1979, p. 1.

24. Findings from the negative income tax experiment also have indicated that one of the things that married couples do with additional income is free themselves of one another (*New York Times*, November 16, 1978, p. 23). See also Center for the Study of Welfare Policy, "Dynamic Analysis of Marital Stability," Research Memorandum No. 58, SRI, Inc., December 1977, revised September 1978.

It also has been suggested that the two-earner family must frequently deal with more tension as a result of the increased demands on a couple's time, and that this also may lead to marital instability. See Douglas R. Sease, "Women at Work: Marital Relations Often Undergo Strain When Wives Get Jobs," *Wall Street Journal*, September 19, 1978, p. 1.

25. Of course, the remarriage rate of divorced women is quite high. One Census survey indicates that 66 percent of women who had been divorced had remarried. For those divorced women who remarried, the median duration of divorce was 3.2 years. (Bureau of the Census, "Divorce," 10). Hence, even with substantial remarriage rates, there will be significant period during which divorced women (and men) will require a separate housing unit.

5 Housing for Single Parents

Robert S. Weiss

In the course of several studies dealing with one or another aspect of single parents' lives, my colleagues and I interviewed over 200 single parents, some of them several times. The interviews did not follow a set outline of questions, but rather were conversational, eliciting from our respondents reports of their experiences in various areas of their lives. The respondents, although they do not together constitute a probability sample of single parents, do include among them the separated and divorced, the bereaved, and the never-married from all income levels. They represent much of the range of single-parent situations.

Among the issues discussed in many of the interviews were problems associated with housing. This was especially the case when respondents' marriages had just recently ended, since then respondents were likely to be confronted with the question of whether to move. Often respondents were deeply ambivalent about the matter. Ambivalence about housing is certainly not unusual: on the one hand, attachments to the place one lives may be strong, and moving would be troublesome; on the other hand, it might be nice to have an extra room or more outside space or to be located nearer a city's services or further from urban problems. However, after marital dissolution ambivalence about housing appears to be especially strong. An owned and cherished house may feel to the newly single parent to be all that remains of security. And yet the house may now seem too large, too difficult to keep up, too expensive, and too much a relic of a life now in the past.

It is not unusual for a separated mother to insist on retaining her family home only to decide, a year or two after her separation agreement has been approved in court, that it would be better to move. Many of those single parents who do remain in their former homes during the first year after their marriages have ended nevertheless move by the second or third year. Widows, it appears, are less likely eventually to move than the separated or divorced, largely because insurance payments sustain their income, but also because they are somewhat less likely to decide on changes in career or lifestyle that would be facilitated by changed residence.

A more detailed description of our samples is given in Robert S. Weiss, *Going It Alone: The Family Life and Social Situation of Single Parents*, (New York: Basic Books, 1979), pages xiv-xvi. Interview extracts reprinted with permission.

Except among the very poor, and except for those situations in which the remaining parent had always been the primary earner, the ending of a marriage results in a severe reduction in the income available to a household. Household expenses, however, remain nearly constant: food may cost somewhat less, but only transportation and clothing costs are significantly reduced. The result is that the parent left to care for the children must meet nearly the same level of expenses with a decidedly smaller amount of money. Single parents often report that for the first time in their lives they find themselves dunned by creditors. One recently separated mother, typical of many, said:

> You have more bills at the end of the month than you have money to pay them. You never catch up. You pay five dollars to the department store, ten dollars to the hospital bill. You put off the bills that can be put off, and you pay the bills that are going to come after you.

Some single parents attempt to reduce the mismatch between income and expenditure by renting space in their homes. Yet this is a solution that can bring with it a new set of problems. By renting out space, the single parent becomes responsible for ensuring that the space is properly maintained. In addition, there is now a new person to be integrated into the household whose personality and lifestyle may be troubling. If expenses still remain unmet, the single parent may decide to give up:

> I advertised for a girl to share the house. And I was really lucky and I found a real nice girl who lived with me for about six months. Then one of the girls I worked with moved in. I had to ask her to leave after she ran into the neighbor's garage with her car, which she was driving drunk. I went through three girls in a year and a half. And it had got to the point where I physically couldn't keep up with working all day, taking care of the baby when I got home, and spending two or three nights in the yard weeding and mowing and, in the winter, shoveling snow. It was just more than I could handle. And the tax assessments were starting to come. I was paying my part of the the street paving. It was just too much. I sold the house.

There might, perhaps, be merit in government-guaranteed, low-cost, "hardship" second mortgages that would permit single parents who own homes to avoid moving until their children are older. Or, perhaps, information and referral services might be developed that would aid those single parents owning homes to manage the problems of renting. However, as things stand, it it often difficult for single parents to remain in homes they own.

Single parents who had lived in rented space when they were married are likely to experience similar pressures to move when their marriages end. Their residences are likely to have represented the best they could afford at a time the incomes available to them were higher. With the ending of their marriages, the residences would be too expensive. In addition, they would have a much weaker sense of identification with their homes than would those who had owned them.

Single parents, like others in search of a new home, generally decide first on the area in which they want to live. A desirable area might be one in which the single parent already lives and so has roots, or it might be an area in which live a sister or brother or the single parent's own parents, or it might be an area where the single parent has friends, or it might be near to the single parent's work or be reputed to have good schools, or it might simply be an area the single parent believes would be interesting or pleasant to live in. There may be two or three areas within which the single parent begins to look for a new home, each with its own combination of attractions and uncertainties:

> You're looking to find something within the price range that's adequate, and in a neighborhood that's not dreadful. I know girls who lived in a neighborhood I wouldn't want to live in, and actually they're not saving any money by the time they've paid for all the extras just to keep the children in the home, or in Cub Scouts, or at the Y, where if they lived in a neighborhood where the children could be out playing, they wouldn't have to spend that extra fifty dollars a week. So the first thing is definitely price, but within an area. The next thing is schools. And then there is the question of aesthetics. And I wanted good public transportation so I wouldn't have to pay for a car.

Some single parents report having been discriminated against at some point in their search. Particularly if they have looked for housing in areas of strong housing demand, where most apartments or houses are rented to married couples, single parents, especially those who are separated or divorced, may find landlords or rental agents reluctant to rent to them. The single parents may be told there is a risk that they will be financially unreliable, or that their social life will be too active for the neighborhood, or that they will be unable to supervise their children. Or, without being given any reasons, they may be turned away when their familial status becomes known:

> You go to people and you say, "I'd like to rent a two-bedroom apartment." And they say, "For how many?" And you say, "Myself and my two children." "Are you a widow?" "No." "Oh. Are you divorced?" And—it's just a few of the people—"Well, gee, I think the rooms would be too small for you."

As it happens, our respondents were all Massachusetts residents, and Massachusetts has a strong antidiscrimination statute on its legislative books that proscribes discrimination on grounds of marital status. Clearly, passing laws against discrimination is only a partial remedy.

Often the first housing decisions of single parents turn out to be mistaken. Some part of the reason for this may be that single parents feel themselves to be less desirable than other possible tenants and so settle for what they can get. But more important, it would seem, is that single parents have neither the time nor the resilience for protracted search. In addition, their emotions may be so unsettled that their judgment is impaired. Moreover, they are not likely to know at first what sort of residence will work for them, and as they become more accustomed to single-parent life, their needs may themselves change. In any event, single parents seem regularly to require a second move or even a third before they finally locate a residence that suits them well enough that, for a few years, they no longer think of moving.

Just as the separated and divorced are more likely than the widowed to move in the first place, so they are more likely to experience repeated moves. The following history, reported by a divorced mother of two, is in outline a common one:

> After my husband left I had to sell my house. The real estate broker told me about an apartment complex that included some three-bedroom townhouses. I just assumed that it would have some married people with kids, but it turned out to be a singles' complex. At first it was fun, because it was just parties constantly. Maybe I needed that right then. Immediately after I moved in, somebody was knocking at my door, "Come on out and have a good time!" I thought, "Gee, this is terrific." But after a while the place really got to seem like a zoo. I mean, people assuming that everything was on a walk-in basis for everybody, because it was all singles. So I decided to move.
>
> I found this woman in a similar situation to mine who had a ranch house. She was moving down to her basement and was going to rent out the upstairs. It was in a super single-family-residence neighborhood. But it had no soundproofing. And my kids made a lot of noise. And she was not a very pleasant person. She got very picky. I was running my fan too long, and she came up to inspect. Little, picky hassles. I stayed there only a few months.
>
> I found the place I'm now living because I knew some people who lived up there. I hadn't heard anything terribly favorable one way or another about it. But I knew there were children. There was a pool. And there is a play area: they have swings and a slide and all that type of thing. And I could have a dog. I don't have the maintenance that I would have if I lived in a duplex or rented a house. I don't have to shovel the snow, I don't have to cut the grass or prune the shrubs. And I don't have to deal with a landlord on a one-to-one basis. I pay my rent and I'm not bothered. There are no personal hassles over anything.

This trial-and-error approach to the location of acceptable housing is enormously costly in energy and morale. But it is difficult to judge whether a government-sponsored information and referral service, say, would be an improvement over the service provided by real estate agents, prospective renters' informal social networks, and the newspaper classified columns. There may perhaps be some need for renters' agents who might help guide renters to residences in which they will want to remain. Yet, how a service of this sort might be structured, regulated, and paid for is uncertain.

The problems single parents report having with places to which they have moved mainly fall under three headings: the neighborhood, the housing, and the landlord or his representative. Let us consider each in turn.

Neighborhoods

Proximity to services can be important for single parents because they have no one at home to look after their children while they run an errand. One single parent, who moved because she felt the crowded and unsafe urban area in which she had previously lived was an undesirable setting for her children, discovered that she had been dependent on living not far from stores:

> Now that I am in a suburban neighborhood, I have to drive everywhere, and that takes time. I'm always getting in and out of that God-damned car and running here and running there and running here and running there.

The neighborhood also must be within easy commuting range of the single parent's work. A nine-to-five work day, with half an hour commuting time on either end, can just be managed by a single parent who also must, in the morning, prepare the children's breakfasts and get them off to school and then, in the evening, prepare their dinners, supervise their evening activities, and get them to bed. A longer commuting time would force the single parent further to skimp on time with the children and might well impose an additional source of fatigue.

The character of relationships with neighbors may be more important to the single parent that it would be to a married parent. The single parent is more likely than would be a married parent to have to ask for occasional favors: perhaps, especially, for availability to the children should the single parent be called away from home. But equally important, the single parent, without an adult ally within the home, is less able to tolerate an unfriendly neighborhood and more easily threatened by antagonism. Mothers without men in their homes may appear to others to be safer to impose on. Some mothers tell of janitors or other maintenance men singling their children out for threats of punishment, although other children who had fathers to defend them had been equally mischievous. In an instructive report, one woman, herself a single parent, described how an unpleasant neighbor's attitudes toward another single parent changed after the intervention of a boyfriend:

> This is our downstairs neighbor. He came up to her apartment yelling about cars. This wasn't the first time that it had happened. He said that she had blocked the driveway and he couldn't get his car in. And she was all for saying, "Okay, okay, I'll take care of it." Her boyfriend was with her and they were in their night clothes watching television. So she said, "I'll get dressed and I'll take care of it." A few minutes later, she hadn't even had time to get dressed, he's back pounding on the door, "Will you do something about that car!" And the boyfriend evidently said, "I don't care how it looks, I'm going to take care of him," because the boyfriend went to the door and I heard him yelling, "You're nothing but a troublemaker!" And he went on with you're this and you're that, and, "I am sick of your coming up here and picking on her." And all of a sudden our downstairs neighbor says, "I don't want any trouble. All right. I don't want any trouble." And he went down the stairs and he's never been up the stairs to pound on her door since.

The very best neighborhood for a single parent appears to be one in which there are other families, so that the single parent's children have playmates, one that is safe, so that the single parent can permit the children to play outside by themselves, and one that is also unquestionably accepting of the single parent. Stable family neighborhoods, whether or not they include other single parents, can be satisfactory, so long as they are accepting:

> Where I am now, almost everyone on the block is a teacher. And there was one family who gave an open Christmas party, no questions, everybody in the neighborhood shows up. Another did carol singing and served eggnog afterwards. And everyone shows up for that. So I lucked out with my neighborhood. There is one other girl there that is a single parent, but everybody else on the block is married. There are kids of all ages, all sizes, kids all over the place. It's very much a community neighborhood and, luckily, I've been taken into it.

Transient neighborhoods are not necessarily undesirable. Some transient neighborhoods foster a sense of mutuality among residents on the basis of the similarity of their life situations. Married-student housing offers one example. However, most transient neighborhoods remain communities of strangers, without the social support necessary for a lone parent.

Some single parents move to a neighborhood in which they have kin. Often this appears to be a good idea. When a marital partnership fails, for whatever reason, relationships with kin can provide a kind of safety net. The children's grandparents or aunts or uncles may look after them now and again and also may provide the single parent with company and moral support. The children have available to them a second home to go to should the single parent for any reason have to be away. Some single parents have been able to work full time only because they lived near enough to the children's grandparents so that the children could go to the grandparents' home on returning from school.

Unfortunately, relatives also can be intrusive and critical. Living too near to relatives makes the single parent's life available to their scrutiny. A formula might be proposed for the proper distance from kin of the single parent's residence: in walking distance, with no heavily trafficked street between, but no less than a block away, and preferably around a corner.

Housing Characteristics

Single parents, like others, want housing that is attractive, in good repair, neither cold in the winter nor unbearably hot in the summer. Like others, single parents want adequate space. It is important that the single parent have a private bedroom. But where a married couple would insist on a private bedroom, a single parent may be tempted to make do with a convertible couch in the living room. This comes about because single parents, as do other parents, believe that older children should have bedrooms for themselves or, at the very least, that older children should be required to share bedrooms only with siblings of the same sex. However, the apartments available to them may have only two bedrooms—or just one. One mother who gave both bedrooms in her two-bedroom apartment to her children had this to report:

> I know a lot of people give the bedrooms to the children and sleep in the living room. That's horrible, because there's never a place that's your own and you get sort of psychologically, "Oh God, I need my own room!" You want to lie down for five minutes in the middle of the day and suddenly you're right in the middle of things. Just as I'd lie down, the front door would open and one of the neighbor's kids would walk in. I mean, there's just no privacy. And there's no such thing as leaving a bed unmade, because you have to rip the bed apart first thing in the morning, to turn it back into a couch.

Apartments in public housing, which is all that many single parents can afford, tend to be limited to two bedrooms. For many single-parent families, two bedrooms are one too few.

The most important room in a single parent's residence is apt to be the kitchen. Much of the time that the single parent and the children are together is time when the parent is cooking or cleaning up after a meal. In many single-parent homes the kitchen also doubles as a workroom, where mending and ironing are done. It is almost essential, for single parents, that the kitchen be large enough to accommodate simultaneously parent and children and their activities.

> The kitchen is very important, because if you are working and a mother, you see your kids at breakfast time and as soon as you get home it is supper time. Any my son was little and needed a lot of sleep. So he was going to bed at seven o'clock. So I would get home at five-thirty or quarter-to-six, and between that time and seven or seven-thirty, I would fix the meal and eat the meal and get him ready for bed, and sometimes have to squeeze in grocery shopping or laundromat or something else. So most of the time we had together was kitchen time.

As the children become older, single parents may need somewhat different housing layouts. When the children are very small, the best housing layout might be a single large room, or near equivalent, for then the parent would never be far from the children, no matter what the parent was doing. A woman who lived in a railway flat with her only son said:

> If I was in the kitchen and my son was in any other room, he could not see me. And if he asked me something or I asked him something, we had to shout to be heard. And it was very difficult to communicate with someone who was out of sight.

However, as the children move into latency and on to adolescence, it becomes more important for parent and children to be able to pursue activities independently: for the children to be able to listen to their music without imposing on the parent, and for the parent to be able to have friends in without requiring the children to go to their rooms. A layout that separates rooms from one another—one perhaps approaching the railway flat—then becomes valuable.

It may seem impossible to accommodate the need of single parents for different organizations of space as their children become older without requiring single parents to change residences. Yet there might be room for exploration of ways in which interior space can be made flexible, in which, perhaps, the one large room most desirable when children are small can be partitioned into two rooms when the children become older. At the very least, single parents might be made aware of the experiences of others so that they can better decide the housing layouts most appropriate to their current family situations.

Landlords, Management, and the Like

Single parents who rent, especially if they cannot afford more than a minimal rental, frequently complain about their relationships with those responsible for their space, both private landlords and administrators of public housing. In this they may not be different from any other group of tenants. Yet the difficulty single parents have in dealing with conflict, because of the absence of an adult ally within their homes, can intensify their feelings of helplessness and frustration.

When single parents have an apartment in a structure in which the landlord also lives, issues of intrusiveness can arise. The landlord may comment on the single parent's lifestyle, the comportment of the single parent's children, or, apparently more rarely, on the way the single parent keeps the apartment. It takes only a single comment, even one that is carefully casual, for the single parent to feel under surveillance.

Single parents living in public housing are sometimes aware of neighbors' interest in their lives but seem not to feel that their lives are being scrutinized by housing administrators. In one instance, however, a neighbor had complained to a housing administrator about the behavior of a mother's former husband at the time he lived with her, and the mother was later made aware that materials dealing with her private life were in a file folder in the administration's office.

Single parents whose landlords live outside their neighborhoods are more likely to complain of inattention than of intrusiveness. Landlords may try to minimize the time and money they give to maintaining their apartments. Most single parents seemed to accept that painting the apartment was their responsibility, but felt unable to deal with the plumbing system, the heating system, or the exterior structure of the building they lived in. One single parent said that her landlord was a pleasant enough man, but that he was letting his property go:

> There are cracks in the windows. The doorknobs are falling off. I write letters and I underline everything that has to be done. And he does nothing. When we had the last snowstorm, the steps were shoveled, but after that they iced up. And I didn't know why they iced up, but my father stopped by and he said, "The gutters are rotten and the water is dripping onto the steps. That's why they are icing up." So I wrote the landlord a letter and I underlined this. So the next day he came up and he put some sand on the steps. But if water is dripping from rotten gutters, it is going to continue, no matter what you put on the steps.

Single parents who live in public housing can find it equally difficult to have repairs made to their residences, even though there is full-time maintenance on the site. The maintenance men feel that, emergencies aside, tenants should take their turn, which is only fair. However, these maintenance men are likely to have little time left after dealing with emergencies, and their list of other requests is apt to be very long. One single parent found it useful to report her defective oven and sticky windows to the Director of Public Housing rather than to the maintenance man in her building. The same sort of problem was dealt with in the same way by a woman who lived in university housing:

> My four-year-old son got very sick. Maybe he should have been hospitalized. I took him to the doctor, and it had snowed that morning, and when we came back the back door had blown open and all the snow had blown onto the kitchen floor. And I couldn't shut the windows in the bathroom. I had never been able to shut them. And I called the head of housing and he said that nothing could be done. And I told him I was going to call the Chancellor, and I did. But in the meantime he had gotten frightened at how angry I was, and he had called the head of maintenance and within half an hour a carpenter was there and he stayed for two days fixing things.

A few single parents we talked with reported that they had been required to leave their space by landlords who wanted the space for themselves or members of their families. One woman spoke bitterly of having painted and repaired her apartment herself, buying her own supplies, after which she was asked by her landlord to move so that the landlord's daughter could have the apartment.

These instances of problems with landlords or with housing management, while they suggest what can go wrong, do not characterize all landlord-tenant relations. A few single parents spoke of landlords who had been friendly and helpful, acting at times as babysitters for their children. But friendly relations with landlords seemed less usual than relationships in which there was tension. Indeed, the existence of a friendly landlord, or one who merely respected the single parent's privacy and provided adequate maintenance, was often thought to be sufficiently noteworthy to be remarked on.

Planning Housing for Single Parents

Single parents, as a group, may have more than their share of difficulties. They are apt to be underfinanced and overburdened; they must meet a parent's responsibilities with a single person's resources. It would be good if their housing could be a source of sustenance for them rather than an additional set of problems.

It is important that planners be aware, as they think about single parents, that single parents often must find housing with little time for search and little opportunity for comparison of alternatives, and that in their encounters with real estate agents, landlords, and neighbors, they have no other adult to turn to for support. They may well still be enmeshed in the emotional aftermath of marital dissolution. They are likely to be imperfectly aware of the importance to them of a supportive neighboring community, of adequate bedroom space, of a responsible landlord. Better understanding of their special needs by planners, as well as others, might reduce the frequency with which their decisions, made under pressure, turn out to have been mistaken.

Part III
Changes in the Rental Market

6 The Uncertain Future of Rental Housing

George Sternlieb and
James W. Hughes

It is only within the post-World War II era that America moved from a nation of renters to one of homeowners. As late as 1940, only 43.6 percent of the nation's dwelling units were owner-occupied. Currently, two-thirds of all Americans own their own homes. The shrinkage in rental tenure and its replacement by homeownership has been viewed as a principal symbol of an affluent society—the triumph of the rise of real incomes and housing purchasing power on the part of most Americans. Yet as the cost of homeownership increases, as real housing-buying power diminishes, and as demographers point to the wave of youthful households emanating from the baby-boom generation (as well as an increasing number of elderly), there has been an expectation that rental housing will once again assume a more formidable position within America's housing-production system. This expectation, however, has been far from realized; indeed, construction statistics indicate that nongovernmentally aided multifamily rental housing starts have approached the lowest levels of the post-World War II years.[1]

What makes this construction shortfall ominous is the fact that, concurrently, rental vacancy rates have reached unprecedented low levels, striking a sudden awareness that the private rental housing industry of the United States is in trouble. Why is there this growing gap between nominal expectation and reality? Why has the market failed to respond to low vacancy rates as traditional housing economics would apparently require? What new factors have been ushered into prominence in this regard?

Throughout the decade of the 1970s, the cumulative effects of a number of forces have melded together to produce a dynamic whose momentum increasingly challenges the historic assumptions underpinning rental housing markets. For the purposes of this chapter, we have isolated five of the more significant phenomena.

1. The emergence of a *postshelter society*.
2. The *cream-skimming* of the rental inventory.
3. The escalation of rental *cost structures* in an inflation-ridden, energy-scarce era.

The author is grateful for the research assistance provided by Deborah Chankin, on whose unpublished directed research paper, "Housing Shortage and Empty Space: Underutilized Housing in Urban America," parts of this article are based.

4. The institutionalization of *rent control* and the proliferation of *condominium conversions*.
5. The prospective coming of age of the *baby-bust generation*.

As these forces mature and self-reinforce one another, there is growing doubt not only about the future viability of the private rental housing industry, but also about its capacity to survive in its more traditional forms.

A Postshelter Society

A dominant rationale for housing choice in America today is no longer shelter from the elements, but rather housing as investment, as a form of tax shelter, and as one of the few successful refuges from an inflationary environment. This has completely restructured the realities of the market, although probably not our rhetoric or the thinking of many housing planners. We have become a postshelter society. Excluded from this new society are those lacking the means—capital resources and taxable incomes—to secure membership. Yet, as we will note subsequently, the fallouts are rapidly slipping from the domain of the private housing market.

The inflation in housing costs for homeowners is essentially counterbalanced by a parallel inflation in real or conjectured capital values. In terms of cash-flow immediacies, homeowners—particularly newcomers to the market—seemingly are willing to devote unprecedented portions of their income to supporting housing acquisition. The alleviatory elements are nominally tax coverage and capital gains potential. Thus, when homeownership is employed as a leveraged investment, its support can be accepted quite realistically as the sum both of nominal shelter costs plus the surrogate quanta of funds that would once have gone into more traditional forms of investment—private insurance, savings accounts, and the securities market.

The rental-housing situation is quite different; there are no tax advantages to the tenancy; rents must be paid from posttax income.[2] Moreover, there is no compensatory investment element offsetting rents. The rental market and its soaring cost structures—both in terms of development and operation—must compete within an environment devoid of the incentives attached to homeownership.

However, such rationalizations have by now assumed the status of an established convention. Indeed, it probably has become a dominant folk wisdom of our time. What has not been fully appreciated, however, is the residual impact this situation has on the rental market—it has generated a very marked cream-skimming of higher-incomed households out of the potential pool of renters.

The Dynamics of Cream-Skimming

Within the overall context of the growth of personal incomes in the United States, there are very significant differences as a function of household configuration. As shown in table 6-1, families, for example, as of 1977 had incomes nearly triple those of unrelated individuals.[3] Within the total family set, moreover, there is a wide range of income variation, which may well exemplify a new class partition within the United States: households with one versus two or more persons working. For example, male-headed households having a wife in the paid labor force had median incomes in excess of $20,000, fully a quarter higher than that for all families. Female-headed households (no husband present), on the other hand, had incomes ($7,765) less than half that for all families.

The ramifications of these partitions are amplified when the occupant characteristics of owned versus rented units are reviewed (table 6-2). Male-headed households (with wife present), which include the most affluent household types, increased by 5.3 million over the 1970-1976 period in the owner-occupied sector; in contrast, the renter-occupied sector lost 1.5 million such households. Other male-headed households had a rate of increase in rental facilities double that of the owner-occupied sector. Similarly, female-headed groups had a far higher rate of growth in rental units than held true in owner-occupied accommodations. This variation in market penetration by household type means that rental facilities are increasingly the refuge of household configurations of lower income—those characterized by more substantial resources are increasingly attracted to homeownership.

Even when disaggregation is undertaken by age sector within various household configurations, it is those with far less income who occupy rental facilities (table 6-3). In sum, therefore, the market penetration of rental units

Table 6-1
Income Changes: Families, Unrelated Individuals, and Households (U.S. Total), 1970-1977, and 1977 Income by Family Configuration

Unit	*1970*	*1977*	*Change: 1970 to 1977* *Number*	*Percent*
Families	$9,867	$16,009	$6,142	62.2
Unrelated individuals	3,137	5,907	2,770	88.3
Households	8,734	13,572	4,838	55.3
Family Configuration				*1977*
Total families				$16,009
Male-head Total				17,517
Married, wife present				17,616
Wife in paid labor force				20,268
Wife employed				20,534
Wife unemployed				13,855
Wife not in paid labor force				15,063
Other Marital Status				14,518
Female Head				7,765

Source: U.S. Bureau of the Census, *Current Population Reports*, Series P-60, No. 118, "Money Income in 1977 of Families and Persons in the United States," Washington, 1979.

Table 6-2
Renter and Owner-Occupied Units: Household Composition, 1970 and 1976
(numbers in thousands)

Household Composition by Age of Head	*1970*	*1976*	*Change: 1970 to 1976 Number*	*Percent*
Total Owner-Occupied	39,886	47,904	8,018	20.1
Two-or-more-person households	35,124	41,626	6,502	18.5
Male head, wife present	30,806	36,108	5,302	17.2
Other male head	1,298	1,629	331	25.5
Female head	3,019	3,889	870	28.8
One-person households	4,762	6,278	1,516	31.8
Total Renter-Occupied	23,560	26,101	2,541	10.8
Two-or-more-person households	17,171	17,541	370	2.2
Male head, wife present	12,759	11,291	−1,468	−11.5
Other male head	1,143	1,730	587	51.4
Female head	3,270	4,520	1,250	38.2
One-person households	6,389	8,560	2,171	34.0

Source: U.S. Department of Commerce, U.S. Bureau of the Census, *Current Housing Reports*, Series H-150-76, "General Housing Characteristics for the United States and Regions: 1976," Annual Housing Survey: 1976, Part A, Washington, 1978.
Note: Numbers and/or percents may not add due to rounding.

increasingly captures the lower-incomed households of American society. Tenant incomes have significantly lagged those of owners.

Cost Structures and Income Lags

The end result of this process of cream-skimming is revealed by the data in table 6-4. From 1970 to 1976, median gross rents increased by 54.6 percent. The median incomes of rental occupants, however, increased by only 28.5 percent. Within the owner-occupied sector, median incomes increased by 48.5 percent, more than one and a half times as fast as that for renters. While median house values increased even more abruptly (88.9 percent) than rents, to those who were homeowners throughout this period, this escalation, rather than being ominous, served to rationalize their homeownership decision. For those who became owners—or wish to become owners—the 88.9 percent increment is a justification for assuming relatively high cost burdens.

Among renters, the median rent/income ratio moved from 20 percent in 1970 to 24 percent in 1976. At this writing, there is some indication that it is over the 26 percent level. The capacity of tenants to absorb higher rent levels is questionable—the level of inflation in operating and construction costs is far in excess of their income increases.

Consequently, the long progression of increased proportions of

Table 6-3
Owner- and Renter-Occupied Household Income, by Household Configuration, U.S. Total, 1976

	Owner-Occupied	*Renter-Occupied*	
Total households	$14,400	$ 8,100	.56
Two-or-more-person households	15,900	9,500	.60
Male head, wife present	16,800	11,600	.69
Under 25 years	12,800	9,800	.77
25 to 29 years	16,200	12,600	.78
30 to 34 years	17,900	13,000	.73
35 to 44 years	19,700	13,200	.67
45 to 64 years	18,600	12,600	.68
65 years and over	8,400	6,600	.79
Other male head			
Under 65 years	15,800	8,600	.54
65 years and over	9,000	6,000	.67
Female head			
Under 65 years	9,600	5,700	.59
65 years and over	7,100	5,100	.72
One-person households			
Under 65 years	8,600	7,800	.91
65 years and over	4,200	3,400	.81

Source: U.S. Department of Commerce, U.S. Bureau of the Census, *Current Housing Reports*, Series H-150-76, "General Housing Characteristics for the United States and Regions: 1976," Annual Housing Survey, 1976, Part A. U.S. Government Printing Office, Washington, 1978.

Note: Numbers and/or percents may not add owing to rounding.

multifamily housing starts that are governmentally aided is not a temporary aberrant; it is merely one manifestation of a new split in the housing market. With the exception of luxury apartment houses and developments that have aspirations toward condominium conversion, there will continue to be an increasing proportion of America's rental facilities that is supported directly or indirectly by government. Adding significant pressure in this direction is the continued ratcheting of energy costs to even higher thresholds, rendering the investment economics of the private rental housing package increasingly dubious.

Rent Control and Condominium Conversion

Other byproducts of sustained inflationary pressures are the attempts by local governments to buffer (and pacify) their constituencies via one of the few avenues open to them—rent control.[4] The classic elements of property rights have changed abruptly from a concentration on landlord privileges to

Table 6-4
Renter- and Owner-Occupied Units, Income, Rent, and Unit-Value Relationships, U.S. Total, 1970-1976

	1970	*1976*	*Change: 1970 to 1976* *Number*	*Percent*
Renter-Occupied Units				
Median gross rent	$108	$167	$59	54.6
Median income	6,300	8,100	1,800	28.5
Median Rent/Income ratio[a]	20%	24%	4%	20
Owner-Occupied Units				
Median House value	$17,100	$32,300	$15,200	88.9
Median Income	9,700	14,400	4,700	48.5
Value income ratio[a]	1.7	2.2	0.5	29.4

Source: U.S. Department of Commerce, U.S. Bureau of the Census, *Current Housing Reports*, Series H-150-76, "General Housing Characteristics for the United States and Regions: 1976," Annual Housing Survey, 1976, Part A. U.S. Government Printing Office, Washington, 1978.

[a]Published ratios.

the protection of tenancy. Regardless of the equities involved, this has made investment in rental property risky. As the uncertainties of securing acceptable cash flows in rent-regulated environments mount, the enthusiasm of private investors has continued to diminish.

Such strictures, in conjunction with the desire to capture part of the withdrawal of more affluent tenancies and to capitalize on the momentum of "homeownership as investment," have led to the phenomenon of condominium conversion, the shift of units of rental tenure to ownership status. Regardless of the dynamics at work—conversion as a takeout mechanism for survival and/or as a very lucrative investment strategy—the end results are similar, a reduced potential for expansion of the private rental housing inventory.

The Baby Bust and Future Demand

The preceding elements can all be viewed as an outgrowth of high endemic levels of inflation and a flight from currencies in general and the dollar in particular. As they converge together, a dynamic has been forged whose consequences are increasingly ominous to rental-housing markets. Yet another independent stricture must be factored into the basic equation—a perception of the coming of age of the baby-bust generation.

The sharp declines in fertility in the past two decades have forced the necessity of acknowledging shrinkage as a basic component of future projections. As the nation proceeds through the balance of the century, there will be sharp contractions in population, first in the 18- to 24-year-old sectors, and subsequently in the 25- to 34-year-old categories.[5] Thus, as the baby-bust generation matures, the number of initial household formations will decline, and with it seekers of rental accommodations. The perception of this impending demand lag raises significant doubts on the use of investment—which requires long periods of time to justify its existence—to meet and satisfy relative short-term needs.

As the housing-buying power of Americans declines and the one-family-unit syndrome—at least for newcomers to the field—becomes more elusive, there will be a growing requirement for alternative mechanisms. Private rental housing, at least in large-scale development, has become the victim of inflation and tax policy. Can it, and should it, be reshaped for the future?

Notes

1. See George Sternlieb and James W. Hughes, *Housing Prospects and Problems* (New Brunswick, N.J.: Rutgers University, Center for Urban Policy Research, *forthcoming*), for an analysis of this trendline.

2. The Internal Revenue Service has recently disallowed attempts by New York State to amend its real property tax law to entitle renters to an itemized deduction for property tax levies (included in their rent payment).

3. Households are generally of two types: primary families and primary individuals. *Primary families* comprise two or more related individuals and are usually subdivided into three types: husband-wife families, male-head (no wife present) families, and female-head (no husband present) families. *Primary individual* households comprise either a single person living alone or two or more unrelated individuals.

In table 6-1, the data for unrelated individuals include persons in group quarters (not in households). The household data comprise both families and those unrelated individuals residing in households (primary individual households). The data in tables 6-2 and 6-3, secured from the *Annual Housing Survey*, are solely for households. However, male-head (wife present) configurations are, by definition, families. Other male-headed, or female-headed configurations can either be families or primary individual households.

4. See George Sternlieb and James W. Hughes, "Rent Control's Impact on the Community Tax Base," *The Appraisal Journal* 47, 3 (July 1979):381-395.

5. For a detailed analysis, see George Sternlieb and James W. Hughes, *Current Population Trends in the United States* (New Brunswick, N.J.: Rutgers University, Center for Urban Policy Research, 1978); and George Sternlieb and Robert W. Burchell, *Multifamily Housing Demand: 1975-2000*, a study prepared for the Joint Economic Committee, Congress of the United States, U.S. Government Printing Office, Washington, 1978.

Part IV
Components of Inflation in Owner-Occupied Housing

7 Housing-Price Inflation in Houston, 1970 to 1976

Barton A. Smith and
Robert Ohsfeldt

During the last decade, increasing attention has been given to the rapid rise in the costs of housing in the United States, especially owner-occupied housing. This increase in housing costs is considered greater than the increase in prices of most other consumer goods and larger than the growth in nominal income (see table 7-1). An increase in the relative price of housing will have two effects on housing consumption: (1) a substitution effect that will reduce housing consumption as consumers shift away from increasingly expensive housing to *relatively* inexpensive consumer goods, and (2) an income effect that will reduce housing consumption as consumers' real incomes decline owing to the large increase in housing prices. Because of the nature of housing as a heterogeneous consumer durable, increases in the relative price of housing also are likely to alter the composition of the typical housing bundle consumed, again reflecting adjustments in consumer behavior to changing prices and real income.

Casual observation of housing-market conditions during this decade indicates that a declining proportion of households can now afford single-family, owner-occupied housing because of the fact that housing prices have increased faster than income. Changes in new housing construction seem to provide evidence that a partial adjustment to the higher relative price of housing has already begun. In particular, new housing construction, especially in urban areas, now tends to be more dense and less luxury oriented. New housing today is typically smaller (than during the 1960s) in terms of both lot size and square feet of living area, even though it is being built in areas of inferior accessibility where urban land rents are presumably low. In addition, many households, now unable to obtain traditional detached owner-occupied housing, are turning to townhouses and condominiums to satisfy their desire for homeownership.

The "Price" of Housing

While some aspects of the changing housing market of the 1970s are predictable and understandable, considerable confusion still exists because the concept of the "price" of housing is so poorly defined in both the

Table 7-1
Comparison of Percentage Changes in Consumer Prices, Housing Values, and Income: United States and Houston, 1970-1976

United States Averages	
Median house value[a]	89%
Consumer Price Index[b]	47
Nominal per capita disposable income[b]	73
Houston	
Mean house value[c]	97%
Consumer price index[b]	52
Nominal per capita personal income (Houston SMSA)[d]	85

[a]U.S. Bureau of the Census, *Current Housing Reports*, Series H-150-75, 1978.
[b]*Economic Report of President 1978*.
[c]Houston Chamber of Commerce 1979.
[d]Bureau of Economic Analysis. *Local Area Personal Income*, vol. 7, 1971-1976.

academic literature and popular usage. Part of the confusion stems from a failure to distinguish between the capital price of housing and the annual cost of consuming owner-occupied housing. While the capital costs of housing have risen enormously during the 1970s, the rise in the annual effective cost of housing has been dampened by such factors as the benefits of favorable tax treatments toward owner-occupied housing and the implicit capital gains to homeownership. However, the annual costs of housing have been pushed upward by such factors as the rising opportunity costs of capital, that is, mortgage interest rates.[1]

While changes in the annual costs of homeownership are both interesting and policy relevant, an analysis of such changes must be preceded by careful examination of the capital costs of housing. In this chapter, the difficulties associated with developing and measuring a useful concept of the capital cost of housing are given primary attention. Recognition is given to the reality that housing is a complex commodity distinguished by a wide variety of attributes and distributed across numerous urban locations of differing amenities. The most popular method of measuring the extent of housing-price change, which involves making simple comparisons of the average transaction price of homes sold between two time periods, is shown to be grossly inadequate and is subsequently dismissed in favor of a complicated but more accurate technique. The popular approach fails not only to adequately control for differences in both structural and neighborhood quality between the two periods, but also to provide the depth of information necessary to fully analyze price changes relevant to consumer decisions. In fact, a key problem with past studies is that price, as applied to housing, has been inadequately developed and defined.

Focus of This Chapter

This chapter first develops a concept of housing price that has universal application to all urban housing markets. Then empirical results are presented focusing on changes in housing prices that have occurred in Houston, Texas during the 7-year period January 1970 to December 1976. Estimates of a housing-price index for an average home in Houston are provided that adequately control for changes in structural and neighborhood quality. In addition to an average price index, the analysis is expanded to examine the extent to which implicit marginal values of the various attributes of the housing bundle (both structure and neighborhood) have changed during this time interval. It is these changes that are expected to alter consumer decisions with respect to the structural attributes bought and urban location selected. In addition, the empirical results indicate the extent of differences in the rate of home-price inflation among houses of different sizes, vintages, and locations.

Houston provides a particularly interesting urban area to analyze because of the rapid change that has occurred in a very short period of time. In the 1970s, Houston experienced exceptional growth and, subsequently, the problems that accompany such growth: a rapid decline in air quality, a sharp increase in crime, and an ominous increase in highway congestion exasperated by the absence of viable mass transit. A high proportion of the migration into the Houston metropolitan area has consisted of upper-middle-class households. Many of these new residents brought with them unusually large amounts of wealth generated from the accumulation of sizable home equities acquired in previous areas of residency. This migration has thus affected the demand both for new dwelling units and for high-quality housing. Together these factors are shown not only to have substantially affected the *average* price of housing in Houston, but also to have altered the metropolitan *structure* of housing prices across both quality levels and neighborhood areas.

Theoretical Background: A Review

Housing: Quantity versus Quality

Traditional economic analysis has not been particularly well developed for dealing with economic problems where quality is the primary choice variable. Typically, standard analyses of supply and demand are defined in terms of *price* and *quantity*. In order to define the quantity of housing, this consumer durable is often thought of as a capital good that produces a flow of "housing services" over time. Within this context, Muth and other economists related the quantity of housing services to the level of *quality* provided by a dwelling unit.[2] House value HV thus becomes the product of the quantity of housing services Q provided by a dwelling unit times the price per unit of housing services P: $HV = P \cdot Q$.

This basic framework has considerable merit because of its simplicity and easy transferability to standard microeconomic theory. By considering the price of housing in terms of the price per unit of housing services (or the price per unit of quality), Muth established an important first step in properly defining price. However, Muth's concept of housing is somewhat limited in its empirical appliction since Q, and therefore P, is not directly nor easily measurable. In addition, this simple construct fails to adequately distinguish between quantity (dwelling units) and quality (units of housing services per dwelling unit).[3] In essence, the Muth model assumes perfect substitutability between quantity and quality, an incorrect assumption that leads to considerable problems in analyzing housing markets and in estimating housing prices or price indices.[4]

Housing and Location Theory

Before considering alternatives to Muth's concept of housing and price, it is instructive to consider the nature of the price of housing within the context of standard analyses of urban price functions. While such an approach is a basic part of urban economics, some of its simplest generalizations have been ignored by those estimating housing-price indices. In the simple model of a monocentric urban area, housing prices are shown to fall with distance from the central business district *CBD* until some point D^*, the edge of the urban area, as shown in figure 7-1.[5] At that location, housing prices reflect the minimum costs of construction, since urban land rents are zero.

From figure 7-1 it becomes immediately evident that there does not exist a single price for housing, but a *price function* related to location.[6] Although consumers face different prices across locations, housing-market equilibrium requires utility for each household type to be equalized across the metropolitan area. Those paying higher interior prices are exactly compensated by the lower costs of commuting to the central business district. Consequently, references to the price of housing are ambiguous.[7]

While the problem of settling on a concept of price within the static equilibrium context of locational differences is complicated, the problem of defining a *change* in housing prices can be even more difficult. Again, within the framework of a simple Muthian urban model, consider a situation in which rising income increases the demand for housing services such that more urban space is required. The Muthian result is an expansion of

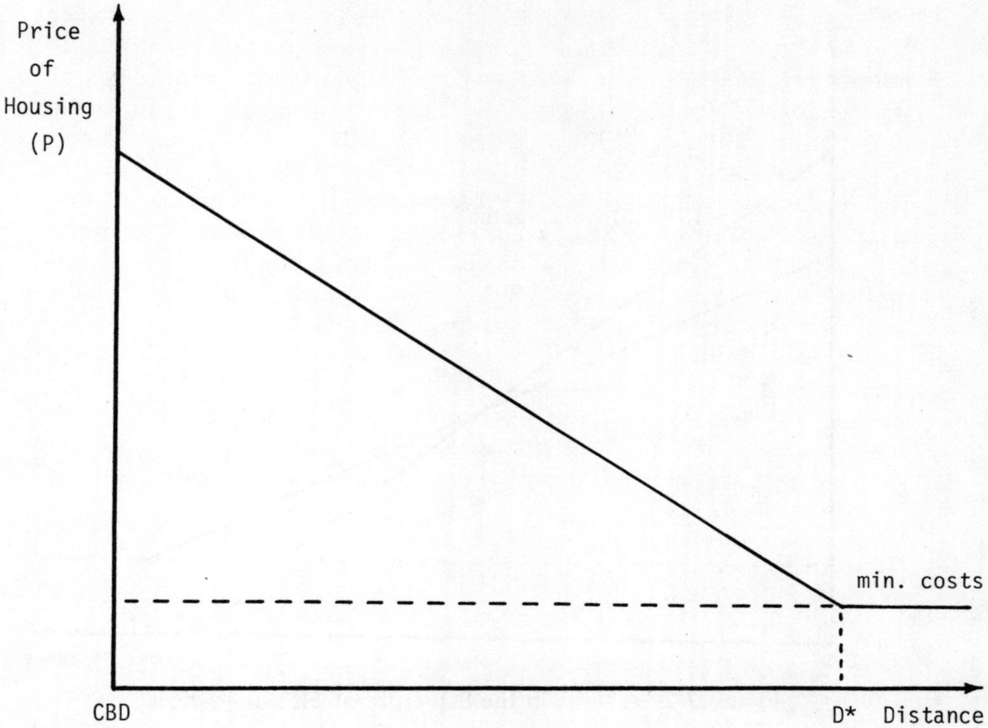

Figure 7-1. An Urban Price Function

the city and a reduction in the price gradient.[8] An improvement in urban transportation (and hence accessibility to the central business district) also will expand the city and flatten the price function. Both examples, one involving a demand increase and the other involving an increase in the effective supply of urban land, can be illustrated by the same diagram, figure 7-2.

Standard partial equilibrium analysis of supply and demand applied to the first example would suggest that the increase in demand should simply lead to a higher price. However, urban theory, as illustrated in figure 7-2, indicates that, in fact, prices fall in some areas and rise in others. Similarly an improvement in transportation and, subsequently, accessibility to the central business district, which will open up new suburban areas for development (an increase in supply), will not simply lower housing prices. Some prices will rise. Such examples are typical of the complications that arise in attempting to describe changes in housing prices over time. Clearly, analyses of price changes must take into account that at any one point in time housing prices differ across locations differentiated by a wide variety

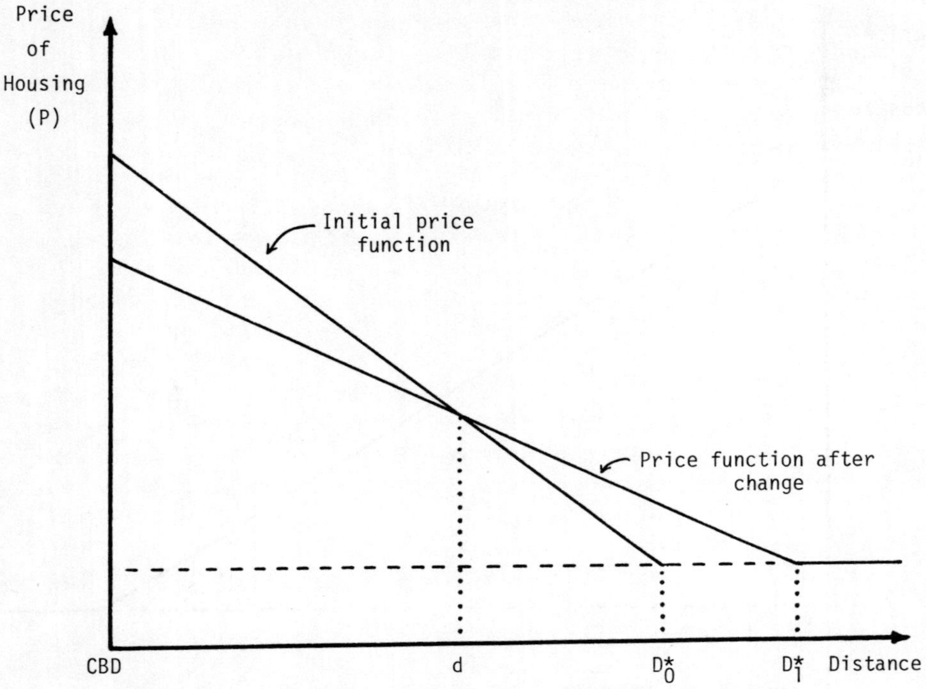

Figure 7-2. A Shift in the Structure of Housing Prices

of amenities (or disamenities), and that over time the entire price structure is likely to change. Any single index will fail to accurately describe potentially complex price changes and will be misleading as a simple index of metropolitanwide housing prices.

Average versus Marginal Price

With the *price* of housing defined as the implicit market price per unit of quality or housing services, the observable market value of a house is the product of this price and the quantity of services: $HV = P \cdot Q$. This price of housing thus is equal to HV/Q. Aside from the problems of measuring Q and therefore calculating P, this concept of price is much too simplistic, since it implicity assumes that the average price per unit of quality is equal to the marginal price of additional quality; that is, $HV/Q = P = \delta HV/\delta Q$.[9] However, the marginal (incremental) cost of an additional amount of living area in the same approximate location could be more or less than the average cost. Assuming that home construction involves significant fixed costs, as exist in other production activities, it may be hypothesized that marginal costs will be lower than average costs. Even though it is the marginal price of housing service (the cost of additional housing quality) that is relevant to consumer decisionmaking, it is almost always the average price (or cost) of housing that is quoted.

The relationship between house value and quality should be written in more general form as $HV = f(Q)$, where average price AP equals house value divided by Q [that is, $AP = f(Q)/Q$], and marginal price MP equals the first derivative of the house-value function with respect to Q [that is, $MP = f'(Q)$]. For illustrative purposes, consider a linear specification of the function f, where $AP \neq MP$; namely, $HV = a + b \cdot Q$. $AP = b + (a/Q)$ and $MP = b$. Changes in the costs of factor inputs could cause b to increase without significantly altering a. Thus the percentage increase in the average price of housing will be less than the percentage increase in the marginal price of housing. However, changes in the value of neighborhood amenities could increase overall home prices across all quality levels without affecting the marginal price for additional quality. The coefficient a rises, but b remains the same.

Figure 7-3 illustrates the necessity of carefully distinguishing between alternative forms of housing-price change. Three HV functions are depicted. Line *aa* represents the initial price function relating house value to housing quality, where HV_0 is the value of a home with Q_0 level of quality. Line *bb* illustrates a case in which the *marginal price* of quality has risen although the total value of a Q_0 home HV_0 is unaffected. However, even though consumers face the same total price for a Q_0 home, because they now face a higher price for additional quality (hence a greater savings for less quality), in the long run consumers are expected to adjust their housing consumption by buying less housing quality. Line *cc* indicates that housing costs at all levels of Q have risen. The result is that a Q_0 home now costs HV_{cc}, but the marginal price of additional Q is unchanged. While such a price change no doubt will result in a real income effect that might result in less housing consumed, the fact that additional quality costs no more than it did initially is likely to minimize the impact of this price change on consumer behavior.

Examples such as these demonstrate the importance of analyzing housing prices from a perspective that recognizes the existance of a price structure for housing across quality types as well as an urban price structure across locations.

The Multidimensional Nature of Quality

For purposes of simplicity, previous examples have considered quality as a single dimensional concept. However, housing provides a wide variety of

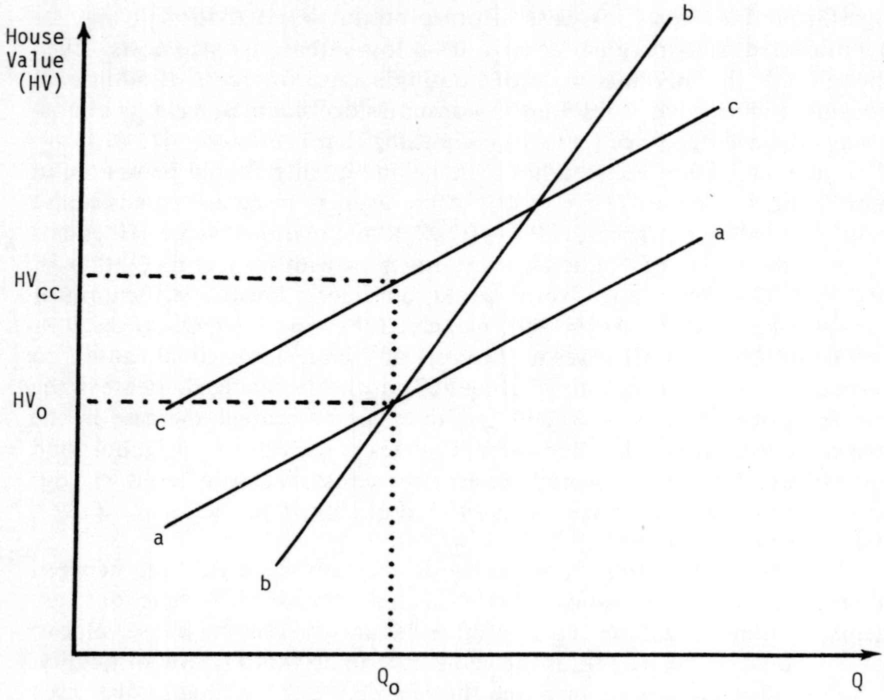

Figure 7-3 Alternative Forms of Housing Price Charges

services and, in the Lancastrian tradition, may be thought of as a composite good that provides a wide variety of services stemming from a multitude of different attributes.[10] Consequently, it becomes necessary to control for differences in housing attributes in order to estimate price indices for a standard (quality constant) housing bundle. To achieve this objective, two approaches are typically used: repeat sales analysis and hedonic regression estimation. The former approach statistically estimates price changes by analyzing the sales prices of houses that had been sold and then resold during the time period studied. However, the use of this method introduces data-selectivity bias and implicitly requires the assumption of identical price changes across locations, which is the most likely explanation for the erratic price indices typically estimated.[11] In the hedonic-estimation literature, the determinants of housing values are statistically estimated as a function of a set of structural and neighborhood attributes.[12] Past efforts using either approach are initially flawed by a failure to provide a rigorous definition of price and, consequently, by a failure to distinguish between *average* and *marginal* price. Typically, studies attempt to estimate a single price index instead of analyzing changing price structures, which entail many prices relevant to any complete analysis of housing markets.[13]

To ameliorate the problems of past studies, several important guidelines should be followed when estimating changes in housing prices. First, one must carefully account for changes over time in the overall structure of housing prices across locations and quality levels. Second, analysts should consider differences in both average housing prices and the implicit marginal values of each important attribute in the housing bundle consumed. Third, separate hedonic regressions must be estimated for each year studied to allow marginal values to change independently over time. Fourth, equation specifications must provide the flexibility necessary to allow marginal prices to differ across neighborhoods and quality levels. Indeed, the estimation of separate equations for broadly defined neighborhoods or quality levels may be the most efficient way to achieve this latter objective. In the following section, it is these basic guidelines that provide the foundation for the approach taken to analyze housing-price inflation in Houston during the 1970s.

Housing Inflation: Houston, 1970 to 1976

Incorporating the concepts discussed earlier, changes in single-family home prices were analyzed for a 7-year period beginning in January 1970. Separate regressions were estimated for 1970 and 1976 in order to maximize the degrees of freedom in the ordinary-least-squares (OLS) regression analysis. Of the alternative specifications attempted, the exponential (or semilog) provided the best fit and most reasonable coefficients. Initially, a single equation was estimated for the entire Houston metropolitan area for both years. Later, several subgroup equations were estimated to expand our understanding of the changes in the general price structure and to complement the findings from the overall metropolitanwide equations. In all cases, both average price indices and marginal price changes are examined and reported.[14]

Data

The data used came from detailed appraisal records and included the actual selling price of each home, the time of sale, the homes' locations, and over fifty characteristics of each dwelling. Of these fifty characteristics, eleven were ultimately used as the primary structural attributes included as explanatory variables. In addition, this data set was augmented by locational data that included several accessibility variables as well as data on crime, pollution, school quality, and census information such as the racial composition of the neighborhood.[15] Special dummy variables were included to account for locational premiums paid to live in independent incorporated cities existing within and surrounded by the city of Houston. A brief description of the variables used in the OLS regression analysis is provided in appendix 7A. the 1970 data set contains 2,111 observations, while the 1976 data set contains 3,585. In no case were any data subgroups analyzed with less than 1,000 observations.

Empirical Results

Table 7-2 presents the estimated regression coefficients for the entire metropolitan area. The R^2's obtained are typical of all regression R^2's, which ranged from .80 to .90. The t values given in parentheses indicated that most coefficients estimated are highly significant statistically with quite narrow confidence bounds.[16]

Table 7-2
1970 and 1976 Regression Estimates of Housing Value for Houston Metropolitan Area

Variable	*1970 Coefficient*	*1976 Coefficient*	*1970 Mean*	*1976 Mean*
Structure				
SQFT	.0379 (30.9)	.0368 (39.6)	15.5	16.5
BATH	.2649 (8.32)	.1840 (8.05)	1.65	1.81
$BATH^2$	−.0405 (5.12)	−.0153 (3.33)	3.14	3.67
LS	.0269 (5.01)	.0308 (4.86)	.967	.882
COND	.0426 (6.94)	.0401 (8.27)	4.02	3.91
AC	.0803 (5.50)	.1260 (12.8)	.523	.671
NGRGE	.0012 (0.22)	.0679 (12.4)	.884	1.58
KIT	.0643 (7.24)	.0740 (11.9)	.899	1.35
FIRE	.1360 (10.2)	.1690 (17.5)	.223	.426
HMAGE	−.0045 (2.88)	−.0001 (0.07)	12.7	12.1
$HMAGE^2$	−.0022 (0.60)	.0037 (1.45)	2.74	2.76
Neighborhood				
BELL	.0248 (0.65)	.2290 (5.53)	.014	.007
WUNI	.1330 (3.73)	.3980 (12.8)	.016	.013
WSG	.608 (1.56)	.1360 (4.11)	.014	.011
ESG	−.0288 (1.77)	−.0136 (0.95)	.091	.067
NOCITY	−.0023 (0.18)	.0333 (3.67)	.219	.347
POLUTN	−.0232 (7.32)	−.0490 (17.8)	7.88	7.40
PCBLK	−.1850 (9.48)	−.2460 (14.7)	.129	.113
PCMEX	−.3020 (7.07)	−.2560 (6.46)	.099	.085
CBD	−.0067 (5.44)	−.0156 (15.7)	10.3	11.7
NFRWY	−.0012 (0.54)	−.0096 (7.18)	1.67	1.97
Constant	5.169	5.920		
$\bar{R}^2$	.861	.870		
S.E.	.197	.198		
N	2111	3585		

Note: t = statistic in parentheses; dependent variable = log house value.

The estimated coefficients associated with square feet of living area indicate that each incremental 100 square feet, *ceteris paribus*, increased the value of a 1970 home by 3.79 percent and a 1976 home by 3.68 percent. Square feet of living area dominates the regression equation, accounting for almost two-thirds of the explained variance in house values. Variables reflecting high levels of quality also add significantly to the equation's explanatory power. This is especially true for the number of baths, fireplaces, kitchen modernization, and central air conditioning. It must be remembered, however, that the coefficients of these variables should be interpreted with care, because their probable correlation with unincluded "quality-type" variables is likely to bias the coefficient estimates upward by incorporating these additional influences.

Changes in coefficients for several variables are especially interesting. For example, in 1970 the presence of central air conditioning added 8 percent to the value of a home, while by 1976 the impact had increased to almost 13 percent. In percentage terms, the influence of pollution more than doubled in 7 years. An increase in pollution by only 10 micrograms increases home values in 1976 by nearly 5 percent. This indicates that over a 40 percent differential exists for similar housing between the lowest- and highest-polluted areas.

Perhaps the most notable change that occurred during the 7 years was the rapid increase in premiums paid for residency within many of the separate but incorporated communities that lie within and surrounded by the city of Houston. The most startling example is West University, a community with ideal accessability located on the near west side. The regression result indicates that homes, *ceteris paribus*, cost nearly 49 percent more in West University. This is a considerable increase over the 14 percent premium that existed in 1970. Of course, these figures underestimate the overall premiums being paid in the area, because one also must include the premiums associated with the superb accessibility of the area, the low levels of pollution, and the nonminority, upper-middle-class status of the neighborhood.

The overall Houston metropolitan results also indicate that housing prices in minority areas are considerably discounted. While the percentage discount in black areas has increased even further during the 7-year period, it appears that the discount in Hispanic areas has moderated some. This latter phenomenon may be due to a more rapid decentralization of the Hispanic population in Houston, where most areas have at least 5 percent Hispanic population and few areas have more than a 40 percent Hispanic concentration.

In 1970 residency 1 mile closer to the central business district added less than 0.7 percent to the value of a home; in 1976 it added 1.6 percent per mile. This means that in 1976 the same home selling for $50,000 at the urban fringe, some 30 miles from the central business district, would sell for nearly $70,000 at a location 20 miles closer. An $80,000 home would sell for about $112,000 given the same improvement in accessibility. Actually, this level of premiums for accessibility is not that abnormal compared with other large U.S. cities. What is unusual, however, is that only 7 years earlier commuting was so relatively effortless in Houston that accessibility premiums paid through the housing market were almost nonexistent.

Average Price Index

To construct the average price index implied by the 1970 and 1976 OLS regressions, a standard technique for decomposing regression equations is used. The average price is given as the difference in the mean value of the dependent variable after adjusting for differences in the means of the explanatory variables (the average level of attributes). This is calculated by summing the differences in the constant terms and the differences in the coefficients weighted by the average level of attributes in the 1970 bundle.[17]

Since the OLS regression was estimated using a semilog specification, this difference, calculated as .561, indicates a 75.3 percent (antilog of .561 minus 1) increase in the average price of housing. Setting 1970 as the base year, the 1976 price index is 1.753.

Marginal Prices

Marginal price estimates are the first partial derivatives of each estimated regression equation evaluated at the means.[18] Then each separate pair of marginal prices (1970 and 1976) is analyzed. Table 7-3 presents estimates of the implicit marginal values or price for twelve important structural and neighborhood attributes. Note that in all cases the percentage increase in marginal prices exceeds the increase in the average price. This means that the price function across quality has become much steeper and that the increase in the slope of the function was greater than the overall upward shift on the entire price structure.

The marginal price of standard variables such as square feet of living area and lot size more than doubled, but this was a relatively modest increase compared with the marginal price of several other attributes. Interestingly, the marginal price of housing attributes is generally lower than the more-often-quoted average price. At the end of 1976, the *marginal price* of additional square feet of living area was only $16 per square foot as opposed to the typically quoted *average price*, which ranges from $32 to $35 per square foot. Although the price of land rose from $0.55 per square foot

Table 7-3
Changes in Housing Prices: Average and Marginal (Houston Metropolitan Area)

	Changes in Marginal (Attribute) Prices		
Attribute	*Marginal Price (1970)*	*Marginal Price (1976)*	*Percent Change*
SQFT	$7.77	$16.0	105
BATH	3756	6652	77
LS	55	134	142
COND	873	1741	99
AC	1636	5471	232
KIT	1318	3213	144
FIRE	2788	7338	163
POLUTN	48	213	347
PCBLK	38	107	182
PCMEX	62	111	80
CBD	138	677	392
NFRWY	24	412	1630
Average price index	1.00	1.75	75

to $1.34 per square foot, this latter figure is still quite small compared with the average price of urban residential land, which in some areas can exceed $6 per square foot.

The marginal price of attributes typically associated with high-quality features of housing such as central air conditioning, modernized kitchen, and fireplaces all increased significantly more than the marginal price of the exterior and interior size variables. However, the greatest increase in housing-price marginals were for neighborhood characteristics. Most noteworthy is the increase in costs for incremental improvements in air quality and accessibility. As much as $21,300 is shown to be paid in 1976 as a premium for residential areas with the minimum level of air pollution. While the costs of improved accessibility are still less than $700 per mile for the average home, this represents a startling 400 percent increase in just 7 years. Furthermore, the premium for more expensive homes is even greater and could exceed $1,500 per mile.

In conclusion, the overall rate of housing-price inflation of 75 percent for the first 7 years of this decade, in light of the general rate of inflation throughout the United States during this period, is large but not enormous. As an investment, housing brought an approximate 8.3 percent annual capital gain, which was not much better than what could have been earned with certificates of deposit, except for the obvious tax advantage of homeownership. Of greater significance were the large increases in the marginal prices of various attributes of single-family dwellings, especially those attributes associated with higher quality and locational advantage.[19]

The rise in home prices is likely to limit the availability of owner-occupied housing to a smaller proportion of Houston's population, but the major constraint faced by new home buyers today is their ability to acquire quality housing in quality neighborhoods with good access to work. It is these homes that have surpassed the reach of the middle-class home buyer in Houston. Prices of the cheapest available *new* housing have increased only about 40 percent during these 7 years, while the price of better-quality housing with superior accessibility has mushroomed in value. As a consequence, Houston is becoming a metropolitan area where only the affluent can live in much of the central city.

Price Indices for Different Housing Types and Different Locations

To examine in some more detail the differences in housing-price inflation for different levels of housing quality and different locations, several sets of submarket regressions were run and averaged, and marginal price indices were estimated. Table 7-4 provides estimates of changes in marginal prices along with the average price indices for six selected housing subgroup categories. For the most part, the results were as expected. Housing prices within the city limits of Houston increased 76 percent, while prices beyond the city boundaries increased only 59 percent. Older housing built prior to 1967 experienced an 81 percent inflation rate, while the newer home prices rose only 57 percent, a rate interestingly less than the growth in personal income. These results are consistent with the metropolitanwide results, which show the greatest amount of home-price inflation occurred in older neighborhoods with good accessibility.

Table 7-4
Estimated Average Price and Marginal Prices of Selected Attributes by Subgroups, 1970-1976

A.

	All Cases			
Attribute	*1970*	*1976*	*Change ($)*	*Change (%)*
SQFT	$7.77	$16.0	8.21	106
LS	55.2	134	78.6	142
AC	1646	5471	3825	232
FIRE	2788	7338	4550	163
CBD	138	677	540	392
POLUTN	47.6	213	165	350
PCBLK	37.9	107	68.9	182
Average	1.00	1.75	—	75

Table 7-4
Estimated Average Price and Marginal Prices of Selected Attributes by Subgroups, 1970-1976

B.

	Old Housing				*New Housing*			
Attribute	*1970*	*1976*	*Change ($)*	*Change (%)*	*1970*	*1976*	*Change ($)*	*Change (%)*
SQFT	$6.78	$11.9	5.12	76	$8.62	$18.5	9.88	115
LS	41.9	114	102	244	92.4	105	12.6	14
AC	1421	5498	4077	287	1007	2424	1417	141
FIRE	1876	7568	5692	303	3845	6912	3067	80
CBD	95.5	1032	937	981	131	482	351	268
POLUTN	36.7	218	181	493	58.4	130	71.6	123
Average	1.00	1.81	—	81	1.00	1.57	—	57
	In Houston				*Out of Houston*			
SQFT	$6.09	$11.8	5.71	94	$11.8	$24.8	13.0	110
LS	40.2	89.2	49.0	122	59.4	173	114	191
AC	1604	5516	3912	244	2001	1776	−225	−11
FIRE	2437	7896	5459	224	2246	4069	1823	81
CBD	204	805	601	295	197	614	417	212
POLUTN	55.1	173	118	214	207	486	279	135
PCBLK	35.5	106	70.5	199	28.9	37.7	8.8	30
Average	1.00	1.76	—	76	1.00	1.75	—	75
	Large Housing				*Small Housing*			
SQFT	$8.95	$13.3	4.35	49	$7.33	$18.5	11.2	152
LS	91.2	219	128	140	50.5	63.8	13.3	26
AC	2267	6747	4480	198	1049	3513	2464	235
FIRE	6543	9676	3133	48	1600	2905	1305	82
CBD	321	1155	834	260	63.4	384	321	506
POLUTN	98.0	474	376	384	21.3	108	86.7	407
Average	1.00	1.61	—	61	1.00	1.84	—	84

The fact that smaller homes experienced a greater rate of inflation than larger homes (84 versus 61 percent) at first seems to contradict the earlier finding that the marginal price of quality had increased substantially, resulting in a steeper price function across structural quality levels. However, of all the structural attributes, the marginal price of additional square feet of living area increased the least. Thus the marginal price of interior room (and to some extent exterior space as well) actually fell relative to the marginal price of other quality attributes, such as central air conditioning, fireplaces, modernized kitchen, and neighborhood quality. It is these attributes that account for the overall increase in the marginal price of quality and hence the steeper price function across quality levels.

In most cases, marginal prices rose at a more rapid rate than the simple average price. Again the price for additional square feet of living area rose less than the price of most other attributes. Particularly interesting is the fact that, even for 1976, the marginal price for additional square feet of housing area is particularly low for older housing in the interior part of the metropolitan area. Given that housing-supply response is highly inelastic in older, fully developed neighborhoods, prices there primarily reflect the nature of housing demand. While it might be expected that the low marginal price for housing space in older, interior areas of Houston are due to the low-income status of households in those areas, a more realistic hypothesis consistent with recent demographic trends is that those paying high location premiums to live close to the central business district are upper-middle-income households with few or no children. Thus their demand for living space is significantly lower.

Another interesting result is that the marginal price for central air conditioning for newer housing falls from over $5,500 to below $2,400, a figure more consistent with the marginal costs of central air conditioning in new construction. The marginal price of air conditioning in other areas no doubt is a result of high demand and the much higher supply costs to convert older housing stocks to central air conditioning. Notice also that the marginal price of air conditioning increased at about half the rate for new housing than for older housing, indicating that the hardware costs of air conditioning have not increased nearly as rapidly as the installation costs, especially in older homes that require new duct work.

The marginal price for improved accessibility is shown to be higher in older, close-in areas, as is to be expected from urban economic theory. However, these areas also experienced a more rapid percentage increase in the marginal price for accessibility, substantiating the facts that the urban price function with respect to distance is becoming increasingly steeper and that the very high rates of housing inflation are occurring in the central city.

The results from the comparison of small and large housing are primarily as expected. In general, all marginal prices are higher for larger homes. In some cases, this phenomenon may be due to technological factors, such as rising costs to air condition larger and larger homes. However, higher marginal prices are also reflective of the much higher house values for the larger homes (remember $MP_i = \hat{B}_i\overline{HV}$). These findings suggest that most housing attributes are complimentary and indicates that hedonic specifications should account for at least some degree of interaction between attributes.

Conclusion

While the rapid increase in home prices in Houston during the 1970s has been given considerable publicity, the rate of housing-price inflation was actually less than the rate of growth per capita personal income. However, the rate of increase in housing prices varies dramatically across locations within the city. Urban-fringe areas experienced only a 40 percent rise in home prices during the 7-year period investigated. More central locations experienced about double that rate, and central locations with high levels of other important amenities experienced rates of housing inflation that approached 200 percent.

These results provide a considerable amount of information with regard to changes that have taken place in the Houston housing market during the 1970s. Premiums for neighborhood quality have risen rapidly. While almost all quality features of neighborhoods are important, it is clearly evident that with Houston's transportation problems, accessibility is one of the most dominant amenities desired. If Houston's transportation problems are not alleviated soon, this trend will surely continue, and it would not be surprising to see this marginal price rise to over $2,000 per mile by 1985 for the average home and over $4,000 per mile for upper-middle-income housing.

Estimates of changes in marginal prices provide some insights with regard to which attributes appear to be most scarce and in what locations. Clearly the results seem to indicate that the greatest scarcities in the Houston housing market are attributes that are *not* produced by the private sector, but are the whole host of public-good amenities provided principally by local government. Furthermore, one would expect that as Houston continues to experience the growing pains of a prosperous city, public concerns over the urban environment, crime rates, congestion, and school quality will exert an increasingly dominant influence on the overall housing market and on location decisions.

Finally, the results indicate a high demand in interior portions of the metropolitan area (as revealed by high average and marginal prices) for housing in general and for high-quality structural and neighborhood attributes in particular. Such demand is being generated by middle- to upper-income households moving back to the city's interior neighborhoods. In fact, recent demographic studies support this conclusion and suggest that the process of gentrification of many older parts of Houston will continue. While this makes the prospects bright for neighborhood revitalization, it further diminishes the ability of low- to moderate-income households to acquire adequate housing, at least in the central city.

In conclusion, then, it must be recognized that housing inflation is not a simple phenomenon that can be adequately described by a single statistic. Housing at "affordable" prices is as much available today as during the 1950s and 1960s. *The problem is the shortage of affordably priced housing in locations where people want to live.* Clearly the continuation of mass-tract building at the urban fringe is not going to alleviate this problem. Rather than a housing shortage, there exists a quality-neighborhood shortage. What is needed is an expansion in the number of high-quality areas, a process for which local government is primarily responsible. Finally, it should be remembered that housing inflation is a two-edged sword. There are gainers and losers. While it has been long recognized that yesterdays owners gain at the expense of todays buyers, we see that the gains and losses also are distributed across households living in various locations. In some locations, capital gains accruing to households fell so short of the city average that any move by these households would probably require them to downgrade the quality of housing bought. Others whose homes increased in value by as much as 200 percent in just 7 years have benefited and now find themselves with housing valued considerably above what their income would typically have enabled them to buy in the past.

Notes

1. See Douglas Diamond, Jr., "Taxes, Inflation, Speculation and the Cost of Home Ownership," working paper, North Carolina State University, 1979.

2. Richard Muth, *Cities and Housing* (Chicago: Chicago Univ. Press, 1969).

3. As a consequence, 1,000 housing service units (HSU) could stem from 50 dwelling units of 20 HSU each, from 10 dwelling units of 100 HSU each, or from any other combination whose product is 1,000 and for which total costs are the same.

4. See Barton A. Smith, "The Supply of Urban Housing," *Quarterly Journal of Economics* (August 1976):389-405.

5. Although Muth and others have demonstrated that the relationship between distance and price tends to be exponential, in the discussion to follow, linear price gradients are assumed for ease of exposition.

6. The slope of the price function is equal to the premium households are willing to pay to live closer (in terms of some measures of distance) divided by either lost size or the amount of housing services consumed: $\delta P/\delta D$ = premium/Q.

7. Attempts have been made to define price in reference to the full cost of housing (the price of a house plus the capitalized value of lower commuting costs), which should be equalized across locations. This solution, however, becomes empirically intractable in an urban area with heterogeneous residents having different preferences, where many neighborhood amenities in addition to accessibility to the central business district are taken into consideration.

8. Recall $\delta P/\delta D$ = premium/Q. With an increase in Q owing to increased demand, $\delta P/\delta D$ will fall (the price function will become less steep). See Muth, *Cities and Housing*, chap. 1 through 4.

9. It is often said that the price of houses in an area is "about $35 per square foot." But does this mean that a home with 2,200 square feet of living area will sell for $7,000 more than a similar home with only 2,000 square feet of living space? In most cases, the answer is no. The $35 per square foot represents the average costs of a home in terms of living area, such as a 2,000-square foot house selling for $70,000.

10. Kelvin Lancaster, "A New Approach to Consumer Theory," *Journal of Political Economy* 74 (April 1966):132-156.

11. See Martin Bailey, Richard Muth, and Hugh Nourse, "A Regression Method for Real Estate Price Index Construction," *Journal of the American Statistical Association* (December 1963); Allen Dobson, "Price Changes of Single-Family Dwelling Units in Racially Changing Neighborhoods," dissertation, Washington University, 1970; Peter Chinloy, "Hedonic Price and Depreciation Indexes for Residential Housing: A Longitudinal Approach," *Journal of Urban Economics* 4 (October 1977); and Raymond Palmquist, "Alternative Techniques for Developing Real Estate Price Indices," University of Washington, 1978, mimeographed.

12. See Zvi Griliches, "On an Index of Quality Change," *Journal of the American Statistical Association* 56 (1961); John Kain and John Quigley, "Measuring the Value of Housing Quality," *Journal of the American Statistical Association* 65 (1970); and M. Straszheim, *An Econometric Analysis of the Urban Housing Market* (New York: Columbia Univ. Press, 1975). For papers specifically addressing the problem of measuring changes in price over time, see John Musgrave, "The Measurement of Price Changes in Construction," *Journal of the American Statistical Association* 64 (1969); Michael Ferri, "Monthly Hedonic Real Estate Price Indexes and the Structural Characteristics of Housing," working paper, University of Kentucky, 1977; James Fallian, Jr., "Cross-Sectional Indexes of the Price of Housing," working paper, 1978; and P. Mieszkowski and A. Saper, "Trends in the Value of Toronto Housing: 1965-1973," working paper, 1978.

13. The single exception is found in Allen Goodman, "Hedonic Prices, Price Indices and Housing Markets," *Journal of Urban Economics* 5 (October 1978). Goodman explicitly recognizes the existence of different price structures over location and time. Unfortunately, he erroneously attributes these differences to disequilibrium and market segmentation.

14. Since the subgroups analyzed represent quite broad categories, the results obtained still must be considered approximate averages. As a consequence, no housing subgroup analyzed more than doubled in value during this period, even though it was known that housing within much smaller geographic areas of special character experienced more than a trebling in value. While the large rates of appreciation in these unique areas are not explicitly reported in the text, they can be obtained for the empirical results reported by substituting into the estimated regression equations the values for variables on home structure and location applicable to these areas.

15. The analysis reported here excludes the crime and school data since these were available only for the city of Houston. (For results obtained where these and other special neighborhood data were used in analyzing the housing market within the Houston city limits, see Barton Smith and P. Mieszkowski, "A Study of Racial Discrimination," report submitted to the Office of Policy Development and Research, Department of Housing and Urban Development, 1979.)

16. One peculiarity is that the age variable stands out as a consistently poor explanatory variable. This is probably due to the extremely low age of the stock of housing in Houston. Furthermore, new housing in Houston, especially in areas where the prairie has not been transformed into a reasonable facsimile of a residential area, appears to sell at a discount.

17. Assuming that the hedonic relationship between house value HV and housing attributes X_i is exponential, the OLS regression specification is

$$\ln HV = \ln \hat{\beta}_0 + \sum_i \hat{\beta}_i X_i + \epsilon$$

Substitution of mean values and total differentiation yields

$$d \ln \overline{HV} = d \ln \hat{\beta}_0 + \sum_i \overline{X}_i d\hat{\beta}_i + \sum_i \hat{\beta}_i d\overline{X}_i$$

Given the Muthian definition of price, differences in HV not attributable to differences in X_i must be due to differences in price. Thus the change in the *average price* of housing is given by

$$d \ln \overline{HV} - \sum_i \hat{\beta}_i d\overline{X}_i = d \ln \hat{\beta}_0 + \sum_i \overline{X}_i d\hat{\beta}_i$$

For a more detailed explanation of techniques for decomposing a regression equation and for details regarding specific applications, see Robert Althauser and Michael Wigler, "Standardization and Component Analysis," *Sociological Methods and Research* (1972); Allen Blinder, "Wage Discrimination: Reduced Form and Structural Estimates," *Journal of Human Resources* (Fall 1973); and Barton Smith, "Determinants of Mexican-American Income," working paper, University of Houston, 1979.

18. The basic transformation required to convert the regression coefficients into estimates of marginal price is the product of the coefficient and the mean house value for the sample:

$$MP_i^{76} = \hat{\beta}_i^{76} \cdot \overline{HV}^{76}$$

19. As a side note it should be mentioned that for estimates restricted to the city of Houston only, the marginal prices of other amenities such as lower crime and higher-quality schools have risen just as dramatically as the price for improved accessibility and clean air.

Appendix 7A: Variable List and Description

Variable	*Description*
Structure:	
SQFT	Square feet of living area (in hundreds)
BATH	Number of bathrooms
LS	Size of lot (in thousands of square feet)
COND	Condition rating (1 = poor, 5 = excellent)
AC	Central air conditioning (yes = 1)
NGRGE	Garage capacity (no garage = 0, one-car garage = 1, and so on)
KIT	Modern kitchen (dishwasher or built-in range/oven = 1, both = 2)
FIRE	Number of fireplaces
HMAGE	Age of housing (in years)
Neighborhood:	
BELL	Housing in Bellaire (yes = 1)
WUNI	Housing in West University Place
WSG	Housing in west-side communities
ESG	Housing in east-side communities
NOCITY	Housing not in any incorporated city
POLUTN	Parts per hundred thousand (suspended particulates)
PCBLK	Proportion of population that is black (census tract)
PCMEX	Proportion of population that is Mexican American (census tract)
CBD	Distance to the central business district (in miles)
NFRWY	Distance to the nearest freeway (in miles)

8 The Effects of Land-Use and Environmental Regulations on Housing Costs

David E. Dowall

During the late 1960s and early 1970s, awareness of the potential adverse environmental impacts of land conversion and the increased predilection for communities to control urban growth lead to the proliferation of land-use and environmental regulations. The revolution in land-use control has occurred at all levels of government. Enactment of the National Environmental Protection Act,[1] increased involvement of state government in land-use regulation,[2] and widespread adoption of growth-management programs and complex procedures for the review of local development proposals have radically altered the process of land-use regulation.

Early reform of land-use and environmental regulation went largely unchallenged. While concern was expressed by development and real estate interests, most groups welcomed increased government involvement, hoping it would effectively check the decline in environmental quality evident in many communities. Early opposition to increased regulation focused mainly on the economic-development and labor-market effects of development restrictions. Initially, little concern was expressed for the potential of increased regulation to generate significant inflationary impacts.

Use of complex environmental and growth-management programs has escalated enormously in the past 5 years. For example, a 1972 study identified eight communities actively engaged in growth management.[3] A 1977 American Society of Planning Officials (ASPO) publication identified over 100 communities that have implemented growth-management programs.[4] In 1973, Petaluma was the only community in the San Francisco Bay Area attempting to control growth. A 1975 state survey of local planning activity identified over thirty communities in the Bay Area attempting to control residential development.[5] As more communities adopted growth-management programs nationwide, attention began to focus on the potential inflationary effects of land-use and environmental regulations. By 1978, the inflationary effects of development restrictions were outlined in two federal studies: the General Accounting Office report "Why Are the New Housing Prices So High, How Are They Influenced by Government Regulations, and Can Prices Be Reduced?" and the U.S. Department of Housing and Urban Development (HUD) report of its Task Force on Housing Costs.[6] The HUD report, while stopping short of recommending federal standards for land-use control, indicated that overregulation of residential development was widespread and adds significant unnecessary costs to housing construction. Since 1978, numerous studies have reported on the effects of excessive and complex environmental regulations.[7]

Although it is unlikely that the federal government will move to restrict the scope of local land-use regulation, pressure for wholesale reform is mounting. During the next several years, land planners can expect increased opposition to development controls and local and national initiatives for regulatory reform. As pressure for reform grows, research assessing the nature and magnitude of the inflationary effects of land-use control is urgently needed. Little research has attempted to systematically identify the range of effects generated by environmental regulation. Available research has focused on particular land-use-control techniques—zoning, for example—and has not attempted to examine the combined impact of simultaneously administered land-use and environmental controls. Subsequent sections of this chapter discuss the range of inflationary effects and, where available, present estimates of the costs of land-use control. The chapter concludes by indicating which land-use-control techniques are likely to be most inflationary and suggesting needed reforms.

Housing-Cost Effects of Land-Use and Environmental Regulation

Communities use a variety of measures to control the location, character, and amount of residential development. Traditionally, communitywide land-use plans, zoning and subdivision ordinances, and building codes have been used to regulate development. As more sophisticated regulations were developed, communities augmented traditional programs with impact-assessment procedures, multiple-permit systems, growth-management timing ordinances, impact fees and taxes, and urban-limit-line designations. Not only have these additions made the regulatory process more complex, they also have introduced numerous effects that lead directly or indirectly to housing-cost inflation.

Examination of seven widely used land-use and environmental regulations has identified four direct and two indirect types of inflationary effects.[8] Presented in table 8-1, these effects are best considered as generic; that is, their relative impact on housing costs depends largely on the level and character of housing demand, the proximity of regulated communities to other jurisdictions, and the degree of restrictiveness cumulatively generated by local land policies.

Table 8-1
Direct and Indirect Effects of Environmental Controls on Housing Costs

Effect on Housing costs	*Land-Use Controls Most Likely to Generate Effect*
Direct Effects:	
Increase in land costs	Zoning, urban limit lines, density constraints, growth-management timing ordinances, and permit programs.
Increase in lot-preparation costs	Subdivision requirements, growth-management timing ordinances, dedication requirements.
Shifting development costs from public to project	Capital-budgeting programs, fees and development charges, dedication requirement, subdivision requirements.
Administrative and delay costs	All land-use controls to some extent. Costs increase with the relative complexity of the regulation.
Indirect effects:	
Facilitating monopoly power	Controls that restrict the number of developers operating in communities will allow builders to charge excess housing prices. Regulations act as barriers to market entry—reducing competition in the housing market.
Market reorientation	Restrictions on development often force developers to reorient their projects to higher-income customers.

Direct Effects

Restrictions on the supply of land and the permissible level of residential development intensity greatly affect land costs. As Ohls, Weisberg, and White have illustrated, zoning regulations, if they restrict the supply of land available for development below that which would be normally exchanged in the market, operate to increase land cost.[9] The supply of residentially zoned land is often limited when communities attempt to maintain environmental quality or fiscal position by designating land for open space or agricultural use, or for more fiscally desirable commercial or industrial use. Stull has shown that communities that shift land to employment-generating use can expect residential land prices to increase as the supply of residential land is reduced and as increased employment raises the demand for residential land.[10]

Direct empirical estimates of the inflationary effects of zoning or other land-use-control-induced land-supply constraints are not widely available. One study has simulated the effect of land-use-policy effects for the London, Ontario land market.[11] Using a model developed for the London area, Davies examined the effect to two hypothetical municipal actions that increased the supply of lots. For 1967, Davies increased the supply of lots by 250 units, about 11 percent. The simulation results suggest a lot-price reduction of about $200 per lot. The price fall is about 4.5 percent. A second simulation experiment for 1973 indicates that the same absolute increase in lots (250) generates a $244-per-lot decrease in prices. In this experiment, the lot increase represents a 15 percent addition to the stock of lots and a 3.4 percent decrease in lot prices. The difference in price effects for the two periods suggests that supply changes vary and depend on overall market conditions. While in both cases the effect on lot price is significant, the effect on house prices is minimal, changing by less than 1 percent.

Estimates of the effects of zoning and land-use-control-determined land supply on housing prices are available and reasonably approximate the impact of land-supply constraints. Using housing-price and land-use data for suburban Boston communities, Stull tested the relationship between land-use control and housing price. After controlling for accessibility, housing stock characteristics, and the quality of public services, Stull found that housing prices were lower in communities with greater proportions of vacant land.[12] An analysis of suburban communities in Alameda and Contra Costa Counties, California found that housing prices were inversely related to the supply of vacant land available for development.[13]

Witte's estimate of the price elasticity of residential sites provides an indirect empirical estimate of the potential price effect of land-supply restrictions.[14] Relying on various parameter estimates, she estimates the price elasticity of residential sites to be -0.7. This inelastic demand will generate lot-price increases if supply is restricted. For example, if we assume that market adjustments occur through price, not quantity, changes (reasonable for the short-run), a community that reduces its supply of lots by 20 percent can expect lot prices to increase by 14 percent.

In addition to reducing the supply of residentially developable land, zoning acts to restrict the intensity of development. Large minimum-lot-size requirements increase the floor price of residential lots. While large-lot zoning reduces the per acres price of raw land, the reduction in price is often offset by higher land requirements. Interpolating from Peterson's empirically determined land-price gradients for Fairfax County, Virginia illustrates the potential cost effect of large-lot zoning. At a distance of 10 miles from the urban center, Peterson found that large parcels zoned 1/2, 1, 2, and 10 units per acre were selling for $5,800, $7,900, $13,700, and $32,000 per acre, respectively. Converting these per acre prices to per lot prices, the per lot prices implied by the 1/2, 1, 2, and 10 units per acre zoning are $11,600, $7,900, $6,850, and $3,200, respectively.[15]

In addition to zoning, other regulations act to restrict land supply and raise land costs. Urban limit lines restrict development to serviced areas. Several communities have implemented limit lines: Boulder, Colorado; Montgomery County, Maryland; Brooklyn Park, Minnesota; and Salem, Oregon. Urban limit lines depress land prices of parcels located outside developable areas and increase prices of developable parcels. In a study of Brooklyn Park, Gleeson estimated that two-thirds of the variation in land price was the result of urban-limit-line designations. As of 1976, the estimated land-price differential was $1,463 per acre. Unfortunately, Gleeson was not able to estimate the overall inflationary impact of the imposition of the limit lines.[16]

Growth-management timing ordinances also contribute to higher land costs. By restricting the amount of residential development per year, control over the pace of construction restricts the amount of land annually developed. Since project location plays a major role in determining community impacts, growth-management allocation systems limit the supply of land likely to receive development permission. Parcels likely to receive approval will sell at higher prices.

A second type of direct cost effect of land-use and environmental regulation is the increase in the cost of lot preparation and subdivision design. Over the years, standards for subdivision design have substantially increased. While generally improving the quality of residential environments, these regulations add significant costs to land development. Numerous regulations act to drive up costs. Growth management has a similar effect. Since all growth-management systems competitively rank development proposals according to a variety of locational and design criteria, developers are willing to provide costly amenities in order to obtain development approval. For example, the Boulder, Colorado Residential Allocation System awards 30 of its possible 100 points to projects that provide open space, extensive landscaping, bike paths, bus shelters, off-street parking, lighting, and other design amenities.[17]

Empirical estimates of the effect of increased subdivision requirements are widely available. In a 1976 study of Jacksonville, Florida, the Urban Land Institute found that changes in water-system design and street-width requirements added, in constant 1976 dollars, $830 to per lot development costs.[18] In a study for the Kaiser Commission, Burns and Mittelbach estimated that excessive subdivision and zoning requirements added 2 to 4 percent to the price of new housing.[19] While it is difficult to differentiate between necessary and excessive subdivision requirements, available evidence suggests that significant cost reduction can be obtained by reducing subdivision standards.

A third direct cost effect of land-use and environmental regulation is generated by local government efforts to shift public-service costs of development onto new projects. Traditionally, communities have shouldered the public-service costs of new residential development. Recently, communities have imposed substantial fees, taxes, and land and infrastructure dedication requirements on new development. As communities become more conscious of the fiscal impacts of land development, efforts to shift costs onto developers will increase (see note 4). In the wake of Proposition 13, this trend has become acute. A recent survey of California communities

munities revealed alarming increases in development fees and taxes.[20] For example, the city of Vallejo, California charges the following fees and taxes for a three-bedroom house: park dedication tax, $275; water facilities tax, $380; sewer hookup fee, $710; storm drain fee, $200; capital improvement tax, $275; school mitigation tax, $435; and bridge construction development tax, $500. These charges total $2,775.[21] In other California cities, charges go as high as $5,000 per unit.

Requirements for dedication of land for school and park sites and for moderate-income housing also add significant costs to project development. A study of Edmonton, Alberta estimated that the land-dedication requirements for moderate-income housing added $243 in per unit costs.[23]

As in the case of subdivision requirements, it is difficult to determine when these fees and charges become excessive. Charges that reflect the actual cost of providing services to new development are reasonable and desirable. However, in many instances, efforts to shift costs appear to be excessive—revenues are used to provide services that benefit the general community.

The fourth direct effect of land-use and environmental regulation results from administrative delays associated with regulatory compliance. With the widespread use of environmental and fiscal impact-assessment and development-permit systems, the time required to obtain development approval has increased tremendously in the past 10 years. A national survey of the length of the approval process found that in 1970, 72 percent of the developers interviewed obtained permission in 7 months or less. Ninety-seven percent obtained approval in 1 year or less. In 1975, only 15 percent of these same respondents obtained permits in less than 7 months; only 42 percent obtained development permission in 1 year or less.[24] A study of the costs of delay in the Houston area estimated that time requirements increased from an average of 22 months during the 1966-1970 period to 27 months for the 1974-1977 period. For projects requiring the establishment of municipal utility districts, time requirements increased from 23 to 36 months.[25]

Unnecessary delays in the development-review process generate several economic costs. Delays result in increased land-holding and overhead costs, development-loan interest costs, exposure to inflation, and opportunity costs of tying-up capital. Costs also depend on when in the development-review process the delay occurs. Several estimates of delay costs are available. In Houston, 1977 monthly constant-dollar estimates of per unit delay costs were determined according to the phase in which delay occurs. For early project tie-ups, costs were estimated to be between $57 and $85 per unit per month. For project-application-related delays, costs range between $76 and $112. For delays in the subdivision development phase, costs were estimated to run between $80 and $121.[26] The overall cost of increased delays in the development-review process in Houston were estimated to add between $388 and $596 to the per unit cost of housing. In California, delays associated with California Environmental

Quality Act compliance were estimated to add between 4 and 7 percent to the selling price of new units.[27] In Hawaii, estimates of delay costs range between $323 and $438 per unit per month.[28] In Edmonton, Alberta, monthly delay costs were estimated to add between $700 and $900 to the costs of new units."[29]

Another impact of complex development-control procedures is the cost of compliance. Preparation of detailed environmental and fiscal impact assessments add significant costs. Muller and James estimate that the per unit cost of environmental-impact-report (EIR) preparation and mitigation are between $100 and $200.[30] As the availability of land declines in rapidly growing urban areas, the costs of environmental-review procedures is likely to increase as developers attempt to develop more environmentally sensitive areas.

Proliferation of complex review procedures, increased citizen involvement in land-use regulation, and growing pressure for the development of sensitive land will increase the costs of environmental compliance and lengthen the regulatory process.

Indirect Effects

In addition to the direct cost effects of land-use and environmental regulations, community control of residential development often (1) confers significant monopoly power on developers and (2) alters marketing and pricing decisions. Monopoly power allows developers to charge excess prices for housing. Increased production costs often force developers to reorient residential projects to high-income markets. Both these effects are the result of the cumulative impact of land-use control.

Regulation establishes monopoly power in a variety of ways. By restricting the supply of land available for development, the potential for market entry and the possibility of increased competition are reduced. If the supply of land is greatly reduced, housing producers may be better able to set housing prices above competitive levels. For example, in Edmonton, Cook found substantial market concentration among developers operating in the city's six restricted development areas. The four largest developers supplied 64 percent of the single-family lots produced between September 1973 and August 1976. Closer inspection of the six city-designated development areas indicates that each is controlled by one developer.[31]

Land-use and environmental regulations that rely on complex administrative procedures act as barriers to market entry. If the level of complexity is great, potential developers will be reluctant to enter local markets. The costs of adjusting to new and unknown administrative programs is high. Developers who have established good working relationships with local planners are more likely to obtain development permission. For example, Hall found that companies that were large and locally based had the highest success rate in obtaining Industrial Development Certificates.[32] Developers that successfully shepard projects through the review process can charge monopoly prices for units as long as local procedures effectively block increased competition. A study of two San Jose, California developers found that after holding constant for increases in labor, materials, and land costs and for increased public requirements and housing quality, between 1967 and 1976, the two developers increased their gross profits (in constant 1976 dollars) by between 158 and 231 percent. The researchers concluded that these excess profits were partially the result of constrained housing supply and the exercise of monopoly power.[33]

Another way local development policy reduces competition is by shifting public-service costs onto developers. While in high-demand areas these costs can be easily passed forward to the consumer, increased front-end costs make it more difficult and expensive to obtain capital financing. Cook estimates that Edmonton's decision to shift the financing of services onto the developer added $7,800 to per unit front-end financing costs.[34] Typically, capital markets discriminate against small firms. As front-end costs increase, it becomes more difficult for smaller developers to remain competitive.

The second type of indirect effect of environmental regulations is the reorientation of residential projects. The previous discussion of monopoly power suggested that developers may increase prices in excess of increased costs owing to limited competition. There is, however, another reason for raising prices. Often developers find that if they raise price to offset increased costs, the marketability of projects declines. Therefore, developers shift the orientation of projects to high-income consumers. Since profit is the result of per unit net revenue times the quantity of units sold, a shift in the design of the project to fewer higher-priced units often will result in higher profits. Development restrictions that limit residential density and increase production costs often force developers to scrap plans to produce high-volume projects and build exclusive high-priced projects. Routinely, land-use controls act to reduce the number of units produced to a level well below allowable limits as developers reorient their restricted projects to exclusive low-density development.[35]

Conclusions and Policy Direction

This chapter has reviewed the available evidence on the effects of land-use and environmental regulations on land and housing markets. While the lack of comprehensive empirical evidence and the importance of local housing-market conditions and development policies makes it impossible to precisely guage the cumulative effects of community-development controls, available evidence suggests that inflationary impacts may be substantial in many areas. The actual magnitude of impacts appears to depend on the degree to which specific regulations restrict land supply and generate production and delay costs.

Of all development-control techniques considered, growth-management timing ordinances are likely to be the most inflationary. Since they act to restrict development to serviced areas, residential allocation systems reduce the supply of developable land. Land costs will increase as developers compete for parcels likely to earn development approval. In competing for development permission, growth-management rationing systems encourage developers to provide high-cost amenities. This practice increases lot-preparation costs and forces developers to reorient projects to high-income customers willing and able to pay for expensive amenities. Administrative costs of growth-management programs are substantial. Since projects must be ranked, development proposals are evaluated infrequently (usually once or twice a year). Evaluation criteria are complex, requiring detailed applications and preparation of costly reports. Most important, growth-management systems inadvertently confer monopoly power on developers of approved projects. All these factors suggest that in high-housing-demand areas, growth-management regulations are likely to generate significant cost effects.

Massive reductions in the supply of land, whether achieved through zoning or urban-limit-line designations can greatly affect land costs. If imposed broadly, downzoning and service-area restrictions rival the inflationary impacts of growth-management techniques. In addition to increasing the cost of land, land-supply restrictions can confer enormous monopoly power on the owners of developable land.

Cost shifting has probably the next most significant impact on housing cost. Recent post-proposition 13 experience in California reveals alarming increases in fees and taxes. If present fiscal trends continue, increased fees and taxes will contribute enormously to housing-cost inflation—possibly eclipsing the inflationary effects of other land-use controls.

While receiving the widest attention in the literature, administrative and delay costs generate substantially lower costs than any of the preceding techniques. It is, however, the one area where efforts for reform are likely to be successful.

Recent trends in land-use and environmental regulation suggest that communities are increasingly relying on growth-management timing ordinances, urban-limit-line designations, downzoning, and cost-shifting strategies. In the San Francisco Bay Area, nine communities have adopted and another eight are considering growth-management ordinances. Thirty-nine of the area's ninety-three communities have downzoned significant portions of residentially zoned land, twenty-three communities have outlined urban-service boundaries, and sixty-eight communities have or are planning to increase development fees and charges.[36] The supply effects of these local land-use policies and programs are significant. Based on projections of residential development, the Bay Area will face extreme shortages of land in the next 10 years. Between now and 1990, the projected demand for land will exceed the available supply by over 10,000 acres in both Alameda and Santa Clara Counties.[37] In the Bay Area, and possibly other growing metropolitan areas, the inflationary impacts of land shortages will become a significant public-policy issue in the 1980s.

Policies for reducing the inflationary effects of local land-use controls will be extremely difficult to implement. Historically, control over development has been viewed as a local responsibility. Proposals for reforming local zoning and land-use control have been offered in the past, but few have been successfully adopted. It appears unlikely that communities will be willing to yield their power to zone or control development to regional or metropolitan governments. Consequently, instead of offering a set of proposals for radical government reform, the chapter concludes by outlining a series of modest reforms aimed at making local communities more cognizant of the inflationary effects of local land-use policies and recommends ways that the regulatory process can be modified:

Land-supply monitoring: One of the most striking discoveries encountered in examining land-use regulation was the total lack of land-supply information. Most land planners have no estimate of local land supply or cost or the ability to anticipate the impacts of changes in land-use regulation. The monitoring of local land supply and cost is urgently needed. Land-monitoring capabilities are needed to assess environmental policies and serve as the basis for balancing housing and environmental objectives.[38]

Regulatory simplification: Overly complex and redundant procedures add unnecessary costs to development. Efforts to reduce delay and application costs must be made.

Reform of subdivision standards: Careful reassessment of subdivision standards is needed. There is much potential for standards reductions without compromising environmental quality.

Reform of fees, taxes, and dedication requirements: Efforts to support public services through the use of development charges and dedications, while appropriate to cover the costs of new development, are increasingly being used to support the provision of communitywide services. Such abuses must be stopped.

Reform of land-use and environmental regulation is likely to be difficult and politically contentious. The greatest potential for needed reform lies in the ability of land-use and environmental planners to recognize the inflationary impacts of excessive regulation and make necessary reforms.

Notes

1. National Environmental Protection Act, Public Law 91-190, 42 USC, section 4331, 1969.

2. U.S. Department of Housing and Urban Development, *State Land Use Activity* (Washington, 1976).

3. American Society of Planning Officials, *Nongrowth as a Planning Alternative*, PAS Report No. 283 (Chicago, 1972).

4. David R. Godschalk et al., *Constitutional Issues of Growth Management* (Chicago: American Society of Planning Officials, 1977).

5. Office of Planning and Research, *Local Planning Survey* (Sacramento, 1975).

6. General Accounting Office, "Why Are New Housing Prices So High, How Are They Influenced by Government Regulation, and Can Prices Be Reduced?" Washington, 1978; U.S. Department of Housing and Urban Development, *Final Report of the Task Force on Housing Costs* (Washington, 1978).

7. For a survey, see David E. Dowall and Jesse Mingilton, *The Effects of Environmental Regulations on Housing Costs* (Chicago: Council of Planning Librarians, 1979).

8. David Dowall et al., *The Effect of Land Use and Environmental Regulations on Land and Housing Markets*, a report prepared for the California Air Resources Board, San Francisco, 1979.

9. James Ohls, Richard Weisberg, and Michelle White, "The Effects of Zoning on Land Value," *Journal of Urban Economics* 1 (1974):428-444.

10. Increases in residential land prices depend on the relative impact of negative externalities generated by manufacturing land use. See William J. Stull, "Land Use and Zoning in an Urban Economy," *American Economic Review* 64 (1974):337-347.

11. Gordon W. Davies, "A Model of the Urban Residential Land and Housing Markets," *Canadian Journal of Economics* 10, 3 (1977):393-410.

12. William J. Stull, "Community Environment, Zoning, and the Value of Single Family Homes," *Journal of Law and Economics* 18 (1975):535-557.

13. David Dowall et al., *The Effect of Land Use and Environmental Regulations*.

14. Ann Witte, "An Examination of Various Elasticities for Residential Sites," *Land Economics* 53 (1977):401-409.

15. George Peterson, "Land Prices and Factor Substitution in the Metropolitan Housing Market," Working Paper No. 0875-02-01 (Washington: The Urban Institute, 1974).

16. Michael E. Gleeson, "The Effects of an Urban Growth Management System on Land Values," Working Paper No. 4, Project on Monitoring Growth Management Systems (Minneapolis: Hubert H. Humphrey Institute of Public Affairs, University of Minnesota, 1978).

17. Boulder, Colorado Planning Department, *Residential Allocation System Application Package* (Boulder, 1977).

18. Urban Land Institute, "Effects of Regulation on Housing Costs: Two Case Studies," ULI Research Report No. 27 (Washington, 1977).

19. Leland S. Burns and Frank G. Mittelbach, "Efficiency in the Housing Industry," in Report of the President's Committee on Urban Housing, *A Decent Home*, vol. 2 (Washington: U.S. Government Printing Office, 1968), p. 133.

20. For an examination of why communities attempt to shift costs, see D.E. Dowall, "Fiscal Impact Rationale for Growth Management," *Annals of Regional Science* 12 (1978):83-94.

21. Office of Planning and Research, *Housing After Proposition 13* (Sacramento, 1979).

22. Elaine Stone, "Impact of Projected Growth on Major Municipal Services," MCP Professional Report, Department of City and Regional Planning, University of California, Berkeley, 1978.

23. Richard Cook, "Lot Prices and the Land Development Industry in Edmonton, Canada," MCP Professional Report, Department of City and Regional Planning, University of California, Berkeley, 1977.

24. Stephen R. Seidel, *Housing Costs and Government Regulation* (New Brunswick, N.J.: Center for Urban Policy Research, 1978).

25. Rice Center for Community Design and Research, *The Delay Costs of Government Regulation in the Houston Housing Market* (Houston: Rice Center, 1978).

26. Ibid.

27. Environmental Analysis Systems, Inc., "The California Environmental Quality Act," prepared for the State Assembly Committee on Local Government, Sacramento, 1975.

28. Hawaii Coastal Zone Management Program, "Red Tape vs. Green Light: A Workshop on Government Permit Simplification, Coordination and Streamlining" (Honolulu, 1978).

29. Richard Cook, "Lot Prices and the Land Development Industry."

30. Thomas Muller and Franklin J. James, "Environmental Impact Evaluation and Housing Costs"(Washington: The Urban Institute, 1975).

31. Richard Cook, "Lot Prices and the Land Development Industry."

32. Peter Hall, *The Containment of Urban England*, vol. 2. (Beverly Hills: Sage, 1973).

33. Urban Land Institute, "Effects of Regulation on Housing Costs."

34. Richard Cook, "Lot Prices and the Land Development Industry."

35. Bernard J. Frieden, *The Environmental Protection Hustle*. (Cambridge: M.I.T. Press, 1979).

36. David E. Dowall, "Land, Housing and Environmental Regulation: An Examination of the Effects of Local Land Use Controls in the San Francisco Bay Area," unpublished manuscript, 1979.

37. Ibid.

38. A proposal for such a monitoring system is outlined in David E. Dowall, "How to Deflate Housing Costs," Working Paper No. 304, Institute of Urban and Regional Development, University of California, Berkeley, 1979.

Part V
The Costs of Open-Housing Policies

9 Low- and Moderate-Income Housing in the Suburbs: The Massachusetts Antisnob Zoning Law Experience

Sharon Perlman Krefetz

Since the mid-1960s, the growing spatial separation of racial and economic groups in our metropolitan areas has been noted with concern by a myriad of government commissions, civil rights groups, planners, lawyers, and social science researchers.[1] The consequences of the virtual absence of low-income people—disproportionately of minority status—from the suburbs and their high concentrations in the central cities are viewed as harmful to society as a whole, as well as to individuals. However, as we enter the 1980s, it is apparent that efforts to open up the suburbs to low- and moderate-income people have met with little success. As a result, the greater opportunities for suitable employment, quality education, and pleasant living environments that suburban locations increasingly offer remain beyond the reach of a sizable segment of our populace, and our cities and suburbs grow ever more separate and unequal.

Blatant, individual-level discrimination by suburbanites has not been the primary obstacle encountered by those attempting to open up the suburbs. Instead, communities have been able to keep out whole categories of "undesirables" by exercising their zoning powers. Arguing that they are simply engaging in "rational land-use planning," many suburbs have ensured that the type and cost of their housing remain well beyond the reach of low- and moderate-income people. Recognizing the aggregate discriminatory effects of such snob, or exclusionary, zoning techniques as large minimum lot size, interior square footage requirements, and bans on multifamily dwellings and mobile homes, advocates of opening up have turned to the courts for redress. However, the results of challenges to the legality of snob zoning practices have been mixed. In the famous 1975 *Mt. Laurel* case (96 N.J. A-11, 1975), the New Jersey Supreme Court decided that zoning laws that have the effect of excluding poor and moderate-income persons violate the state constitution, and moreover, the court decreed that communities must share in the provision of housing on the basis of regional needs. More recently, though, in 1977, the U.S. Supreme Court ruled in the *Arlington Heights* case (98 U.S. 752, 1977) that it is not unconstitutional for a suburb to refuse to change zoning restrictions whose practical effect is to block construction of racially integrated housing for low- and moderate-income people as long as that is not the sole intent of the laws.[2]

The uncertainties and high costs in time and money that court challenges involve, combine with the recognition that even the encouraging *Mt. Laurel* decision left to the state the critical task of working out a proposal to increase the supply of low- to moderate-income housing, has prompted some observers to suggest that the key to successful resolution of the exclusionary zoning problem lies in state legislative action.[3] For despite protestations that their local autonomy cannot be infringed upon, localities are, in fact, legally the creatures of the state, and the zoning power of local governments is a gift of the states—and a relatively recent one at that, dating back to the 1926 Supreme Court *Euclid* decision (272 U.S. 365, 1926). Thus a straightforward and, in the final analysis, probably necessary approach to getting more low- to moderate-income housing built in the suburbs may be to secure a reassertion of state governments' authority in zoning and land-use matters in order to override local restrictions that impede its construction.

Can this sort of state-level action produce low- and moderate-income housing in the suburbs? Is this a viable approach for the 1980s? A decade of experience in Massachusetts, the only state that has passed legislation specifically aimed at opening up the suburbs, should be instructive.

Chapter 774 of the Massachusetts Acts and Resolves of 1969 provides "for the construction of low or moderate income housing in cities and towns in which local restrictions hamper construction." Chapter 774, or the "Antisnob Zoning Law" as it was soon dubbed, was not passed in response to a court mandate. Rather it was proposed by a group of young, liberal legislators who were concerned about the growing urban crisis, especially the shortage of housing for low- and moderate-income people that had been documented in various government reports. Detailed accounts of the controversy their proposal sparked and the political maneuverings that secured passage of the bill can be found elsewhere.[4] For present purposes, the intentions of Chapter 774's architects and the mechanisms they devised to realize them must be elaborated.

The Antisnob Zoning Law was aimed at stimulating and facilitating activity to produce subsidized housing in the suburbs—activity by the suburbs themselves as well as by developers interested in building such housing. Although the details of the bill were compromised repeatedly in order to secure passage, the backers of Chapter 774 were hopeful that its final provisions would achieve this goal.[5] The main components of the legislation contain distinct innovations that reflect its drafters' awareness of the need to overcome barriers that have typically hampered the construction of low-and moderate-income housing in the suburbs.

First, Chapter 774 creates a procedure whereby qualified developers (the local housing authority, a nonprofit organization, or a limited-dividend corporation) can apply to one local authority, the Zoning Board of Appeals (ZBA), for a comprehensive permit to build subsidized housing.[6] This would replace the usual long, complex, and costly process of securing separate approvals from a multitude of local bodies, for example, health, planning, building inspector, and town council. This streamlining and simplification was intended to appeal to developers, who, not unrealistically, think of time as money. Brief time limits for arriving at decisions were also set, with the ZBA required to hold a public hearing within 30 days of receiving an application from a developer and to then grant or deny the comprehensive permit within 40 days of the hearing.

Second, the Antisnob Zoning Law grants developers the right to appeal adverse ZBA decisions (either outright denials of permits or approvals with qualifications deemed uneconomic) to the state for a possible override. Instead of being forced to either abandon the proposal or face a lengthy, expensive, rancorous court battle to try to pursue it, this provision gives developers immediate recourse to present their case to a special body, the Housing Appeals Committee (HAC), set up within the state Department of Community Affairs (DCA). The HAC is composed of two members appointed by the governor to represent local communities, one DCA official, and two members appointed by the DCA commissioner. Upon determining that a local denial was unreasonable or not consistent with local needs, the HAC is empowered to require the ZBA to grant a comprehensive permit to the developer immediately. To avoid costly delays, time limits were also attached to this component of the legislation: the HAC is required to hold hearings withing 20 days of receiving an appeal application and must render its decision with 30 days after hearings end, unless both parties involved agree to an extension.

Third, the bill sets standards for determining whether local denials are consistent with local needs. In so doing, Chapter 774 effectively establishes housing goals, or fair-share quotas, for all communities, which, if met, would exempt them from the law. A zoning board denial of the comprehensive permit would be consistent with local needs if (1) 10 percent of the community's housing stock was already low- or moderate-income housing, (2) 1.5 percent of its land area was already used for such housing, or (3) the proposal in question would in any one year result in the start of construction of such housing in more than 0.3 percent of the town's land area or 10 acres, whichever is larger. This section of the legislation was aimed at inspiring communities to take the initiative in developing subsidized housing in order to satisfy any one of the three standards and thereby become invulnerable to the Chapter 774 process. (When the legislation was passed, only three communities, Boston, Brockton, and Holyoke, met any of the criteria.)

Some of the particulars of the law make it a less than perfect solution for all the vexing problems of suburban exclusion. For example, it is a passive approach, with the onus on developers to make a proposal in order to start the proceedings. ZBA's tend to be quite conservative and therefore predisposed towards denying comprehensive permits. Planning boards might be a more enlightened bodies in which to vest local decision-making power. A 10 percent-existing-units standard is arbitrary and permits the most exclusive towns with the largest (and hence most restrictive) lot zoning requirements to satisfy quotas more easily. Nevertheless, in theory, at least, the Antisnob Zoning Law broke new ground in the battle against exclusionary zoning, and its provisions were hailed by advocates of opening up the suburbs as a landmark step and a model for emulation.[7]

Since the passage of Chapter 774 ten years ago, there have been 111 proposals (in 82 communities) to build a total of 14,639 units of low- and moderate-income housing under its provisions.[8] Most of these proposals have been made in Boston suburbs, where the need for subsidized housing is, indeed, great, and where virtually no such housing existed prior to Chapter 774's enactment.[9] In a further reflection of responsiveness to need, roughly two-thirds of the units proposed have been for the construction of primarily family housing, (with some including elderly units, too); one-third exclusively for the elderly. The comprehensive permit provision of the law does seem to have stimulated activity aimed at opening up the suburbs; a number of subsidized-housing developers have reported that the streamlined, simplified application process it created did encourage them to make proposals.[10] However, only twenty-four of these proposals were approved by local zoning boards with no or minor modifications; eighty-five were denied, either outright ($N = 47$) or effectively ($N = 38$), by being approved with uneconomic conditions attached; in nine cases other action, that is, withdrawal, was taken. Significantly, the vast majority of the applications approved (twenty out of twenty-four) were proposals for elderly housing, while the majority of those denied (fifty-five out of eighty-five) were for family housing.[11]

The comprehensive permit component of the Antisnob Zoning Law, thus has had some positive effects, largely limited to facilitating the construction of elderly housing. Suburban officials apparently do not object to the idea of creating housing opportunities in their comunities for senior citizens on fixed incomes. This is probably because the elderly are seen as both deserving and unthreatening. As one observer has snidely remarked, "Old people as a rule are not dangerous. They do not, as a rule, produce children."[12] But the comprehensive permit process has been largely ineffective in the case of family housing. When this category is involved, most exclusionary suburbs have demonstrated that "they'd rather fight than switch."[13]

The consistent pattern of local denials of permits for family housing projects clearly points up the need for the state appeal and override provision of the law, and the disposition of cases by the Housing Appeals Committee has been striking: local denials of Chapter 774 proposals have been upheld in only four of the thirty-nine appeals the committee has so far reviewed. The state has, almost without exception, found local refusals to accept subsidized housing for families to be unreasonable and/or inconsistent with local needs.

However, despite the promise suggested by Chapter 774's principal provisions, the direct impact of the law in terms of actually getting low- to moderate-income housing units built and occupied has been, at best, limited. To date, only about 3,600 units have been completed, and approximately 2,000 additional ones have been approved and are either in the final planning stage or under construction. These figures, even when combined, are quite modest.

The Antisnob Zoning Law has probably helped produce a small number of additional units of low- and moderate-income housing by inspiring some communities to undertake activities on their own. For example, several of the most affluent and heretofor exclusionary of Boston's suburbs, Wellesley, Sudbury, Lincoln, and Southborough, have recently built their first low- to moderate-income housing projects (all but Lincoln's being housing for the elderly only).[14] However, such actions have been on a small scale and not widespread. The more typical suburban response to the Antisnob Zoning Law has been no response. Instead of trying to meet their fair-share quota and become invulnerable to the law, most communities have assumed an ostrich-like posture and ignored Chapter 774's existence altogether. The only localities that have met the 10 percent subsidized units criterion since the law was passed have generally been the older, poorer cities and some inner-ring working-class suburbs in which internal pressures and the need for public housing are high.[15]

Thus far, then, the Antisnob Zoning Law has a limited, though not altogether inconsequential, impact on the creation of low- and moderate-income housing in Massachusetts suburbs. That this law has resulted in the construction of more such housing than would have been built in its absence is clear and suggests that its backers were on the right track, particularly in foreseeing the need for the comprehensive permit and state override provisions. That such a modest amount of housing has been built, even with these provisions, is also apparent and suggests that the barriers that need to be overcome in the battle to open up the suburbs are greater than Chapter 774's enlightened designers perceived.

A variety of factors have hampered the effectiveness of Chapter 774, but all have had one common denominator: increased time and/or costs creating serious obstacles to project viability. As noted earlier, the drafters of the Antisnob Zoning Law were well aware of the costly effects of a long, drawn-out process and therefore tried to provide safeguards to ensure speedy, efficient proceedings. They did not, however, foresee just how willing and able suburbs would be to engage in activities to render these safeguards ineffective. The first and foremost factor accounting for the Antisnob Zoning Law's limited impact has been the persistent resistance to it by suburbanites.

As indicated earlier, most communities presented with Chapter 774 project applications for family housing projects have denied them. Upon appeals to the HAC, nearly all these denials have been ruled invalid, and local ZBAs have been ordered to grant the comprehensive permits requested by the developers. The matter has not, however, ended there, with suburbs accepting HAC rulings and reconciling themselves to the imminent construction of the unwanted housing. Instead of complying with the HAC orders, most of the suburbs involved (twenty out of thirty) have gone to court to challenge not only the specific HAC decision, but the legality of the Antisnob Zoning Law itself. Such challenges have succeeded in adding on an average of 10 additional months (the range is 3 to 27 months) to the 4 months total time Chapter 774's architects envisioned elapsing from initial application to the ZBA to rendering of the HAC decision.[16]

Significantly, the first two HAC decisions to be appealed to the courts, by the towns of Hanover and Concord, took 20 months and 17 months, respectively, to clear the courts. When these cases were finally decided jointly, by the Massachusetts Supreme Judicial Court in March of 1973, proponents of the Antisnob Zoning Law won a major victory, for the court not only upheld the power of the state to superecede local zoning laws, but "decided every conceivable issue raised in favor of an expansive interpretation of the statute, [and] went out of its way to note in passing the favorable side of issues that were not raised by the statute."[17]

Nevertheless, despite these rulings and the refusal of the U.S. Supreme Court to hear a case (*Winchester*) challenging the constitutionality of Chapter 774, communities have continued to appeal HAC decisions to the courts. The facts that the developer in the *Hanover* case (363 Mass. 339, 1973) found it impossible to go ahead with his project because of increased expenses and that action on the Concord project has been held up because of subsequent complications created by Conservation Commission requirements (see subsequent discussion) have no doubt helped convince communities of the continued worth of such ventures.[18]

Thus, although no community has won a favorable ruling from the courts (HAC decisions have been upheld in all the dozen or so cases that have been heard so far), by dragging out proceedings, dampening enthusiasm, and increasing the costs (in construction and legal fees) to developers, a number of suburbs have succeeded in getting proposals scrapped. In this way they have, in other words, lost the battles, but won the war. In playing a game in which time is money, suburbs are at an obvious advantage.

Costly delays in Chapter 774 proceedings caused by this resistance have not been the only obstacles limiting the law's ability to produce more low- and moderate-income housing. While waiting for Chapter 774's legality to be established by the State Supreme Court, would be developers of such housing were dealt a severe direct financial blow: federal funds expected to support their efforts dried up, when in January of 1973, President Nixon imposed a moratorium on federal support for the construction of new subsidized housing. This was soon followed by the cessation, in 1974, of state funding for such housing construction as a result of bonding problems experienced by the Massachusetts Housing and Finance Agency. Furthermore, at about the same time that government subsidies were vanishing, housing construction costs were beginning to soar. Low- and moderate-income housing developers thus faced skyrocketing increases in building materials, land, and labor costs with no government sources available for funding.

Insufficient funding of the state agency charged with administering Chapter 774 appeals cases, the Department of Community Affairs, also contributed to delays in their processing. Because of budget cuts made by Governor Dukakis and continued by Governor King, the support staff and funds of the Housing Appeals Committee have, since 1974, been substantially reduced. The two principal HAC staffers have numerous other ongoing responsibilities that take them away from vigorous factfinding and speedy pursuit of Chapter 774 appeals applications.

Nonmonetary delay-causing problems also have attenuated the bill's impact. HAC proceedings have been lengthy not only because of inadequate funding, but also because of the outlook of the bureaucracy involved and systematic constraints within it. Exceptionally high turnover in DCA commissioners—seven different agency heads in the 10 years since Chapter 774 was enacted—has created and exacerbated problems in the administration of the law, since each change in agency head has necessitated a period of adjustment that has repeatedly slowed down the work of the department's staff. A reorganization into the Department of Communities and Development with a new thrust toward economic development also had to be weathered. Moreover, as part of an agency with ongoing relations to, and the need for cooperation and support from, localities apart from Chapter 774 dealings, the HAC staff has sometimes intentionally moved slowly with appeals proceedings. The aim has been to get the parties involved to work out an agreeable compromise on their own, rather than imposing a disagreeable decision on localities. HAC has generally moved less expeditiously than Chapter 774's backers intended, rarely imposing the

30-day limit the law requires for reaching a decision. Instead, hearings have frequently been held up or suspended by HAC officials to encourage local negotiations. Although these negotiations have sometimes resulted in settlements, they also have led to abandonment of some projects by frustrated developers.

Environmental-protection legislation passed after the enactment of Chapter 774 also has played a role in lengthening the time required to secure final approval to build Chapter 774 housing. The Wetlands Protection Law enacted in 1974 instructed local conservation commissions to review proposals for local construction that might affect wetlands and granted them power to veto projects they judge a threat. Because these reviews were not supposed to be undertaken until all other relevant permits had been approved, they have dragged out Chapter 774 proceedings in a number of cases. It has been especially frustrating for developers who have weathered long HAC and court appeals, which finally gave them the go-ahead, to find their project stalled yet again, or vetoed altogether, by a conservation commission. This is precisely what led to the final withdrawal of the developer in the Concord case and in the more recent Chelmsford case, which involved one of the largest proposals for family low- and moderate-income housing (459 units). Similarly, the 1974 Massachusetts Environmental Policy Act's requirement that all public agencies submit environmental-impact statements to the Secretary of Environmental Affairs for approval of projects also has added a few months to the Chapter 774 process in several cases.[19]

It is ironic that all these problems began at about the same time, or just shortly after, the first serious tests of the Antisnob Zoning Law had cleared the courts, validating it and strengthening its potential impact. All things considered, it is easy to see why the Antisnob Zoning Law has produced such a relatively small amount of housing. Indeed, in view of these numerous obstacles, it is rather remarkable that Chapter 774 has yet had any impact at all.

Some of the problems encountered in trying to implement the Antisnob Zoning Law during the last 10 years have already been resolved or could be overcome with relative ease. Federal and state subsidies for low- and moderate-income housing have been resumed in the past few years, and as a result, construction of at least one sizable stalled Chapter 774 project for family housing has begun (in Scituate). The Wetlands Act was recently modified to allow conservation commission reviews of proposals to proceed while comprehensive permit applications are being considered, and similar alteration to the timing of environmental-impact reviews could be made. Bureaucratic contributions to the delays in Chapter 774 proceedings could be lessened by a legislative or judicial mandate that the HAC adhere strictly to the law's deadlines and by an increased budget allocation to provide HAC staff with the means to comply. Court reform, as proposed by the Cox

Commission and recently adopted by the Massachusetts legislature, should help to lessen, if not eliminate, some of the backlogs that also have helped draw out Chapter 774 proceedings.

With these changes effected, the Massachusetts Antisnob Zoning Law could, in the next decade, produce considerably more low- and moderate-income housing in the suburbs than it has in the past. However, none of the changes will stop suburbs from lengthening proceedings by slugging it out in court, thereby causing developers' costs to rise and projects to be abandoned. Unless and until suburban resistance is overcome, or at least substantially reduced, it seems unlikely that Chapter 774 will result in opening up for many low- or moderate-income families. For the antisnob zoning approach to end these detrimental delay tactics in Massachusetts or in any other state in the 1980s and beyond, the *reasons* for such intense suburban opposition must be understood and addressed.

Most opposition by suburbanites to proposals for subsidized housing for families probably stems from fear: fear that "a bad class of people" (read: black, AFDC mothers with hordes of unruly children) will occupy it and threaten their valued way of life, or fear that no matter how nice the occupants may be (even if they're white and well-behaved), they will raise the tax rate by requiring costly public services, especially education for their children.

Although public-opinion polls reveal that racial attitudes have become more liberal over the past two decades, there is still considerable evidence that many whites hold stereotyped, negative views of the personal characteristics of blacks, who are widely perceived as the primary occupants of public housing, which also has a negative image.[20] Furthermore, while support among whites for the abstract principles of racial justice is high, surveys reveal significant disapproval by whites of concrete government action to guarantee the rights of blacks. And predictably, suburban residents are more opposed than their urban counterparts to government action in the housing field.[21] Emotional, irrational, prejudice-based fears, which undoubtedly play an important role in suburban resistance to the Antisnob Zoning Law, cannot be allayed easily, but some could perhaps be lessened by publicizing the success stories of completed Chapter 774 projects and other subsidized family housing units, for example, those in Beverly and Lincoln. Far from being eyesores or becoming instant slums, these developments are attractively designed, well-maintained, and occupied by an income and racial mix of people that has by no means lowered the quality of life in their communities. The second cateogry of fear, that based on the belief that increased costs necessitated by such housing will come out of the pockets of local homeowners, cannot be alleviated without a fundamental alteration to the Antisnob Zoning Law's approach, for this fear derives from rational—and real—economic calculations: subsidized housing units, especially those for families, *do* require services that cost far more than the meager revenues that payments in lieu of taxes provide municipalities.[22] While astutely and wisely recognizing that unreasonable costs to developers would impede the building of low- and moderate-income housing, the architects of the Massachusetts Antisnob Zoning Law consciously chose to dismiss as invalid the role of economic considerations in suburban exclusionary behavior. Service and support costs incurred by localties were explicitly excluded from Chapter 774's definition of reasonable grounds for a ZBA's denial of a subsidized housing proposal. However, given the realities of the current system of heavy reliance on property taxes to finance local services, such concerns cannot be dismissed cavalierly, especially not in Massachusetts, where property taxes are the highest in the nation, and especially not now that the "Proposition 13 property tax revolt" is in high gear and local "tax cap" fever is spreading. Under these circumstances, as a number of students of suburban politics and exclusion have observed, it is in the rational self-interest of suburban officials to do all they can to resist efforts at opening up.[23]

The Chapter 774 experience makes clear that a negative-incentive "stick" approach such as the threat of state intervention will not alone overcome this resistance. Positive financial incentives must be provided to local communities to gain acceptance for family low- and moderate-income housing. The "carrot" needed is a guarantee that the local costs of servicing such housing will be offset by the state and/or federal government. As we have argued elsewhere, problems inherent in the property tax, for example, its regressivity and visibility, make communities dependent upon it ill-equipped to serve as agents of redistribution, and opening up the suburbs is clearly a redistributive measure.[24] The federal income tax, for all its shortcomings, provides the largest, most progressive and equitable source of funding, with state income or sales taxes second best.

Creating an arrangement to help local communities meet the costs of subsidized housing thus seems the most critical change required to increase the Antisnob Zoning Law's ability to get family housing built in the suburbs. However, one cannot be sanguine about the prospects for achieving this reform. Having states compensate localities for the costs of supporting such housing is not a new idea. Several years ago, two prominent advocates of opening up the suburbs proposed that states establish an Urban Development Fund to do this, and bills introduced in the Connecticut and Wisconsin legislatures since the enactment of Chapter 774 have included provisions for state financial incentives to gain local cooperation.[25] Such a fund has yet to be created, and the Connecticut and Wisconsin bills died in committee. So positive incentives from the states do not seem likely. Nor are they likely to come from the federal government. Congress has gone on record in support of the dispersal of subsidized housing, but the major tool designed to accomplish this, the 1974 Housing and Community Development Act, with its Housing Assistance Plan and "expected to reside" requirements, relies solely upon a negative-incentive approach.[26] And although the Carter administration did renew federal support for the construction of low- and moderate-income housing, its proposed budget for fiscal year 1980 actually reduced federal spending for housing.

The reluctance of state and federal politicians to undertake costly housing programs for low- and moderate-income people is, to be sure, understandable in the current economic climate, in which housing costs have become a serious concern for many of their middle-class constituents. In such a climate, it is asking quite a lot to expect elected officials at either the state or federal level to allocate more funds for subsidized housing. Nevertheless, if more than lip service is to be paid to achieving the goals of an integrated society and "a decent home and a suitable living environment" for all Americans, the necessary financial support for programs designed to open up the suburbs will need to be committed. The Massachusetts experience with the Antisnob Zoning Law demonstrates that the reassertion of state power to override local restrictions is a necessary, but not sufficient, means to accomplish these goals.

Notes

1. See, for example, *Report of the National Commission on Urban Problems: Building the American City* (Washington: U.S. Government Printing Office, 1968); *Report of the National Advisory Commission on Civil Disorders* (Washington: U.S. Government Printing Office, 1968); *Report of the President's Committee on Urban Housing: A Decent Home* (Washington: U.S Government Printing Office, 1969); *The President's Task Force Report on Suburban Problems* (Cambridge, Mass.: Ballinger, 1974); Charles A. Krause, "Rights Movement Aims at U.S. Suburbs," *Washington Post*, May 15, 1976; Paul Davidoff, Linda Davidoff, and Neil Gold, "Suburban Action: Advocate Planning for an Open Society," *Journal of the American Institute of Planners* 36 (January 1970); Charles M. Haar and Demetrius Iatrides, *Housing the Poor in Suburbia* (Cambridge, Mass.: Ballinger, 1974); Richard F. Babcock and Fred P. Bosselman, *Exclusionary Zoning* (New York: Praeger, 1973); R. Robert Linowes and Don T. Allensworth, *The Politics of Land Use* (New York: Praeger, 1973); Anthony Downs, *Opening Up the Suburbs* (New Haven, Conn.: Yale Univ. Press, 1973); Joseph P. Fried, *Housing Crisis U.S.A.* (New York: Praeger, 1971); Michael N. Danielson, *The Politics of Exclusion* (New York: Columbia Univ. Press, 1976); and John F. Kain and Joseph J. Persky, "Alternatives to the Guilded Ghetto," *The Public Interest* (Winter 1969).

2. In a striking parallel, the Supreme Court recently ruled that veterans preference in Civil Service hirings and promotions is not unconstitutional. The Supreme Court has thus made clear that it is unwilling to deal with discriminatory situations for minorities or women unless they have come about intentionally.

3. For problems encountered in New Jersey in trying to develop a viable plan for requiring communities to take action to construct low- and moderate-income housing on a regional-need basis, see Jerome G. Rose and Robert E. Rothman (eds.), *After Mount Laurel* (New Brunswick, N.J.: Transaction Books, 1977); see also, Fred Bosselman and David Callies, *The Quiet Revolution in Land Use Controls* (Washington: U.S. Government Printing Office, 1971, pp. 164-186), prepared for the Council on Environmental Quality; and Leonard S. Rubinowitz, *Low-Income Housing: Suburban Strategies* (Cambridge, Mass.: Ballinger, 1974).

4. See Sharon Perlman Krefetz, "The Massachusetts Anti-Snob Zoning Law: Who Wanted What, Who Got What, and So What?" paper presented at the Northeastern Political Science Association Annual Meeting, 1977; Karen Schneider, "Innovation in State Legislation: The Massachusetts Suburban Zoning Act," Radcliffe College Honors Thesis, 1970; Martin A. Linsky and Robert L. Turner, "Watch Out Suburbs—Here Come the Cities," unpublished manuscript, 1970; Margaret Power, "Metropolitan Policy and State Politics," Ph.D. dissertation, M.I.T., 1974; "Chapter 774: Anti-Snob Zoning," author unknown, Harvard-M.I.T. Joint Center for Urban Studies paper, October 1975; and Sylvia B. Perlman, "The Massachusetts Anti-Snob Zoning Law: Its Drafting and Passage," graduate seminar paper, Florence Heller School, Brandeis University, April 1976.

5. The legislation went through fifteen drafts in subcommittee, where its backers "tried to meet every legitimate objection of local communities except the inviolability of local zoning" (Schneider, "Innovation in State Legislation," p. 19).

6. Detailed discussions of the key provisions of Chapter 774 can be found in James Breagy, "Overriding the Suburbs," Citizens Housing and Planning Association Report, Boston, May 1976, p. 12; Paul M. Vaughn, "The Massachusetts Zoning Appeals Law: First Breach in the Exclusionary Wall," *Boston University Law Review* 54 (January 1974):37-77; and reports by the state's two largest regional planning commissions: "The Impact of Chapter 774," Central Massachusetts Regional Planning Agency, April 1971, and "Chapter 774: Four Years Later," Metropolitan (Boston) Area Planning Council, August 1974.

7. Bosselman and Callies, *The Quiet Revolution*, p. 164. For more critical views of the legislation, see Breagy, "Overriding the Suburbs"; Vaughn, "The Massachusetts Zoning Appeals Law"; and Samuel A. Sherer,

"Snob Zoning: Developments in Massachusetts and New Jersey," *Harvard Journal on Litigation* (1970):246-270.

8. Figures on the total number of Chapter 774 applications made and housing constructed are, unfortunately, not necessarily precise because systematic records are only kept for cases appealed to the Housing Appeals Committee (61 to date). Figures reported here are from a survey of Massachusetts municipalities (to which 336 of 351 responded) conducted by the Citizens Housing and Planning Association in 1978-1979. See Lisa Ruben and Constance Williams, "The Use of Comprehensive Permits for Housing Lower Income Households in Massachusetts," preliminary draft, August 1979.

9. The Massachusetts Legislative Research Council reported this in 1967 and estimated the shortage in the Boston area alone to be about 35,000 units for low- and moderate-income households.

10. Allan G. Rodgers, "Snob Zoning in Massachusetts," *1970 Annual Survey of Massachusetts Law* (Boston: Boston College Law School, 1971), pp. 487-497; and McDonald Barr, "The Massachusetts Zoning Appeals Law: Lessons of the First Three Years," Department of Community Affairs (DCA), Boston, August 1972.

11. Indeed the type of housing involved was a much better predictor of local response to a Chapter 774 proposal than community characteristics such as size, growth rate, educational level, or racial composition. See Krefetz, "The Massachusetts Anti-Snob Zoning Law," pp. 28-31.

12. Calvin Trillin, "U.S. Journal: Mt. Laurel, N.J.," *The New Yorker*, February 2, 1976, p. 71.

13. Danielson, *The Politics of Exclusion*, p. 305.

14. The undertaking of these projects cannot, of course, be attributed directly or solely to the influence of Chapter 774. Discussions of the need for low- and moderate-income housing in Lincoln were actually begun in 1963. See Polly Jackson's account of the Lincoln undertaking, "The Development of Housing for Low and Moderate-Income Households in a Suburb: A Case History," Massachusetts League of Women Voters and the Citizens Housing and Planning Association, 1978.

15. For example, Springfield, New Bedford, and Lowell; Chelsea, Malden, and Cambridge. Approximately twenty communities now meet Chapter 774's 10 percent quota.

16. Breagy, "Overriding the Suburbs," pp. 42-43.

17. Ibid., p. 40. The ruling also held that DCA could and should issue administrative regulations for Chapter 774 proceedings. This enabled some of Chapter 774's advocates to tighten up and revise the law a bit. The Massachusetts Law Reform Institute, for example, proposed numerous items for inclusion in the new regulations, virtually all of which were adopted by DCA and included in its 1974 Rules and Regulations.

18. According to HAC staff head Maurice Corman, trying to obtain stipulation (to agree to a compromise) from the developer and the municipality is preferable to ruling against the locality because it eliminates lengthy court appeals, which so frequently result in the demise of projects (interview with author, September 5, 1979).

19. Breagy, "Overriding the Suburbs," pp. 52-56.

20. For analyses of these trends, see D. Garth Taylor, "Housing, Neighborhoods, and Race Relations"; Thomas F. Pettigrew, "Racial Change and Social Policy"; and Reynolds Farley et al., "Barriers to the Racial Integration of Neighborhoods: The Detroit Case"; all in *The Annals* 441 (January 1979).

21. Frederick Wirt et al., *On the City's Rim: Politics and Policy in Suburbia* (Lexington, Mass.: Lexington Books, Heath, 1972), pp. 109-115.

22. One calculation of the "cost-revenue posture of alternative land uses" in a New Jersey suburb in 1975 has estimated the annual net deficit created by a subsidized low-income apartment with 4.2 occupants to be about $2,000; of this total, about $1,850 is in educational costs for 1.6 pupils. Robert W. Burchell and David Listokin, "Response to Supreme Court of New Jersey Questions," in James W. Hughes (ed.), *Methods of Housing Analysis* (New Brunswick, N.J.: Rutgers Univ. Center for Urban Policy Research, 1977), pp. 414-415. While the exact figures will vary in different suburbs, this estimate is sobering.

23. Danielson, *The Politics of Exclusion*, pp. 43-47; Babcock and Bosselman, *Exclusionary Zoning*, p. 3; Trillin, "U.S. Journal," p. 69. Robert Wood in *Suburbia: Its People and Their Politics* (Boston: Houghton Mifflin, 1958) perhaps overstated the case when he wrote: "Given the nature of the property tax, it is difficult to criticize suburban officials who are fortunate enough to have desirable locations for exploiting their position. To do otherwise when government costs are rising steadily—to be liberal in their attitude toward lower-income newcomers, to strive for heterogeneous neighborhoods, to welcome citizens regardless of race, creed, or color—is to invite financial disaster. If the town fathers are to be faithful to their economic trust, they must practice discrimination" (p. 217).

24. See Sharon Krefetz, *Welfare Policy-Making and City Politics* (New York: Praeger, 1976).

25. Paul and Linda Davidoff, "Opening Up the Suburbs: Toward Inclusionary Land-Use Controls," *Syracuse Law Review* 22 (1971):525; see also Rubinowitz, *Low-Income Housing*, p. 95. The fact that the Massachusetts Antisnob Zoning Law did not involve any contribution of funds by the state may help explain why it passed while these other proposals were defeated.

26. The limits of this recent approach by the federal government have already been demonstrated. In response to HUD's threat to refuse water and sewer grants and other funds for community development, a number of suburbs, for example, Windsor Locks, Connecticut and Union Township, New Jersey, have said they would rather do without them than be required to plan for low- and moderate-income housing. See, "Fortress Suburbia," *New York Times*, August 21, 1977. Furthermore, HUD's monitoring and enforcement of this policy has been less than vigorous. See Robert E. Mitchell and Richard A. Smith, "Race and Housing: A Review and Comments on the Content and Effects of Federal Policy," *The Annals* 441 (January 1979):181-184.

10 Racial Discrimination: Some New Empirical Evidence

Barton A. Smith

Discrimination and Housing Policy

One of the more pervasive problems in urban housing markets is discrimination against minorities, limiting their access to both housing and neighborhood amenities. Prior to the Civil Rights Act of 1968, blatant acts of discrimination were observed. Suppliers of housing (sellers or landlords) simply refused to deal with blacks and openly said so. The result, or so it appeared, was that blacks were forced to consume inferior housing and were segregated into ghettos that offered inferior neighborhood amenities. Since the mid-1960s, the more open and explicit forms of discrimination have gradually disappeared. However, new evidence suggests that they are likely to have been replaced by more subtle, yet just as effective, forms of discrimination. This phenomenon has created two important challenges for policymakers: (1) developing programs that can buttress the law against discrimination in housing (Title VIII of the Civil Rights Act), thus making it a more meaningful piece of legislation; and (2) monitoring progress that is being made against discrimination in housing markets. In addition, decisionmakers need to be able to sort out the difficulties that minorities have in acquiring "a decent home and suitable living environment" which are due to discrimination as opposed to those which are due to inferior purchasing power. Clearly the development of appropriate policies to solve the low level of consumption of quality housing and neighborhoods by minority households depends crucially on knowledge of the exact cause of the plight that affects such a large portion of America's minority population.

Recent Empirical Literature

During the 1950s, the existence of discrimination was obvious, and studies related to race and housing primarily sought to document the severity of its impact on minorities. Today discrimnation is considerably more difficult to document, and analyses of discriminatory impacts have been used extensively as evidence that discrimination still exists. Unfortunately there are few rigorous analyses that enable direct inferences to be made about the existence and extent of explicit discrimination from differential housing-consumption outcomes for minorities and nonminorities. Furthermore the process whereby blacks and other minorities are now discriminated against and segmented in segregated all-minority neighborhoods is not well understood. Arguments in support of current theories are for the most part conjectural and anecdotal.

The Title VIII Fair Housing Evaluation recently conducted by the Department of Housing and Urban Development (HUD) is perhaps the only exception, providing some *direct* evidence regarding the nature and extent of discrimination in today's housing markets. As reported in *Measuring Racial Discrimination in American Housing Markets*, HUD analysts suggest that despite fair-housing legislation, there exists "definitive evidence that blacks are discriminated against in the sale and rental of housing" and that "substantial racial discrimination was observed."[1] However, the analysis of the HUD data, based on "housing audits" performed in selected metropolitan areas, is far from complete. The fact that many whites also received inferior treatment is left unexplained, and the concept of *net discrimination* (defined as the difference in the percent white minus the percent black that received favored treatment) is not obviously policy relevant. Nonetheless, while further research is required to understand all the implications of the HUD audit experiment, it does clearly demonstrate that today's discrimination has become extremely subtle and is quite difficult to directly document, phenomena that are likely attributable to a large extent to Title VIII enforcement itself.

While direct evidence is sparse, a voluminous literature exists providing indirect evidence of discrimination, such as those documenting differentials in the housing-consumption patterns of minorities. In the absence of stronger evidence, those differentials which cannot be explained by normal market conditions or by the economic status of minorities are presumed to be due to discrimination. Thus the recent empirical literature focuses on the nature and magnitude of distorted housing-market impacts on minorities as the dominant means of documenting and monitoring the continuing existence of discrimination. Unfortunately, however, this empirical literature does not provide a foundation for consensus. In fact, a considerable amount of confusion still exists over the nature and extent of today's minority housing problems. Indeed, conclusions from among some of the best recent analytical work are quite contradictory. Furthermore, while casual observation reveals that minorities are highly segregated and consume significantly lower-quality housing than the overall population, the causes of these phenomena are still very much open to question, despite the fact that identifying those causes is essential to policy development.

Research Goals and Objectives

This chapter provides a greatly reduced summarization of a recent study (hereafter referred to as the *Smith/Mieszkowski study*) of discrimination in urban housing markets and subsequent differentials in consumption outcomes between racial/ethnic groups.[2]

The purpose of this study was to reexamine some of the basic issues surrounding discrimination in housing markets and the observed phenomena purported to be consistent with the presence of discrimination. While both blacks and Mexican-Americans are analyzed, the primary focus is on black households. Three issues dominate this research. First, the potential of housing-price differentials between blacks and whites is examined. Second, the apparent underconsumption of housing by black households is analyzed. Finally the relationship between tenure choice (owner/renter) and race is reappraised.[3]

The initial stimulus for this study was the existence of a considerable amount of conflicting evidence provided in the literature. Equally important was the fact that the formulation of national policies to deal with racial issues obviously requires a much better understanding of the performance of urban housing markets. Issues with respect to minority access to adequate housing are very complex and intertwined with a host of other problems. Indeed, given the breadth of the problem faced, it is not obvious that housing policies alone can totally solve these problems. In many instances it now appears that, alone, explicit housing programs may be insufficient to provide long-run solutions to housing problems. Policies and programs with respect to employment, income redistribution, fiscal equity, crime, public services, education, and transportation also have a bearing on the solution of minority housing problems. Furthermore, it must be realized that many problems faced by minorities in housing markets are not unique to them, but are problems faced in common with all lower-income households.

Government policy obviously plays an important role in the entire urban system. Fair-housing efforts are bound to affect the desegregation of schools, the availability of public services, the access to labor-market opportunities, and the viability of small neighborhood businesses. For example, non-HUD policies that aim at other urban problems are certain to impact HUD program efforts. Furthermore, fair-housing policies will impact other HUD objectives and concerns, such as community development and neighborhood revitalization. Conversely, these concerns and subsequent policies are bound to impact HUD's attempt to promote equal opportunity in housing.

While recognizing the breadth of the problem, the research summarized here had no intention of providing a comprehensive description of the broad social problems discussed earlier. To the contrary, it was conducted on the firm belief that comprehensive answers are often based on a series of incremental gains in our awareness of particular issues. Nonetheless, while the analytical beginnings of this research are narrowly focused, they do provide the foundation upon which further research may more successfully be pursued to shed light on issues of neighborhood stability, racial transition, resegregation, and gentrification and on such policies as those involving fair-housing enforcement and community-development strategies. It is fully recognized that more research is needed to increase our understanding of urban housing markets and the process whereby minorities are adversely affected. However, at this point it appears essential that clarification and corrections, when necessary, be made in the current empirical literature before broader questions are addressed. As consensus is reached with regard to empirical findings, the analyses of causes or processes will be given much clearer direction.

Racially Oriented Housing-Price Differentials

One major research objective of the Smith/Mieszkowski study was to reexamine the question of whether blacks pay more for housing than whites. Several theoretical models of housing-market discrimination suggest that minorities faced with restricted supply would be forced to pay higher prices for housing. Other models, based on the assumption of the dominance of white prejudice, predict that whites will pay premiums to live in all white areas and thus "pay the price" for their prejudicial attitudes. The empirical literature, however, is quite mixed, providing neither answers to the theoretical questions (the cause of the problem) nor satisfactory answers to the simple empirical question of fact: Do blacks pay more? In the current literature, just as many studies show a negative correlation between housing prices and race as there are studies that indicate the opposite.[4]

Methodology

In this study, *housing* is explicitly defined as the private good consumed, including both structure and land, but excluding neighborhood. This definition of housing is consistent with the general literature and was considered more appropriate, since it provides a rational dichotomy of the housing consumption bundle: the *private good*, house, produced by the private sector, and the *public good*, neighborhood, produced indirectly through externalities generated from private-sector decisions and directly from public-sector programs. While the question of price differentials is thus focused around the costs of the private good, differentials in neighborhood attributes that clearly affect housing prices are fully considered. Using detailed housing and location data for both Houston and Chicago, separate hedonic housing-price equations were estimated for various areas defined by their racial composition. From these equations, price differentials were obtained.

Findings

For both Houston and Chicago, it was found that housing prices (the price of housing of equivalent quality) in black areas appear to be lower than housing in all white, non-Hispanic areas. In comparison to the all non-minority area, housing prices were found to be 21 percent less in predominantly black areas, 16 percent less in integrated areas, 10 percent less in nonminority areas threatened by minority immigration, and 7 percent less in nonminority areas bordering minority neighborhoods but not perceived to be imminently threatened by racial transition. The results for Chicago were very similar. Equally interesting, the price differentials found for both Houston and Chicago appear to be explained for the most part by differences in neighborhood amenities.

In addition to overall price differentials found in both cities, significant differences were found to exist among neighborhoods in the marginal prices of various housing attributes. While these results do differ somewhat between Houston and Chicago because of basic differences in the extent and pattern of the segregated black ghettos in each city, some generalizations still can be made. Areas impacted by racial factors tend to have lower marginal prices for structural attributes usually associated with quality. However, blacks appear to pay higher prices for exterior space (lot size) and interior space (square feet of living area and number of rooms).

Perhaps the most interesting and significant evidence provided in the overall text of the Smith/Mieszkowski report is that the *house-value function*, defined as the relationship between the total value of housing paid and the quality of housing purchased, is quite different for blacks and whites. The black house-value function appears to have a higher intercept term but lower slope coefficients. This means that the black and white house-value functions intersect, suggesting that given the constraints that segment the urban housing markets in both cities, self-segregation of minorities is to be expected. This self-segregation is not, however, due to direct preferences, but to the economic incentives provided by the implicit price structure that exists in racially segmented markets. These findings suggest a somewhat different model of the relationship of minorities in urban housing markets than currently accepted. The price differentials found are much more consistent with the original border models of Muth and Bailey, suggesting that whites pay for their prejudices.[5] Differences in the marginal prices of housing attributes found by blacks is consistent with de facto self-segregation. Lower prices for quality and higher prices for exterior and interior space are also very much consistent with apparent differentials in housing demand, where blacks appear to have relative higher demand for the latter two components of housing.

Rate of Appreciation

For Houston, time-series as well as cross-section data were available, enabling the analysis of rates of appreciation between 1970 and 1977 for various neighborhood types. Rates of appreciation were estimated for the following six types of areas:

White (upper middle class)	152.7%
White	101.8%
Border	117.1%
Border (threatened)	79.8%
Integrated	92.8%
Black	84.1%

While even black areas experienced high rates of appreciation, these results indicate that given housing as an investment as well as a consumption good, the "effective prices" blacks pay for housing is actually higher.[6] This follows from the previous finding that prices across neighborhoods are approximately equivalent after controlling for neighborhood attributes; yet as shown earlier, the rate of return in the form of capital gains from homeownership is almost double in white upper-middle-income areas.

These results are important beyond the fact that blacks do not appear to be achieving equivalent returns on housing investment. In 1970, Houston housing prices were quite low relative to the nation. During the last decade, the higher rates of appreciation reflect a catching up of the Houston housing market. However, because white areas experienced much higher rates of appreciation, black households will find it progressively more difficult to acquire owner-occupied housing in predominately white areas, because their equities will be insufficient to allow for upward mobility to higher-quality houses in white areas. This finding appears to be substantiated by recent evidence indicating that while many all white areas of Houston are experiencing minority migration, further integrating the city, very little of this minority immigration is to owner-occupied housing. Black movement in predominately all white areas is almost exclusively into the large number of relatively new apartment complex units scattered throughout most of these areas. Thus the differentials in appreciation rates found in this study suggest that homeownership by minorities in nonminority areas is going to become less likely, despite fair-housing efforts.

The Underconsumption of Housing by Black Households

Findings

Despite the fact (contrary to current wisdom) that blacks pay less for housing, the empirical results of this study indicate that blacks underconsume housing by an amount that ranges from 10 to 30 percent. That is, given the same economic status, a black household is likely to spend 10 to 30 percent less on housing, a finding that is consistent with most previous empirical studies.[7]

Analyses of the demand for key housing attributes show that blacks primarily underconsume housing *quality*, defined in terms of the age of housing along with a single hedonic weighted variable of several attributes normally associated with housing quality. Blacks, *ceteris paribus*, tend to purchase housing that is about 35 percent older and has about 22 percent less quality than housing consumed by their white counterparts. Thus, while there may be some connection between the apparent underconsumption by blacks and the prices they face, evidence here indicates that it is not likely to be the most important explanation. The two primary features of housing, exterior space (lot size) and interior space (square feet of living area and number of rooms), for which they pay a higher price are not found to be underconsumed by blacks.

These findings, however, are considered tentative at this point for several reasons. First, alternative income variables used change the results rather dramatically, even to the point of completely eliminating any underconsumption effect for some specifications.[8] Second, the results are quite sensitive to interactions among age, marital status, and wealth. Finally, there appears to be a very strong correlation between the underconsumption effect and the type of mortgage instrument used. Currently the underconsumption effect appears to be a phenomenon primarily found in the FHA market. Needless to say, a considerable amount of additional research is needed to sort out all the aspects of this effect and to ascertain its cause.

Wealth and Homeownership

The analysis of housing-consumption patterns clearly demonstrated that wealth and previous homeownership are particularly important in the consumption of owner-occupied housing. Together they explain more of the variation of housing expenditures than does income. The results of the inclusion of a wealth variable are rather robust in light of other specification problems. This seems to underscore the concern expressed over the high appreciation rates in predominately white areas. Since equity accumulation is one of the primary means of wealth accumulation, lower appreciation rates in black areas mean less wealth accumulation and subsequently greater difficulty in acquiring owner-occupied housing. Furthermore, because of either past discrimination or low economic status, blacks traditionally have been found to have a higher propensity to rent. Given the importance of wealth (and homeownership in the wealth-accumulation process) and of past homeownership in enabling households to purchase single-family housing, the achievement of goals associated with increasing owner-occupancy among minorities may becoming increasingly remote.

Underconsumption and Segregation

The importance of mobility into nonminority areas also was illustrated in the research findings by the fact that blacks who had "broken the racial barrier," so to speak, and had acquired owner-occupied housing in virtually all white areas appear to consume the amount of housing expected given their economic credentials. While these results strongly suggest that integration per se may be an important tool in achieving other minority-oriented housing goals, further investigation is needed with regard to the prices minorities pay in white areas, the financing used, and the attributes of the households that either allowed or stimulated them to acquire housing in white areas. In other words, integration may not be such a simple solution if, in fact, blacks that do acquire owner-occupied housing in white areas are unique from the black population in general or if they have to pay an exorbitant price for the luxury of living in white neighborhoods.

The consumption patterns of blacks found in the Smith/Mieszkowski research are consistent with several hypotheses regarding race and housing markets. However, together with the findings regarding price differentials, these results seem to be most consistent with prejudice models of segmented urban housing markets.[9] If, indeed, prices are lower in black areas and the black house-value function rises with quality much more steeply than for whites, the consumption patterns found are consistent with utility maximization of black households unconstrained by nonmarket forces. Low prices in the ghetto coupled with the high incremental costs of acquiring better-quality housing outside the ghetto could create strong incentives for blacks to purchase the lower-quality housing in the ghetto, thus fostering both underconsumption and segregation.

Blacks and Homeownership

Sample Representativeness

Logit analysis was used to examine the extent that blacks of similar economic status are more likely to rent. An extremely important methodological finding was that the results obtained were very sensitive to the representativeness of the sample analyzed. A search of the literature shows that no one as yet even discusses this issue. Alternative sample distributions from the Houston data demonstrate that one can get almost any result desired. Preliminary results using the National Longitudinal Survey data and Survey of Economic Opportunity data also indicate that presumptions of representativeness in these samples is misdirected and that estimates from an unweighted sample of these national data bases produce biased results.

The results considered most accurate in this study are based on a sample created to be representative of the Harris County (Houston Metropolitan Area) population with respect to race, tenure (owner/renter), and income.

Findings

While further exploration is still warranted, the best estimate is that if wealth is controlled for in the estimating equation, blacks appear to have an 8 to 14 percent lower probability of owning, *ceteris paribus*. These results are somewhat lower than estimates of previous studies.[10] However, the exclusion of wealth as an independent variable raises the black/white differential to over 20 percent, a figure that is surprisingly high given that previous tenure (owner/renter) was still controlled for.

More experimentation with alternative specifications is still needed in order to maximize our ability to explain differences among past studies. Preliminary results seem to indicate that specifications with respect to such important independent variables as income and wealth are quite important. There appears to be a threshold point (that is, a minimum income and wealth level) before the probability of ownership is significantly different from zero. The nonlinearity (even in the logs) of income and wealth needs to be pursued in further research. In addition, alternative explanations of this apparent tenure distortion need to be explored. One possible next step would be to integrate other research on redlining and lending patterns, on segregation, and on the joint tenure/expenditure decision in order to achieve a better understanding of this phenomenon.

Reasons for the Apparent Tenure Distortion

In many ways the results obtained from this part of the research effort are not particularly surprising given the other findings with regard to housing prices and consumption patterns of blacks in the owner-occupied market. Low- to moderate-income blacks may find homeownership out of the question because of the apparent higher discounts on black incomes that was found (presumably because of greater variability and instability). In addition, middle-income blacks may find renting the cheapest way to acquire better neighborhoods. Many middle-income blacks who desire to break away from the ghetto, as well as the inferior quality neighborhood there, may find that renting quality apartments is a more viable alternative to achieving their demands for improved neighborhood quality than paying white owner-occupied premiums.

However, before hasty conclusions are made with respect to these findings, it should be mentioned that some caution is needed in interpreting the empirical results from the traditional perspective. Instead of blacks underconsuming housing and experiencing abnormally low ownership rates, it could easily be said that whites overconsume housing and tend to have an abnormally high propensity to own. Within the context of a Muth/Bailey model of prejudice, whites not only may be willing to pay more to live in exclusively white areas, but also may, in fact, overconsume owner-occupied housing in order to achieve their racial-prejudice objectives.

Synthesis of Findings

Conclusions with Regard to Methodology

The scope of the research undertaken was limited to a review and reexamination of three basic empirical propositions: blacks pay more than whites for housing; blacks underconsume housing; and blacks of similar economic status as whites have a greater tendency to rent. As a byproduct of the research efforts to analyze these three questions, important conclusions were made regarding appropriate methodological approaches in analyzing hypothesized segmented housing markets.

Empirical work that purports to examine differences in submarkets must first analyze those submarkets separately and then proceed with the desired comparisons. In relation to price differentials, single-equation estimtes using either dichotomous variables for racially defined areas or continuous variables indicating the area's percent minority are shown in the full text of the Smith/Mieszkowski study to be incorrect specifications and highly prone to produce erroneous results. It is also demonstrated that it is essential that differences in neighborhood characteristics consumed jointly with housing be adequately controlled for. The previous literature has been severely limited by the state of the art regarding the capitalization of neighborhood amenities into property values, a limitation that is just now beginning to be seriously addressed by housing-market researchers.

As economic theory has predicted for some time, analyses of consumer behavior must include the correct budget constraint. This is particularly true with respect to housing demand and the analyses of differences between races. Not only is it essential that some form of permanent income be used instead of actual income, but wealth also should be included as a separable part of the budget constraint. In addition, nonlinearities with respect to both expenditures and tenure choice as a function of income and wealth require careful consideration. Without exception, the past race and housing literature has failed to adequately control for these aspects of the budget constraint that constitute the primary elements of economic status.

Finally, this research demonstrated that the analyses of questions of dichotomous choice (such as the owner/renter decision) are extremely sensitive to the representativeness of the data samples used. It was shown that virtually any result regarding tenure choice (ownership versus renting) can be obtained by using alternative samples of the same basic data set. Remarkably, none of the previous research published to date has even addressed itself to this question, despite the fact that some of the past studies that have investigated differentials in black/white ownership rates use blatantly unrepresentative samples.

Empirical Findings

This study provides rather strong evidence that blacks *pay less* for housing than whites. However, if differences in the quality of neighborhood amenities are considered, the black/white differential appears to virtually disappear. In addition, when differences in rates of home appreciation are included in the analysis, the effective price for housing faced by blacks appears to actually be higher. This latter result must be carefully interpreted, however, since it is not known whether the "1970 market" or the "1977 market" were equilibrium markets. It could easily be argued that further rises in housing prices in white areas were required to sustain the racially segmented housing market as a reflection of strong white prejudices.

Blacks are found to underconsume housing in comparison to whites of similar economic status, although this result is quite sensitive to alternative definitions of economic status (that is, income and wealth). This latter phenomenon clearly warrants further investigation, since at present, conclusions regarding underconsumption are at best imprecise and since a better understanding of the role of alternative budget constraints could have extremely important policy implications. While blacks are found to underconsume housing in general, they consume similar levels of exterior and interior housing size, but much smaller levels of housing quality and neighborhood quality.

Blacks also are found to have a higher probability of renting, even after controlling for wealth and past tenure. These findings are more robust to alternative definitions of income and wealth and continue to exist after the sample used is adjusted to be representative of the overall population distribution.

Policy Implications

The findings of this research lend themselves to at least some tentative conclusions relevant to policy. The empirical results suggest that strong forces exist to promote self-segregation of blacks even in the absence of explicit housing-market exclusion. Given the relative prices that exist with respect to housing quality and neighborhood quality, it appears that in many cases it is likely that it is in the self-interest of blacks, *given market conditions as revealed by housing prices,* to acquire low-price housing in the ghetto rather than pay white premiums, which in part may be attributable to white prejudice. Thus the results found in this research are more consistent with the Muth/Bailey models of prejudice, although the standard border models need not be implied. While it is suggested that white flight is the primary means by which white prejudice is expressed, the results are also consistent with the existence of stable integrated areas under certain conditions, a conclusion that is at odds with current wisdom. However, the results also provide a basis upon which explanations of reverse tipping may occur, not so much because blacks are *driven* out of rehabilitated areas, but because too many alternatives exist where blacks do not have to pay white premiums for housing.

While such a hypothesis of racial market segmentation suggests that whites pay for their prejudices, this does not mean that the *implicit* barriers to blacks acquiring housing in predominately white areas do not impose real social costs on society as a whole and leave urban areas fragmented and polarized. This indicates that perhaps policymakers should reconsider integration as a *direct* goal and objective and pursue policies that promote integration within a framework that truly recognizes the mechanisms that cause segregation. The fact that blacks living in white areas consume housing at similar levels as their white counterparts also suggests the possible importance of integration as an explicit goal or direct tool to achieve equal outcomes for both whites and blacks in the same metropolitan housing market.

Finally, the results found in this research suggest that HUD needs to evaluate the role FHA home financing plays in the segmentation of housing markets. Blacks almost exclusively use FHA (or VA) financing to acquire owner-occupied housing, and it is these blacks, for the most part, who appear to underconsume housing. In addition, it appears that the availability of FHA financing in minority areas has not affected the lower ownership rates among blacks.

Notes

1. See Ron Wienk et al., *Measuring Racial Discrimination in American Housing Markets: The Housing Market Practices Survey* (Washington: Department of Housing and Urban Development, 1979).

2. Barton Smith and P. Mieskowski, "A Study of Racial Discrimination," report submitted to the Office of Policy Development and Research, Department of Housing and Urban Development, 1979.

3. In the Smith/Mieskowski report, past studies of each issue are reviewed and critiqued, the important conceptual and empirical problems are summarized, and alternative approaches to the analysis of each question are explored. Because of space limitations, much of this detail could not be provided in this chapter. Interested readers are encouraged to read the full report, available from HUD.

4. Among the published studies that indicate that blacks pay less for housing are Martin Bailey, "Effects of Race and Other Demographic Factors of the Value of Single-Family Homes," *Land Economics* 42 (1966); Mahlon Straszheim, "Housing Market Discrimination and Black Housing Consumption," *Quarterly Journal of Economics* (1974); Mahlon Straszheim, *An Econometric Model of the Urban Housing Market* (New York: NBER, 1975); C. Daniels, "The Influence of Racial Segregation on Housing Prices," *Journal of Urban Economics* 2 (1974); Anne Schnare, "Racial and Ethnic Price Differentials in Urban Housing Markets," *Urban Studies* 13 (1976); and Brian Berry, "Ghetto Expansion and Single-Family Housing Prices: Chicago, 1968-1972," *Journal of Urban Economics* 3 (1976). Among those who find no significant price differentials are Victoria Lapham, "Do Blacks Pay More For Housing?" *Journal of Political Economy* 79 (1971); Ann Schnare and Raymond Struyk, "Segmentation in Urban Housing Markets," *Journal of Urban Economics* 3 (1976); and H. Nourse, "The Effect of Public Housing on Property Values in St. Louis," *Land Economics* 42 (1966). But many others find that blacks pay more, including C. Rapkin, "Price Discrimination Against Negroes in the Rental Housing Market," *Essays in Urban Land Economics* (Los Angeles: Univ. of California Press, 1966); R. Ridker and J. Henning, "The Determination of Residential Property Values with a Special Reference to Air Pollution," *Review of Economics and Statistics* 44 (1967); J. Kain and J. Quigley, "Measuring the Value of Housing Quality," *Journal of the American Statistical Association* 65 (1970); J. Kain and J. Quigley, *Housing Markets and Racial Discrimination: A Microeconomic Analysis* (New York: NBER, 1975); John Yinger, "The Black-White Price Differential in Housing: Some Further Evidence," Institute for Research on Poverty, Discussion Paper No. 308-75, Univ. of Wisconsin, 1975; R. Gillingham, "Place to Place Rent Comparison Using Hedonic Quality Adjustment Techniques," BLS Discussion Paper No. 7, 1973; T. King and P. Mieskowski, "Racial Discrimination, Segregation and the Price of Housing," *Journal of Political Economy* 83 (1973); and Garret Vaughn, "Some Recent Evidence on the Supply of Urban Housing to Non-whites from Neighborhoods Undergoing Racial Change," *Journal of Economics and Business* (1975).

5. R. Muth, *Cities and Housing* (Chicago: Univ. of Chicago Press, 1969); R. Muth, *Urban Economic Problems* (New York: Harper and Row, 1975); M. Bailey, "A Note on the Economics of Residential Zoning and

Urban Renewal," *Land Economics* 35 (1959); and M. Bailey, "Effects of Race and Other Demographic Factors on the Value of Single-Family Homes."

6. For a good analysis of housing prices where a wide variety of costs of ownership are considered and adjusted for, including differentials in appreciation rates, see Douglas Diamond, "Taxes, Inflation, Speculation and the Cost of Home Ownership," working paper, North Carolina State Univ., 1979.

7. Kain and Quigley, *Housing Markets and Racial Discrimination*, and M. Straszheim, "Housing Market Discrimination and Black Housing Consumption," are among the most well known studies that document the underconsumption of housing by blacks. Both are particularly noted because of the extensiveness of their treatment of this topic.

8. Six alternative definitions of income were used in the Smith/-Mieszkowski study. Each was consistent with the broadly defined concept of permanent income that is generally accepted as the correct budget constraint relevant to household-consumption decisions.

9. For discussions of the arguments concerning the validity of models of prejudice versus models of discrimination, read and compare Paul Courant, "Racial Prejudice in Search of a Model of the Urban Housing Market," *Jornal of Urban Economics* 5 (1978); P. Courant and J. Yinger, "On Models of Racial Prejudice and Urban Residential Structure," *Journal of Urban Economics* 4 (1977); J. Yinger, "The Black-White Price Differential in Housing: Some Further Evidence"; J. Yinger, "Prejudice and Discrimination in the Urban Housing Market," mimeographed, Harvard Univ., 1978; and B. Smith, "A Re-evaluation of Models of Discrimination and Prejudice in Urban Housing Markets," working paper, Univ. of Houston, 1979.

10. See J. Kain and J. Quigley, *Housing Markets and Racial Discrimination*; M. Straszheim, "Housing Market Discrimination and Black Housing Consumption"; R. Struyk, "Determination of the Rate of Home Ownership of Blacks Relative to White Households," *Journal of Urban Economics* 2 (1975); Birnbaum and Weston, "Home Ownership and the Wealth Position of Black and White Americans," *The Review of Income and Wealth* 20 (1974); and E. Roistacher and J. Goodman, "Race and Home Ownership: Is Discrimination Disappearing?" *Economic Inquiry* 14 (1976).

Part VI
Policies for Low- and Moderate-Income Housing

11 Housing Allowances and Demand-Oriented Housing Subsidies

John M. Quigley

Supply-and-Demand Subsidies

Public subsidies for housing can be classified as supply- or demand-oriented. *Supply-oriented policies* subsidize directly the *construction* or rehabilitation of dwelling units for occupancy by deserving households. They directly produce additional dwelling units for occupancy by households who meet certain program criteria. Indirectly, by increasing the housing supply, they may reduce prices in the short run for those existing dwelling units which are substitutes for the newly constructed or rehabilitated units. *Demand-oriented policies* subsidize the housing *consumption* of deserving households. Such policies stimulate directly the purchasing power of selected households. They thus provide only an indirect stimulation to the construction sector, and by increasing effective demand, they may bid up prices in the short run in those housing submarkets in which the subsidized households compete.

During the past half century, the principal federal housing subsidies have been demand-oriented; that is, they have stimulated demand directly by reducing the price of housing for certain classes of households. The demand subsidies—the treatment of mortgage interest, property tax payments, and capital gains from housing on personal income tax returns—amounted to $9.59 billion in 1977.[1] The subsidies are given only to a certain class of households, namely, to homeowners who itemize deductions. The amount of the subsidy for each recipient household is proportional to its marginal tax rate and to the quantity of housing it selects. The tax subsidy is equivalent to a voucher (or a housing allowance) given to each household in this class. The voucher entitles the recipient to a specified percentage reduction in the price of housing, with larger-percentage reductions going to households with higher taxable incomes.

The administrative cost of this program is negligible. The subsidy is calculated annually when tax returns are filed, and vouchers are issued monthly in the form of reduced withholding taxes. It is estimated that these vouchers are equivalent, on average, to a reduction of 15 percent in the price of owner-occupied housing.[2] Of the $9.6 billion in vouchers issued in 1977, however, about $4.0 billion (or 42 percent) was redeemed by households with annual incomes in excess of $30,000.[3]

By comparison with these demand-oriented subsidies, which accrue principally to middle- and upper-income households, federal subsidies for lower-income households have been almost completely supply-oriented; that is, payments have been made to those who built or substantially rehabilitated dwelling units for occupancy by low-income households at reduced rents. Before 1974, only a few federal programs subsidized the demanders of low-income housing or were not tied to newly constructed units.[4] Since the passage of the Housing Act of 1974, the principal federal housing assistance programs to low-income households have included public housing, homeowner assistance (Section 235), new construction/rehabilitation (Section 8), and existing housing (Section 8). With the exception of the latter program and a small fraction of public housing (leased under Section 23), all other subsidies for low-income households are tied to increases in the overall supply of housing. Deserving households, in this case households with particularly low income levels, are subsidized by making payments to suppliers who contract to produce a new or substantially rehabilitated dwelling unit for occupancy at reduced rents.

The Section 8 existing housing program also provides for payments to housing suppliers to permit occupancy by low-income tenants at reduced rents. As the name suggests, however, the dwelling units provided by landlords may be from the current stock of standard housing and need *not* be rehabilitated or newly built units. Under this program, a household receives a commitment from the federal government to pay part of its rent and then uses this entitlement to seek its own housing. Tenants have some financial incentives to seek housing that meets minimal quality standards and also rents for less than the so-called fair market rent (they are able to keep some of the difference). Recipients are limited in choice; they cannot spend more than 25 percent of their incomes on rent; they cannot occupy a unit that costs more than the fair market rent; and they can choose only units owned by landlords who participate in the program.

This program is demand-oriented in the sense that it subsidizes rent-paying ability without tying it to increases in housing supply. Nevertheless, it is clearly more restrictive than the housing vouchers given to homeowners.

As of June 1978, it is estimated that 2,120,000 low-income housing units are provided by supply-oriented programs and only about 328,000 low-income households are assisted by demand-oriented programs. It is anticipated, however, that the relative importance of demand-oriented subsidies will increase under current programs. For example, it is estimated that the "processing pipeline" currently includes subsidies for an additional 356,000 low-income households under the Section 8 existing housing program compared with 804,000 additional units under supply-oriented programs.

Nevertheless, for about 85 percent of the low-income households currently assisted by federal housing programs, the subsidy is still tied to the production of a brand new or substantially rehabilitated dwelling unit.[5]

When compared with existing programs of housing subsidy, the concept of housing allowances is thus not radical or even particularly novel. The principal difference between housing-allowance proposals and the current array of housing subsidies is the payment of allowances to *poor* households. This housing-allowance concept represents the confluence of two distinct social programs. Through a variety of supply-oriented programs (beginning with public housing in the early 1930s), the federal government has sought to ensure safe and decent housing for the poor. At the same time, and only tangentially related to housing concerns, a variety of income-transfer entitlement programs has emerged. A housing-allowance program melds the two.

A major criticism of current housing programs is the glaring inequity caused by the limited availability of subsidized units, so that equally needy households receive differential treatment. Further, the limited supply of subsidized units has meant that the most needy—usually defined in income terms—are not necessarily the first served. This has led to the charge that the programs are inefficient in that they do not accurately target subsidies according to need.

Welfare programs have been subject to a different sort of criticism. Because of the incentive structure built in through eligibility rules, there can be very large work disincentives. Any work disincentives are magnified by complicated interactions among the eligibility rules for different support programs, including those rules governing current housing subsidies and traditional welfare programs.

These criticisms have led to reform movements both in the housing and the welfare area; housing-allowance plans represent an appealing reform. The inequities of housing programs are attacked by targeting subsidies to needy families, through entitlement subsidies to housing potential consumers based on need criteria (that is, household income and the cost of standard housing). The work disincentives of welfare plans are reduced by a negative income tax scheme designed to eliminate "notches" in payment schedules and, in general, reduce marginal tax rates on work income.

The Experiments

Up to June 1, 1979, the federal government has spent more than $120 million under the Experimental Housing Allowance Program (EHAP)—a large-scale program that combines some features of a feasibility study or demonstration with several features of a true social experiment.[6] The EHAP program consists of three separate experimental programs—the

Housing Allowance Demand Experiment (HADE), the Housing Allowance Supply Experiment (HASE), and the Administrative Agency Experiment (AAE).

Under the HADE program, which comes closest to being an experiment in the scientific sense, some 1,200 households in each of two local housing markets (Pittsburgh and Phoenix) were offered various experimental payments—under differing payment formulas and earmarking restrictions—for a 3-year period. The behavior of these households and a sample of control households was monitored for a period of 2 years. Public expenditures for this experiment were $29 million—$3.6 million in transfer payments to low-income households, $14.0 million in program administration, and $10.4 million in research.[7]

Under the HASE program, all households in two local housing markets (South Bend and Green Bay) who met specified eligibility criteria were offered housing-allowance subsidies under a single-payment formula with a uniform earmarking restriction. Households were offered these subsidies for periods of up to 10 years. So far, public expenditures for this experiment have exceeded $72 million—$25.6 million in transfer payments, $10.0 million in program administration, and $36.5 million in research.

Under the AAE program, four different types of agencies administered housing-allowance subsidy programs for 2 years in eight local markets. These subsidy programs were available to all renter households who met specified eligibility criteria under a common payment formula, but with local variations in earmarking restrictions. The overall budget for this experiment was more than $19 million—$7.1 million in transfer payments, $2.8 million in program administration, and $9.2 million in research.

Why Conduct Experiments?

The immediate reaction of most economists, schooled in notions of consumer sovereignty, is "Why not simply give money?" The answer to this question seems twofold and interrelated. In the first place, there may be physical externalities in housing consumption that warrant overriding recipients' choices. These externalities, for example, may come from neighborhood effects if the social cost of slums is imposed on others. Despite the fact that many individuals seem to regard these externalities as self-evident, they are not well supported by scientific evidence. There is little or no evidence, for example, that the incidence of bad health, safety, or social pathology is affected by housing conditions as distinct from income conditions.[8] Second, and perhaps of more importance, a subsidy program tied to housing consumption has ample historical precedent and may be more feasible politically than a pure cash transfer. Donor sovereignty is not inconsistent with paternalism.

If considerations of housing consumption per se motivate the notion of housing allowances, it still does not follow that an expensive set of experiments is necessary. Indeed, if social scientists could provide policymakers with reliable estimates of the price and income elasticities of demand, it would be possible to forecast or simulate directly the effects of certain allowance programs. For example, the long-run effects of an unconstrained transfer targeted to housing need and the long-run effects of percent-of-rent subsidy similar to that given to homeowners depend only on these two parameters. For a variety of technical reasons, however, there is still considerable uncertainty about the values of these parameters.[9] Thus a significant portion of the research sponsored by the HADE experiment is devoted to providing better estimates of these key relationships by analyzing the behavior of those Pittsburgh and Phoenix households receiving unrestricted percent-of-rent payments (price subsidies) or unrestricted payments geared to the gap between current income and the cost of standard housing (income subsidies).

There is also considerable uncertainty about the responsiveness of housing supply in the short run to increases in demand, that is, about the value of the supply elasticity of housing services. Despite this uncertainty, however, it does not follow that the $72 million supply experiment is really necessary to the choice among allowance policies geared to housing-gap or percent-of-rent payments. Clearly, in the short run, a large-scale commitment to demand-oriented subsidies *would* drive up prices. Just as surely as supply is unresponsive in the short run, however, it is responsive over the long term. No serious scholar or policymaker would propose a crash program of housing allowances, regardless of the outcome of the supply experiment, nor could one be dissuaded from a phased program on the basis of any experimental results indicating price effects in two local markets. Indeed, the obvious way to phase in a program of demand-oriented subsidies would be to begin with a national program for the elderly poor—a group that has been the target of other federal assistance programs (including particular housing programs) and represents only a small fraction of overall housing demand.

The one clear-cut case in which the results of these experiments are critical to policy design is the consideration of tied subsidies, that is, programs that require households to live in units with particular characteristics in order to receive subsidy payments.

The crucial issues in experimental design involve the kinds of housing restrictions imposed. If the restrictions are very loose (or nonexistent), the program is simply a negative income tax program (with the feature that a housing-gap transfer recognizes regional cost of living differences as reflected in local housing prices and a percent-of-rent transfer reflects differences in tastes for housing). In a situation in which housing restrictions are initially binding for a proportion of the population, those households who already meet the restrictions—who previously expressed a taste for standard housing—again receive a simple income transfer. For those who do not initially meet the standards, the program is a combination of a pure transfer program and an in-kind benefits program; the pure income transfer equals the gross transfer payment less the cost of upgrading to meet the standards.

Since particular requirements are more binding, and since there is less upgrading by eligible households, a housing-allowance program incorporating restrictive standards looks more like a general welfare, or income-transfer, program with eligibility based on household tastes for a given type of housing. The inequities of past housing programs, determined by supply constraints on available units, are replaced by inequalities determined by housing tastes—tastes that are hardly immutable. The effectiveness of any particular form of housing allowance as both a welfare program and a housing program, relates directly to these questions.

Issues in Evaluation

There are two very different ways of evaluating the overall effects of an unrestricted housing-allowance program, either a housing-gap or a percent-of-rent payment. On the one hand, the results can be evaluated in terms of their effectiveness in stimulating increased housing consumption by low-income households; on the other hand, the results can be summarized in terms of reducing the high rent burdens faced by poor people. A program could be viewed as successful if it furthers either of these objectives. Note, however, that a subsidy program will *always* indicate an improvement in one or the other of these dimensions and that *no* program can further both objectives.

A price subsidy will always be more effective in stimulating housing consumption than an income subsidy of the same amount, but it will have a smaller effect on relative rent burdens. In general, if the housing consumption of low-income households is highly responsive to price, then a percent-of-rent subsidy would be viewed as relatively effective, but it would have little effect on the rent burdens of low-income households. Conversely, if housing consumption is insensitive to price, then percent-of-rent allowances are relatively ineffective in stimulating consumption, but they will greatly reduce the rent burdens of low-income households.

If, on the basis of the HADE research, estimates of the demand parameters (price and income elasticities) are available, the effect of housing-allowance programs on housing consumption and rent burdens can be forecast. However, the desirability of any particular program will depend on the policymakers' views about the importance to the larger society of these different outcomes—an *increase* in the housing consumption of poverty households who currently live in slum conditions, or a *decrease* in the large fraction of their small incomes which must be devoted to shelter. Changes in rent burdens relate most directly to the welfare goals of a cash transfer, while increases in housing consumption relate most directly to the housing goals of such a transfer.

Undoubtedly, the most complex problems in evaluation relate to notions of standards and tied subsidies. The imposition of a requirement that households must live in standard housing to qualify for assistance presupposes some common and precise definition of minimally adequate housing. An evaluation of the effects of tied subsidies, moreover, presupposes some conceptual model of household demand for the characteristics of housing.

Unfortunately, neither of these conditions is met. The appropriate physical or occupancy standard is not well defined. (Should fenestration requirements be included in the definition of standard housing? Should ceiling heights?) Second, for any definition, the standard is not easily measured, and verification is both expensive and intrusive. Third, even if measurement is possible, the relationship between household preferences and any specific standard is problematic. Little is known about the relationship between various types of incentives, on the one hand, and decisions to participate and to upgrade or move, on the other hand.

Two basic types of information are needed from the experiment: (1) What is the response of households to different kinds of housing requirements and transfer payments? (2) What are the costs of particular entitlement programs keyed to these differences? For standards requirements that are more restrictive, larger subsidies are required to induce households to participate. For any given set of standards and payments, some projections of long-run program costs could be made on the basis of HADE and HASE experimental results.

Again, however, the normative choice among standards cannot be made on the basis of any experimental evidence. Policymakers will have to decide whether standards dealing with narrowly defined physical components are more important than standards dealing with the quality of the schools servicing those dwelling units.

Notes

1. U.S. Congressional Budget Office, *Federal Housing Policy: Current Programs and Recurring Issues* (Washington: U.S. Government Printing Office, 1978), p. 44.

2. Edwin S. Mills, "Economic Analysis of Urban Land Use Controls," in P. Mieszkowski and M. Straszheim (eds.), *Current Issues in Urban Economics* (Baltimore: Johns Hopkins Press, 1979), p. 531.

3. U.S. Congressional Budget Office, *Federal Housing Policy*, pp. 40-43.

4. These programs include relocation payments to households displaced by renewal programs (cash payments to small numbers of low-income households for periods of up to 4 years); Section 23 leased public housing (cash payments to housing authorities for leasing existing housing for occupancy by low-income households); and rent supplements (cash payments to private suppliers to make up the difference between reduced monthly rents and the amortization of the cost of new construction. Neither of the latter two programs made payments directly to low-income households, however, and under neither program could a recipient household transfer the subsidy if it moved to another unit.

5. Figures in this paragraph are derived from program summaries in U.S. Congressional Budget Office, *Federal Housing Policy*.

6. Federal expenditures are currently projected to be about $170 million by the time the entire set of experiments is completed. U.S. Department of Housing and Urban Development, "The Experimental Housing Allowance Program: A 1979 Report of Findings," mimeographed, April 1979, pp. 1-5.

7. Expenditures for all parts of the experiment were obtained from Mr. Garland Allen, U.S. Department of Housing and Urban Development.

8. Many studies have indicated that the incidence of bad health is correlated with bad housing. This is, of course, beside the point.

9. This uncertainty arises principally from two sources: first, the costs of relocation indicate that the appropriate notion of income is some long-run, or permanent, or normal concept; second, housing prices are never observed in the market (market rents are in the units of price times quantity).

12 The Section 8 Rental-Assistance Program: Costs and Policy Options

Mahlon R. Straszheim

The Section 8 existing housing program closely resembles a housing-allowance program and offers many of the efficiency advantages of such an approach.[1] Households deemed income-eligible are allowed to search for an available housing unit. The government establishes an upper limit on the rent that can be paid for a unit, the so-called fair-market rent, which determines the level of benefits under the program. The tenant's contribution to the rent is limited to a fixed percentage of income, (either 15 or 25 percent, depending on income and family size), with the remaining rent paid directly to the landlord by the government. In addition to receiving better-quality housing, households' housing payments as a share of income are reduced. Since the government is not the direct supplier of housing, the problems of public ownership and management of the supply of housing that have plagued many previous housing programs are avoided. The opportunities for the household to search for a unit largely eliminates the inevitable economic welfare losses when households are placed in particular housing units through some sort of administrative process.

The Section 8 existing program is intended to provide subsidies to eligible households occupying existing units deemed in decent, safe, and sanitary condition. The specific provisions defining acceptable quality units in the regulations include specific requirements with respect to plumbing, heat, electricity, and other physical characteristics of the unit. All units must meet these standards unless the local public housing authority proposes an alternative quality standard that is accepted by HUD.

The Section 8 new construction and substantial rehabilitation programs are construction programs. The substantial rehabilitation program entails units with major structural repairs and is designed to provide housing that is essentially comparable to new units. The financial arrangements between tenant and landlord and the tenant's housing costs are identical in existing, new construction, and substantial rehabilitation—in each case 25 percent of income. The major differences in the three programs involve the nature of contracting arrangements between the government and housing suppliers. HUD area offices advertise the opportunity for potential developers to build units in particular geographic submarkets at rents below published fair-market rents, and they select projects from among those proposed by developers. Developers of approved proposals are responsible for financing their units and for all activities related to tenants that public housing authorities conduct in Section 8 existing housing programs, including advertising available units, screening applicants, verifying income eligibility, selecting tenants, and determining the subsidy required and tenant contribution. The financial incentives for developers include some financial relief for vacancies and HUD commitment to increase contract rents over the life of the 30-year contract to offset increases in operating costs. If the sponsor can be confident that eligible households will be available in the future so as to avoid vacancies, the commitment to increase contract rents over time removes most risk from the project.

The Section 8 program now supports approximately 1 million households and is rapidly becoming one of the largest housing programs. A summary of the principal federal housing programs appears in table 12-1. There has been very little expansion in conventional public housing in recent years, and most of the other major federal assistance programs other than Section 8 are contracting. The costs of the Section 8 program also have grown quite considerably. These costs are summarized in table 12-2. Since the federal government is entering into long-term contracts with landlords and owners, present commitments have budgetary implications for many years. In fiscal year 1979, the government estimated it would spend approximately $1 billion to make first-year commitments to 230,000 units. The estimated cost over the life of the contract for these units, so-called budget authority, is $24.6 billion. Each year of expansion of Section 8 entails a

Table 12-1
Principal Federal Housing-Assistance Programs, 1979

Program	*Units Available for Assistance End of FY 1978*	*Estimate of Increase in the Number of Units Receiving Federal Assistance, FY 1979*	*Estimated Number of Units to which New Commitment Is Made, FY 1979*
Section 8	666,603	231,397	231,650
Section 235 homeownership	261,866	−21,866	12,344
Rent supplement	171,598	−1,598	0
Section 236 rental housing assistance	544,515	−2,515	0
Public housing	1,173,000	−16,000	17,000
Total	2,817,582		

Source: U.S. Congress, House of Representatives, Hearings before a Subcommittee of the Committee on Appropriations, 96 Congress, First Session, Department of Housing and Urban Development, Independent Agencies Appropriations for 1980, April 1979, pp. 633-668.

Table 12-2
Section 8 Rental-Assistance Program Budgets

		FY 1976	FY 1977	FY 1978	FY 1979 (Estimate)
I.	Net unit reservations:				
	New construction	157,092	145,272	99,342	129,362
	Substantial rehabilitation	18,971	24,124	22,703	51,882
	Existing	314,518	161,581	135,472	123,118
	Total	490,581	330,977	257,517	304,362
II.	Units made available for occupancy:				
	New construction	6,348	20,867	46,059	110.000
	Substantial rehabilitation	468	4,134	7,685	15,000
	Existing	85,199	274,537	159,724	106,500
	Total	92,015	272,538	213,468	231,650
III.	Cost of new units committed:				
	Annual contract authority for new unit reservations ($ bill)	$ 1.214	1.047	.924	1.115
	Budget authority to fund units reserved over life of contract	$18.051	23.764	22.887	24.651
IV.	Cost of program activity ($ bill), cumulative to date:				
	Units available and leased (000s)	130.5	459.6	666.6	943.0
	Annual contract authority for all currently leased units ($ bill)	$.301	1.098	1.832	2.231

Source: U.S. Congress, House of Representatives, Hearings before a Subcommittee of the Committee on Appropriations, 96 Congress, First Session, Department of Housing and Urban Development, Independent Agencies Appropriations for 1980, April 1979, pp. 633-668.

roughly similar commitment. For fiscal year 1979, the annual subsidy costs of all Section 8 units were estimated to be $2.2 billion.

Decisions regarding the nature of redistribution from taxpayers to recipient households in Section 8 and the distribution of benefits among eligible households involve both vertical and horizontal equity. When funds are limited, it becomes increasingly difficult to achieve horizontal equity, the condition wherein all eligible households have an equal opportunity to obtain the same level of benefits.

This chapter examines the role of fair market rents and income-eligibility rules as they affect program cost and benefits. It then reviews fair-market rents as a determinant of benefits to recipients and program costs to taxpayers. Income-eligbility rules are reviewed last, followed by concluding observations on selected policy issues.

The Role of Fair-Market Rents

Fair-market rents are the basic determinants of the level of housing benefits received by participating households. Housing prices and the quality of units are closely related in most markets. To establish fair-market rents for existing units at any given level in a given submarket is to exclude all units that rent for more than the fair-market rent and to make potentially available all units of lesser quality. If fair-market rents are set at low levels, available units may prove to be inferior to the independently established housing-quality standards. Landlords may not have a financial incentive to upgrade units to meet quality standards. High fair-market rents result in a larger subsidy being borne by the nonrecipient population, and vice versa.

The level of fair-market rents also affects the attractiveness of the program to households with different income levels, and hence participation. As noted later, income-eligibility rules are such that millions of households, many with quite substantial incomes, are eligible for Section 8; the level of fair-market rents has an important role in determining which of these households will desire program participation. In actual practice, the level of fair-market rents is sufficiently low in many markets that the housing available is of lower quality. Low fair-market rents may limit the interest of all but the poorest households in program participation, and in actual practice, the level of fair-market rents has been one of the major factors in determining the income distribution of participating households.

The level of fair-market rents also affects the distribution of income transfers among eligible households. A higher fair-market rent, and hence larger subsidies to recipients, creates a larger difference in real income between eligible households who receive the real income transfer and nonparticipating but eligible households who do not. Determining appropriate fair-market rents therefore involves normative judgments regarding the nature of income redistriubtion from taxpayers to recipients, and also the distribution of income among eligible households.

Concern for whether fair-market rents for existing housing are adequate in any market should be viewed in this context—that fair-market rents essentially define where along the continuum between housing quality and price the limits of the Section 8 existing program are to be drawn. If fair-market rents are lowered, unit quality declines and greater search costs for households will be incurred. Similarly, for the Section 8 new construction and substantial rehabilitation programs, the level of fair-market rents involves a decision about what quality unit is to be provided. The debate over fair-market rent levels involves a basic issue of horizontal equity: should Section 8 program coverage be expanded by subsidizing only the most modest (and cheapest) standard quality rental units, or should the program allow inclusion of more typical rental units, thus providing for subsidy of a better grade of housing and truly solving the housing inadequacies of the recipients at the expense of those additional households who might otherwise be served under the former concept?

Two characteristics of urban housing markets much complicate the administrative task of establishing appropriate fair-market rents. First, housing units are multidimensional products with many characteristics (for example, age of structure, neighborhood quality, condition of plumbing, and so on) that households value. In order to determine appropriate fair-market rents, it is necessary to specify the housing-quality level desired for recipients along these many quality dimensions.

The second complexity is that housing markets in a given urban area are geographically segmented. Market prices for units offering similar housing services have been shown to vary widely within Standard Metropolitan Statistical Areas (SMSAs).[2] Since dwelling structures are very durable, markets in reasonably close geographic proximity may exhibit widely different prices for the same (or similar) dwelling attributes. In essence, this variation in prices is traceable to the fact that demand curves in particular markets often shift more rapidly than the supply of units. Prices may vary as much as 100 percent across submarkets within a given SMSA.

If prices vary across submarkets, establishing a single fair-market rent for an entire SMSA, or for counties within SMSAs, will provide an incentive for households to select lower-priced neighborhoods. To the extent that fair-market rents are below market rents of units in neighborhoods with better public services or amenities, or neighborhoods with higher-income households, or predominately white neighborhoods, entry is discouraged in these areas. Fair-market rents may discourage socioeconomic or racial integration in this circumstance. Geographic variation in prices implies that it will be necessary to define different fair-market rents for many small geographic submarkets in order to encourage participation of Section 8 households in all submarkets.

The need to establish different fair-market rents for many small geographic submarkets that reflect variations in market rents for units of different sizes creates a very complex administrative task. Analysis of prevailing rents as a basis for setting fair-market rents must therefore carefully consider all quality characteristics of properties. To collect the necessary information in local markets on rents and housing quality and to statistically analyze the data is an expensive and difficult task. Local public housing authorities or other local officials have the most direct information about prices but generally are not trained to do the requisite statistical analysis. In addition, they have an interest in demonstrating that market rents are high in their community, because a higher fair-market rent would then make it easier for households to find units.

It is of course true that the program could function quite adequately from an administrative point of view regardless of whether differences in fair-market rent schedules by geographic submarket correspond precisely to differences in market prices across submarkets. In any given submarket, units that rent below the fair-market rent because of their quality will be made available. As long as fair-market rents are sufficiently high that many units are potentially available relative to the number of units that local housing agencies can fund, participating households will be able to find units. If the fair-market rent is sufficiently high, units will satisfy the quality standard. Households would receive higher benefits in markets with high fair-market rents relative to market rents and lower benefits in other markets. However, program equity requires that households in different geographical areas have the same opportunity to acquire a target quality dwelling unit deemed appropriate to the program. This can be accomplished only if fair-market rents are established in each submarket at a level adequate to acquire a unit of that quality level in each submarket. The administrative problems of establishing appropriate fair-market rents arises principally because of a desire to achieve program equity, as just defined.

The enabling legislation requires that HUD establish fair-market rents by unit size and geographic submarket, without providing specific definitions of structure type and geography. In determining geographic boundaries, that is, the number of submarkets, the tradeoff exists between administrative cost and horizontal equity. Because of the spatial variation in housing prices in urban areas, the use of a larger number of market areas with small geographic boundaries makes it possible for fair-market rents to be more closely matched with market prices; however, administrative costs are increased when a large number of submarkets are used. Because of data unavailability, the costs of data collection, verification, and processing, and related problems and costs of administering an elaborate monitoring of market rents in many geographic markets, there is a limit on the number of submarkets that can be used. In the existing housing program, the county has been the basic area for defining market areas, although many counties have the same fair-market rent. In the case of the new construction program, fair-market rents are defined for 510 market areas, generally multicounty areas.

The fair-market rent schedules for existing housing include rents for units by bedroom size (that is, number of bedrooms), and separate schedules are published for elevator and nonelevator buildings. In the new construction program, fair-market rents are defined for five structure types and for each bedroom size. An illustrative schedule for fair-market rents for the Boston SMSA is shown in table 12-3.

Establishing appropriate fair-market rents within a submarket requires that an assessment be made of the type of housing recipients should consume and the supply prices of different types of units. The establishment of a single fair-market rent for all housing in a given market allows households

Table 12-3
Fair-Market Rent Schedule, Boston, 1978

	Number of Bedrooms				
Structure Type	*0*	*1*	*2*	*3*	*4 or more*
Existing housing:					
Elevator	$259	$293	$314	$401	$453
Nonelevator	$235	$266	$316	$364	$411
New construction:					
Detached	—	—	—	—	—
Semidetached/row	—	$382	$447	$567	$627
Walkup	$295	$372	$404	$434	$500
Elevator: 2-4 Sty.	—	—	—	—	—
5+ Sty.	$316	$396	$467	—	—

Source: *The Federal Register* 43 (March 29, 1978).

free choice of a unit of any size, age, quality, or structure type. Small, older units would be available at the lowest rents. To establish different fair-market rents for each type of unit, each reflecting market prices for that type of unit, implies that units of different types are available at the same price. For example, by setting separate fair-market rents for units with different numbers of bedrooms, equal to market rents of units with different numbers of bedrooms, HUD has sought to make various size units available to Section 8 participants at an equal cost (25 percent of the tenant's income). This is, in essence, an equity decision, that the number of bedrooms is a quality attribute of housing for which tenants will not be charged. All other quality attributes implicitly have a price; if the household acquires a unit with more of one attribute (for example, number of bathrooms), it will likely obtain less of some other (for example, no air conditioning) in order that the unit's rent fall below the fair-market rent.

Initial fair-market rents were established in 1974 based on the 1970 Census of Population data on gross rents. Periodic adjustments have been made using Consumer Price Indices (CPI) for residential rent and fuels to update for inflation. Initial fair-market rents for one-, two-, and three-bedroom units and the three published annual revisions, which incorporate all changes in fair-market rents made at the date of each annual revision, are summarized in table 12-4. The sample of cities is the sixty SMSAs covered in HUD's Annual Housing Surveys. In 1975, initial fair-market rents for one-bedroom units were $147.91, while three-bedroom fair-market rents were 33 percent higher. There was concern in 1975 that fair-market rents were inadequate for larger units, and hence fair-market rents for larger units were increased disproportionately more than for smaller units in a number of markets in the period since 1975. In 1978, the fair-market rents for three-bedroom units exceeded those for one-bedroom units by 43 percent.

Table 12-4
Fair-Market Rents, Selected SMSAs

	1975	*1976*	*1977*	*1978*
Existing housing by number of bedrooms:				
One	$147.91	$163.28	$182.11	$196.98
Two	174.56	193.54	214.33	235.23
Three	200.42	222.79	249.93	278.53
New construction:				
Fair-market rent	$272.40	$286.34	$314.78	$351.49
Annual percentage changes:				
Fair-market rents	N.A.	5.1%	9.6%	11.9%
Rent component of consumer price index[a]	N.A.	5.4%	6.9%	6.5%
Fuel and utilities consumer price index[a]	N.A.	9.0%	11.2%	7.3%
Construction materials wholesale price index[a]	N.A.	7.1%	8.6%	10.3%

Note: Sixty SMSAs are included in HUD's Annual Housing Surveys, 1975, 1976, and 1977; N.A. means not applicable.

[a]U.S. Department of Labor, Bureau of Labor Statistics, *Monthly Labor Review* tables 23 and 27, 1975-1979.

Fair-market rents for two-bedroom new construction units in buildings without elevators for the market areas that most clearly correspond to those for existing housing are also summarized in table 12-4. Fair-market rents for new construction were increased 9.6 percent in 1977 and 11.9 percent in 1978. These increases are one of the contributing factors to the acceleration in the rate of new construction starts in the Section 8 program since 1977.

A comparison of fair-market rents for the existing and new construction programs must adjust for the 2-year trend factor built into fair-market rent schedules for new construction. Current fair-market rents for new construction reflect rents that will be charged when the building is completed, assumed to be 2 years from date of approval. Current fair-market rents for new construction will apply to units available in 1980. Existing housing fair-market rents in 1978 are increased by 15 percent as an estimate of fair-market rents in 1980.[3] The results in table 12-5 reveal that the new construction fair-market rents are about one-third higher, implying that subsidies to households will be nearly twice as high in the new construction program. These differences in fair-market rents and subsidy costs must be paid over many years. The net present value of federal subsidy for households in new construction units over the life of the program therefore become quite considerable.[4]

The new construction program's costs compare least favorably with existing housing in the largest cities. Higher land costs and longer construction periods make new units more expensive in the older and larger cities. The

Table 12-5
Comparisons of Fair-Market Rents, Two-Bedroom Units, New Construction versus Existing Housing, Selected SMSAs

	Fair-Market Rents (FMRs)	
SMSAs by Size	*Existing*[a]	*New Construction*[b]
> 2 million	$300.53	$426.48
1-2 million	267.53	341.76
500,000-1 million	265.73	334.60
< 500,000	249.45	304.40

Note: Sixty SMSAs are included in Annual Housing Surveys, 1975-1977.
[a]FMRs for existing units in 1978.
[b]FMRs for new construction, two-bedroom walkup unit.

larger cities also are more likely to have a larger supply of older units suitable for recipients if fair-market rents are set such that landlords have incentive to provide maintenance. These cost comparisons do not, of course, adjust for quality differences between units under the new construction and existing housing programs.

Statistical analysis of market rental data from the Annual Housing Survey in twenty-one cities reveals that fair-market rents were set in 1976 at levels, which are somewhere below the median of the distribution of available units with respect to quality. For smaller units, fair-market rents are near the median of all rents, and hence participants could obtain units approximately comparable with those occupied by persons at the twenty-fifth percentile of the entire income distribution. (The average income of owners is much above that of rental households.) For larger units, of three bedrooms or more, the comparisons of market rents to fair-market rents are less favorable from the point of view of potential participants. For larger units to rent below fair-market rents, the unit must have only one bath, be at least 30 years old, or have other small quality deficiencies.[5]

Statistical analysis of these same data also show that there is considerable variation in rents in different submarkets within SMSAs. In some SMSAs, fair-market rents tend to price households out of higher-quality, higher-priced neighborhoods. The combination of low fair-market rents relative to prices in better-quality neighborhoods and the provision that limits what the household can spend on housing to the fair-market rent encourages households to select units with more structural quality but in lesser-quality neighborhoods. That fair-market rents deter Section 8 households from entering better-quality areas is likely consistent with political views of most taxpayers, who appear willing to subsidize better-quality housing for the poor, but seem unwilling to encourage socioeconomic (or racial) integration.

Income Eligibility and the Distribution of Benefits

The statute makes all households with incomes less than 80 percent of the median income in their area of residence eligible. Administrative decisions regarding definition of regions and adjustments for family size have important effects on who qualifies for assistance. The analysis that follows examines the effects of place of residence, income, and family size on eligibility using Annual Housing Survey data for twenty-one SMSAs. The extent to which the eligibility rules make households with high housing-cost burdens eligible and exclude those with low rent-income ratios is analyzed.

As will be seen, the income eligibility rules are such that a very large number of households are eligible for Section 8. Since budget allocations to date have been sufficient to serve only a small number of households, only a small percentage of potential eligible households will receive benefits. This circumstance creates potential problems of *horizontal equity*, the extent to which persons at a given income level are treated similarly. If all persons are equally well informed of opportunities to participate and participants are chosen from applicants randomly, horizontal equity might be achieved even if many persons are eligible and funds are limited. In practice these conditions are never met. In Section 8, certain groups are more likely to be informed, and to be selected.

The most important administrative regulations defining income eligibility involve family size and place of residence. One possible objective in establishing income-eligibility limits by region is to make all households with real incomes below a stated level eligible for the program. Since money incomes among counties vary dramatically, and are much lower in nonurban areas, a single national income-eligibility limit would tend to exclude most urbanized areas.[6] However, to adjust for cost-of-living differences in order to relate money income levels in each region to a target level of real income is difficult. Most analyst have concluded that after adjustments for cost of living, real income variation is much less than money income differences across regions. Studies by Hoch, Coelha, and Gholi, and Henderson all show that real income variation across cities or Census regions is relatively slight, in the 10 to 15 percent range.[7] Larger differences in real incomes exist between rural counties and urban areas.

HUD has established income-eligibility levels in each county at 80 percent of the median family income in the county. This procedure implies an approximately equal proportion of households in each county will be eligible (all those with incomes below 80 percent of the median for the county); that is, it ignores differences in real income across counties or any possibility that one county that has a lower money income may be deserving of more assistance than another county with higher nominal income. In the poorest counties, many households with incomes above the Section 8 eligibility limit of 80 percent of the county median income will have incomes below the national average. Conversely, the income-eligibility limit was as high as $15,000 in wealthy urban counties in 1976.

This procedure avoids the political problems of deciding which are the neediest counties. If the program is largely to be focused on urban areas, where real income differences between cities are indeed slight, as suggested previously, it is reasonable to avoid the administrative, conceptual, and political costs of trying to measure and adjust for differences. The political difficulties of establishing a program that directs most of its monies to a select few counties, based on assessments that one area's real income level is slightly above or below income in another, is quite evident.

The definition of income eligibility also makes adjustments for family size. A family of four is eligible if income is 80 percent of the county median household income. For a one-person household, the eligibility limit is 56 percent of median family income; household income may be as high as 100 percent of median family income for a family of eight persons or more. These relationships among family sizes and income-eligibility levels are the same nationwide.

In order to determine in practice how the eligibility rules affect who will be eligible, and in order to ascertain whether significant subgroups of the eligible population are being excluded as the program is currently designed and administered, it is necessary to empirically describe the eligible population. It is possible to develop approximate estimates of the income-eligible population using data from the 1975-1976 Annual Housing Survey data. Median income for each SMSA was translated into income-eligibility levels by family size, using the HUD family-size adjustments as described earlier. The numbers of households who would be eligible under the Section 8 rules for each family-size class for each SMSA were tabulated. This analysis provides a summary of the effects of the Section 8 income-eligibility rules, under the assumptions that the Annual Housing Survey data accurately reflect household incomes and market prices in the market in question, and assuming that HUD would establish income-eligibility levels consistent with the reported income data.

The results are shown in table 12-6. On a nationwide basis, 47.2 percent of rental households are income-eligible. The analysis of Section 8 income-eligibility rules as they relate to family size reveals that a higher percentage of larger families were income-eligible than of smaller families. Seventy-two percent of six-person households were eligible versus 42 percent for two-person renter households. There is no legislative expression that suggests that larger families are to be favored.

Rent burdens by family size also have been analyzed. Larger families in general had lesser rent burdens than smaller familes. (Although families of all sizes who were income-eligible have sizable rent burdens.) Of the eligible households, 80.3 percent had rent-income ratios in excess of 0.25, with the mean rent-income ratio for income-eligible househlds at 0.40. The

Table 12-6
Rent Burden of Eligible and Noneligible Households

City	Percentage of Renters Income-Eligible	Rent-Income Ratios of Income-Eligible Households > 0.25	Rent-Income Ratios of Income-Eligible Households < 0.25	Rent-Income Ratios of Non-Income-Eligible Households > 0.25	Rent-Income Ratios of Non-Income-Eligible Households < 0.25
Population > 2 million					
Chicago	42.7%	81.8%	18.2%	11.9%	88.0%
Philadelphia	49.4	80.3	19.6	20.8	82.4
San Francisco	47.4	84.2	15.7	17.4	82.5
Subtotal	46.0	82.4	17.6	16.1	84.5
Population 1-2 million					
Atlanta	49.4	73.2	26.7	13.6	86.3
Cincinnati	47.4	70.3	29.6	6.7	93.2
Kansas City	45.8	69.7	30.2	11.3	88.6
Miami	47.6	93.4	6.5	36.0	63.9
Milwaukee	44.4	81.0	18.9	10.3	89.6
New Orleans	43.8	75.2	24.7	9.9	90.0
Patterson	45.1	78.4	21.5	15.6	84.3
Portland	46.3	85.2	14.7	11.5	88.4
San Bernadino	59.8	76.4	23.5	6.6	93.3
San Diego	49.4	88.3	11.6	22.1	77.8
Subtotal	47.9	78.4	21.5	14.6	85.3
Population 500,000-1 million					
Columbus	47.7	79.2	20.7	9.8	90.1
Hartford	47.8	82.3	17.6	11.5	88.4
Rochester	47.8	84.6	15.3	11.2	88.7
San Antonio	46.9	68.3	31.6	17.4	82.5
Springfield	46.8	84.4	15.5	15.3	84.6
Subtotal	47.4	80.0	19.9	13.0	86.9
Population 250,000-500,000					
Colorado Springs	51.3	78.8	23.8	9.0	90.9
Madison	48.0	88.8	11.1	12.1	87.8
Newport News	44.1	75.9	24.0	9.8	90.1
Subtotal	48.0	82.1	18.7	10.5	89.4
Total	47.2	80.3	19.7	14.4	85.7

Source: Author's tabulations from U.S. Department of Housing and Urban Development, *Annual Housing Survey*.

highest rent-income burdens are for smaller households. The mean rent-income ratio of noneligible renters is 0.20, and only 20.8 percent of noneligible households have rent-income ratios in excess of 0.25. It is evident that the eligibility rules are capturing the great majority of households with high rent burdens, not surprising given that almost half of all renters are income-eligible. These data on rent-income ratios reveal a serious plight for a considerable number of renter households. To the typical income-eligible household with a preprogram rent-income ratio of 0.40, participation in Section 8 will constitute a sizable transfer of real income.

To summarize, the current income-eligibility limits for Section 8 are quite high, such that approximately one-third of all households are eligible. However, most of the households receiving Section 8 benefits are quite poor. The mean income of recipient households was $3,535, ($3,155 for elderly households and $3,720 for nonelderly households). Eighty-two percent of participating households are identified as very low income.[8] Only a fourth of participating households have wage and salary earnings, the great majority living on welfare or retirement benefits. These income levels are well below the income-eligibility limit discussed in this section. The preponderance of quite-low-income households among those actually participating reflects the level of fair-market rents and outreach effects of local housing agencies. To date, the Section 8 program should receive high scores in its capacity to reach the low-income population.

Concluding Observations

The Section 8 rental assistance program should receive high scores for its success in providing benefits to very-low-income households. Short of an unrestricted income transfer, the Section 8 program comes very close to achieving an efficient outcome. The reliance on market incentives and household search for a unit are important characteristics that assure this result. Such an approach is to be much preferred over programs in which the government is directly supplying units or placing households in units on the private market. Developing administrative procedures for matching households with housing units cannot hope to operate as well as the market. In this regard, a most important component of a successful program is an informed recipient population, who will shop for the best available unit. Informed shopping will cure most potential problems, particularly that of the government subsidy being wasted on inferior-quality units or being used to subsidize landlords by paying above-market prices. The Department of Housing and Urban Development and local housing agencies should continue in their efforts to educate potential recipients and assist them in the search process.

HUD need offer no apologies that the Section 8 existing housing program is an income-transfer program rather than a housing program because it has not built new housing. Critics have suggested that since about half the households who participate stay in place, the Section 8 existing program is doing little to add to the housing supply. Others have recommended that emphasis be directed to the new construction program. Each of these views seems misdirected. The high cost of the new construction program was noted earlier. It is difficult to imagine widespread support for a program that builds new units for our poorest citizens, at a cost in excess of that paid for housing by a majority of taxpayers. To raise the income limits and place middle-class households in Section 8 new construction units is to abandon assistance for the real needy. Conversely, to attempt to hold down costs of the new construction program by building very-low-quality units on poor sites is also pointless. The Section 8 existing program is a vehicle that provides both housing benefits and income assistance. While supply adjustments take time, all empirical evidence indicates that the private market will offer better-quality housing at higher rents. Public subsidy of rents for poor households is an effective use of the older housing stock and is a policy that will ensure maintenance of such units. Such benefits will accrue to those households who stay in place as well as those who move.

Modifications in fair-market rents and income eligibility could be envisioned which would provide added program benefits. Establishing a single fair-market rent for an entire SMSA is likely to exclude participants from many geographic submarkets and certain suburban submarkets. While it would create added administrative costs, establishing separate fair-market rents for distinct areas within SMSAs would create more opportunities for poor households to enter better-quality neighborhoods. This policy would, of course, face considerable political opposition.

The income-eligibility rules raise complex policy questions. The size of the program is a constraint that precludes it from aiding more than a tiny fraction of currently eligible households. Participants receive large benefits, while equally needy nonparticipants are not aided. As the program becomes better known, larger numbers of applicants could create rationing problems.

There are several solutions to the implied horizontal inequity other than increasing program size. It would be possible to achieve greater horizontal equity by dramatically lowering fair-market rents, at the same time eliminating or lowering housing-quality standards. The effect would be to reduce the appeal of the program to any but the lowest-income sector. Presumably a higher proportion of this group could then be aided.

Alternatively, reducing income-eligibility limits would directly reduce the number of eligible households and tend to reduce the mean income of participants. Lowering the income limits also would result in eligible households having higher rent-income ratios as a group than under the current rules. However, this approach has distinct disadvantages. The size of the real income transfer received by participants relative to the average rent burden of income-eligible households who were not participating would be increased. As a result, lowering the income-eligibility limit would increase the difference in real income between participating and nonparticipating income-eligible households. This difference might be regarded as inequitable to nonparticipants.

A third alternative would raise the tenant's contribution as a fraction of his or her income. This would reduce the size of the potential participating population in the sense that a greater percentage of those income-eligible households would have nothing to gain by participation. The average income of participants would be reduced. By reducing the subsidy cost per household, it would be possible to assist more households for the same budget. For example, raising the tenant contribution to 30 percent of income would exclude approximately 11.6 percent of present income-eligible households.

Of these several choices, lowering fair-market rents or raising the tenant's share would seem the most desirable. If lower fair-market rents will not support housing of sufficient quality, the choice of raising the tenant's contribution to 30 percent of income should be considered. It would seem difficult to justify on social welfare grounds the need to limit tenant's housing payments to only 25 percent of income (as opposed to 30 or 35 percent) when the program as currently funded assists only a tiny fraction of the renter households with rent payments in excess of 35 percent of income. It also should be noted that housing payments as a share of income have risen considerably in the unassisted housing market in recent years as interest rates, land costs, and utility costs have increased dramatically.

Notes

1. Section 8 of the Housing and Community Development Act of 1974 (Public Law 93-383. August 22, 1974).
2. Mahlon Straszheim, *An Econometric Analysis of the Urban Housing Market* (New York, Columbia Univ. Press, 1975); Ann B. Schnare and Raymond J. Struyk, "Segmentation and Urban Housing Market," *Journal of Urban Economics* (April 1976):146-166; John Kain and John Quigley, *Housing Markets and Racial Discrimination* (New York, Columbia Univ. Press, 1976).
3. Actual contract rents in particular markets may lie below fair-market rents because the "rent reasonableness test" is applied. This test requires that no rent be approved if it exceeds market rents of comparable unassisted housing units, regardless of the level of fair-market rents. In practice, contract rents have closely approximated fair-market rents.
4. Congressional Budget Office, Congress of the United States, "The Long-Term Costs of Lower-Income Housing Assistance Programs," Washington, 1979.
5. Irene Malazemoff and Mahlon Straszheim, "The Section 8 Rental Assistance Program," mimeographed, 1979.
6. In 1977, per capita income ranged from $8,535 to $11,430 for the richest ten counties, that is, 21 to 63 percent above the national average,

and from $3,859 to $5,213, or 26 to 45 percent below the national average, in the ten poorest counties. U.S. Department of Commerce, Bureau of Economic Analysis, News Release, June 15, 1979.

7. Irving Hoch, "City Size Effects, Trends and Policies," *Science* 193 (September 1976):856-863; Phillip Coelha and M.A. Gholi, "The End of the North-South Wage Differential," *American Economic Review* 61 (December 1977):932-937; J.V. Henderson, "The Sizes and Types of Cities," *American Economic Review* 64 (September 1974):640-656; Peter Mieszkowsky and Mahlon Straszheim (eds.), *Current Issues in Urban Economics* (Baltimore: Johns Hopkins Univ. Press, 1979), pp. 9-15.

8. U.S. Housing and Urban Development, Lower Income Housing Assistance Program (Section 8), Nationwide Evaluation of the Existing Housing Program, Technical Supplement, Washington, 1978.

13 The Housing-Assistance Plan: Promise and Reality

Karen S. Christensen and *Michael B. Teitz*

In the early 1970s, an important change occurred in the relationships between the federal government and states and localities in the United States. Congress replaced many discretionary aid programs with formula allocations of federal funds on the basis of such social indicators as population and poverty. The form of these entitlement grants ranged from the almost unrestricted formula of general revenue sharing to the programmatically bounded Title XX for social services. The Housing and Community Development Act of 1974 provided an intermediate, hybrid form.

On the one hand, its Community Development Block Grant (CDBG) component replaced seven categorical programs, such as Urban Renewal and Open Space, with a single grant to be used for any of the purposes permitted by the previous programs. Cities (with populations over 50,000) no longer received funds through HUD's discretionary approval of competing applications, but rather through entitlement.

On the other hand, the housing-assistance programs were not reconstructed into the form of block grants to localities. However, they were profoundly transformed by the act's Section 8 program, which brought multiple forms of assistance (new construction, rehabilitation, and rent support) for multiple beneficiaries (low- and moderate-income families, elderly, and handicapped) under a single umbrella. For the first time, program allocations were made under a single program that was informally fungible. Furthermore, HUD began to use a formula for preliminary allocation of housing funds, although final distribution depended on effective demand by developers responding to HUD Area Office advertisements of fund availability.

The 1974 act also required that all localities participating in the CDBG program prepare a Housing Assistance Plan (HAP) that would describe local housing needs by types of households in need of assistance and would formulate local housing goals and proposals for achieving them. The HAP, then, could be seen as serving two purposes. First, it could stimulate local

The authors wish to acknowledge the work of the other members of the research teams that carried out the studies referred to in this chapter. In addition, Deborah Kogan and Roger Montgomery were especially insightful in their criticisms and suggestions. The authors are, of course, responsible for this chapter's contents.

housing planning and link it to HUD delivery of housing assistance, a gap painfully evident to observers of the historic relationships between HUD and assisted housing developers, which substantially excluded local governments. Second, the HAP could connect housing assistance with CDBG activities that would logically be used to support housing objectives in many localities.

Clearly, the 1974 Housing Community Development Act embodied profound changes in the philosophy and logic of housing and community-development policy in the United States. The HAP and the related housing-assistance allocation formulas constitute key elements of a new policy insofar as they imply shifts in responsibility and relations among levels of government.

We believe that development of a genuinely national housing policy requires a programmatic and institutional structure in which national goals and resources can be conveyed to localities, yet can be adapted to the extraordinary diversity of political, economic, and social conditions that exist in a country as large as the United States. Although it can be argued that the absolute level of resources devoted to housing assistance has never been sufficient to respond to the scale of need, it is equally important that the strategies and means for delivery of assistance be responsive to national and local policy objectives. HUD's experience with high-volume, uncontrolled programs, such as Sections 235 and 236, makes this lesson clear. The 1974 act was a landmark attempt to articulate and coordinate housing and community-development programs so that they would constitute a national system that would more equitably respond to needs. We want to ask, in general terms, how has this innovation worked?

This chapter explores the outcome of the HAP requirement and its associated innovations. It is based on an evaluation of the HAP as it evolved in eight metropolitan areas during the first 2 years of the program and a study of housing distribution in another set of metropolitan areas for the latter period.[1] However, our purpose is less to present the results of our research than to use them to reflect on the evolution of a major innovation in subsidized-housing-allocation policy and to explore some of its implications for the future.

The rest of the chapter consists of three parts. The first section describes the new housing planning and allocation structure and the purposes embodied in the 1974 act against the back drop of the housing system it replaced. The second section dicusses the outcomes and evolution of the HAP innovation thus far. Finally, we conclude with a more speculative assessment of the future of the allocation of federal housing resources and local participation.

The New Structure for Housing Planning and Delivery

The 1974 Housing Community Development Act offered a new structure to resolve the dilemma of disjointed attacks on urban problems in a system of inherent diversity. Before exploring three key aspects of this ingenious legislation, however, it must be recognized that interpretations of the act's purposes may vary. The administration submitted several proposals for a block grant, and Congress, along with vested interests, altered the form and institutional roles many times before an acceptable version was enacted. The act was the product of compromise among many views, rather than a coherent, single blueprint. Nonetheless, our interpretation of the act's design is supported by the logic of the act and is clearly established in its language.

Community-Responsive Housing Resources

Prior to the act, national housing assistance was administered almost without regard to local conditions and preferences. A number of programs, such as Sections 221(d)3 and 236, operated outside local-government purview, depending on direct HUD and developer negotiations. Even public programs, administered by semiautonomous housing authorities, operated largely on an ad hoc basis, applying for federal assistance when funds were available, and without regard to the intentions or ongoing activities of other local agencies, the needs of the community as a whole, or political accountability. A locality's choice of categorical program frequently depended on fund availability rather than on housing need. For example, when Section 312 rehabilitation loan funds were depleted but Section 202 funds were ample, aggressive housing authorities built more for the elderly, regardless of their locality's relative needs or priorities. The fragmented administrative structure and the categorized programs, however, combined to create disincentives for discovering a community's housing priorities at all. For example, redevelopment agencies pursued Urban Renewal grants focusing on the needs of target areas rather than the entire community, while housing authorities addressed only those housing needs susceptible to programs they administered rather than the community's full range of housing problems. In short, the centralized, categorical provision of federal housing resources, reinforced by fragmented local administration, precluded responsiveness to diverse community conditions and preferences.

The act's design reversed this pattern through several interlocking provisions. First, general-purpose local government rather than private developers, HUD officials, and semiautonmous agencies would determine the housing assistance it received. As a CDBG recipient, general local government would prepare the housing-assistance plan and could use Section 213 to block any proposed housing that might be inconsistent with that plan. Thus fixing authority in local government would ensure housing tailored to unique local conditions and preferences.

Second, Section 8 provided a block of resources unfettered by the vagaries of congressional and administrative manipulation of categorical funds. Unlike the narrow, single-purpose programs, Section 8 can be used for a variety of housing types: new construction, rehabilitation, rental subsidies to needy households, and a variety of beneficiaries—elderly, handicapped, family, poor, and moderate-income households—in any combination. Moreover, since the funds are easily divisible, different combinations can be created at very low levels. For example, one community might specify rental allowances for the elderly, while an adjacent community might specify rehabilitation for families.

Third, this new potential for community-responsive housing programs gave meaningful incentives for comprehensive local housing planning, including thorough assessments of citywide housing needs and market conditions and consideration of multiple strategies to meet locally determined priorities. The Housing Assistance Plan would document these needs, goals, and strategies as local policy and as the definitive guide for HUD's provision of housing resources. Moreover, with the insurance of locally responsive housing assistance, communities could link that assistance to supportive local actions, such as zoning changes, or CDBG-funded neighborhood improvements to create a comprehensive housing strategy.

Thus the act's design remedied the defects of the prior, disjointed housing-assistance system by replacing it with an entirely new form: a decentralized, yet locally integrated, housing system. By giving general local government the authority and the means to achieve a coherent housing strategy, the new system would create both comprehensive, politically accountable integration and responsiveness to diverse local conditions and preferences.

Suburban Responsibility for Housing

Prior to the 1974 act, suburban participation in assisted housing was minimal. The fragmented structure of governance in metropolitan areas provides plentiful social, political, and economic inducements to income stratification. As a result, central cities tended to house the very poor and rings of suburbs exhibited fine differentiations of income and social class. This structure is inimical to low-income housing in the suburbs.

Former HUD programs and developer practices only reinforced this pattern. Middle-income HUD-insured programs located in compatible suburbs, while public housing for the very poor located in central cities. Urban Renewal programs reconcentrated the central city very poor through either new subsidized center-city replacement housing or indirect relocation to remaining center-city slums with still-affordable rents. The courts have been uneven in ruling on this set of outcomes, finding, for example, in Arlington Heights that restrictive zoning was acceptable so long as its discriminatory result was unintended, while finding in Gautreaux that

HUD must provide assisted housing outside center cities and in Mount Laurel that suburbs are responsible for housing a share of the region's poor.

The 1974 act ingeniously designed a carrot-and-stick to ensure subsidized housing in the suburbs at their own request. Substantial community development block grant money offers most cities an irresistible inducement to participate, since the CDBG funds may be used for multiple, politically attractive activities (for example, parks, water, and sewers), and few communities—or their elected officials—can politically afford to reject them. The Housing Assistance Plan (HAP) is one of the few conditions on the grant. On the face of it, the HAP requirements for assessing local housing needs and setting reasonable goals for meeting them seem innocuous. Yet once participating, suburbs are inextricably bound to subsidized housing. In the extremely unlikely event a suburb found no poor of its own to assist, it must still address the needs of the poor, who, by reason of employment, would be expected to live there if affordable housing were available.

To supplement this primary device for ensuring suburban responsibility for housing, the act stressed a metropolitanwide (rather than exclusively local, and so fragmented and to some extent competitive) approach to housing. Not only does the act require HAPs to be consistent with areawide planning, but it also conditions receipt of Section 701 funds on creation of a housing element. Since areawide planning organizations are customarily financially dependent on Section 701 funds, they must develop a metropolitan housing plan acceptable to HUD if they are to survive. The areawide planning organization's mediating position means that it must develop a metropolitan housing strategy that is tolerable to its member jurisdictions (including potentially resistant suburbs) and at the same time promote dispersion of assisted housing to meet HUD objectives. Therefore, the areawide planning organization is compelled to devise a means for increasing subsidized housing in the suburbs that is politically tenable.

Taken together, the design elements of CDBG carrot, HAP stick, and politically sensitive areawide strategies can create strong pressures to counter structural deterrents to housing assistance in the suburbs.

National Concerns

As implied, prior to the 1974 act, national housing efforts were fragmented into categorical programs administered through a disjointed complex of field officials, private developers, and special-purpose local agencies. This program structure precluded national housing planning, coherent strategies, and control over the distribution of subsidies.

The old system was hardly goalless, however, since each categorical program contained goals. Rather, the fractionated goals defied ordering and interconnection, because they were funded and administered separately. One congressionally popular program—for example, Section 202 for the elderly—might be amply funded, while another—for example, Section 235 for homeownership for poor families—might be moribund as a result of highly publicized scandals. The old system of mortgage-insurance manipulation and fragmented sets of goals, subsidies, and institutions prevented comprehensive national housing planning and concerted strategies for achieving multiple goals.

Since the distribution of housing funds depended not only on the uneven funding and administration of the various programs, but also on the unpredictable demand from various developers and local housing authorities, it was effectively out of anyone's or any institution's control. The only certainty was that all money appropriated would be spent—somewhere, somehow—rather than reverting to the Treasury. Experienced, sophisticated developers and aggressive housing authorities and redevelopment agencies, skilled at grantsmanship, secured the lion's share of resources. This sort of quasi-market for housing subsidies reeked with inefficiencies and inequities, since funds were distributed not according to housing need, but according to such criteria as "proven track record" or "quality of proposal," which (partly in order to spend quickly) rewarded experience. Thus expeditious subsidy recipients received more, while needy areas without skilled housing entrepreneurs received little or nothing.

Old sys'.

In the aggregate, the distribution and eventual location of assisted housing was unplanned and not directly responsive to housing needs, but it was hardly random. Housing assistance located according to the entrepreneurial skills of developers and special-purpose local agencies. Because of lower land costs, larger, more sophisticated central-city staff interests, and programmatic (for example, Urban Renewal) orientations, subsidized housing tended to locate in inner-city slums. Notwithstanding these causes for locating subsidized housing where the greatest concentrations of the very poor already lived, the quasi-market forces distributing housing resources resulted in grosser inequities from a national perspective. Some central cities and some regions of the country garnered much more assisted housing than did equally needy others.

The 1974 act reformed the system in ways that served national interests in coherent housing planning and equitable distribuion and dispersion of housing resources. It replaced the quasi-market system for allocating housing subsidies with a system of decentralized rational planning, need-based formula distribution of resources, and a set of programmatic and planning devices to promote the national goal of dispersion of assisted housing. The key national principle was equity.

The HAP served the national goal of equity in two crucial ways. First, every community (over 50,000 population) prepared a HAP. Thus, every community's housing needs and goals would be equally valid, in contrast with the old system, which responded to some and altogether ignored others. Second, each HAP considered all housing needs, citywide. Thus the needs of poor families and those of the elderly would be equally valid, and the needs for rehabilitation and those for new construction would be equally valid, in contrast with the old system, which, through the disjointed funding and administration of categorical programs, addressed different sorts of needs inequitably.

While the actual needs assessments and planning were intended to be a local responsibility, they were cast in a framework that ensured attention to national concerns of equity and housing dispersion. The HAP's first tables, establishing housing needs, were categorized to focus on the full range of housing concerns, and the subsequent goals, while adjustable to local preferences, nonetheless were required to respond to these needs. Finally, HAPs were to identify locations for subsidized housing that avoided impaction. Thus the decentralized planning would simultaneously increase responsiveness to diverse local conditions and serve national objectives.

The act required HUD to distribute Section 8 housing resources according to a fair-share principle. The national fund would be divided equitably among regions (and subsequently redivided among communities) according to housing needs determined by such objective indicators as poverty and overcrowded housing. Such formula allocations would ensure that distribution would be both comprehensive and equitable. The new system's emphasis on objective, equitable distribution of resources in no way connotes that all needs would be met, but rather that all needs would have equal chances and all kinds of needs and all locations would be equal. However, the principle of formula allocation did not imply an absolute local entitlement: there was no housing block grant.

The national objective of dispersion of housing assistance is addressed at several levels within the legislative design for the new system. Most directly, each community's HAP must specify locations for housing that avoid impaction of low-income housing. Beyond this city-level focus, the system of housing assistance addresses interjurisdictional dispersion of housing assistance by expressly serving the suburbs, thereby promoting greater housing choice for low-income people. The design of the Section 8 housing program itself constitutes the system's third element of promoting dispersion. By concentrating on market-level rents, the new construction and rehabilitation programs were designed to encourage a mixture of low-income subsidized tenants and regular-market-rate tenants within individual Section 8 projects. Furthermore, the Section 8 existing housing component promotes dispersion by permitting low-income people to find suitable market-rate housing wherever they like.

In short, the act overturned the former system to create decentralized planning and at the same time to ensure national goals, standards, and controls over the distribution of housing resources. In so doing, the national government asserted its own responsibility for equity and dispersion of housing subsidies.

The Role of the HAP

This interpretation of the 1974 Housing and Community Development Act as a radical response to systemic problems of housing assistance has shown the HAP as the crucial link among complex elements in the new design. The HAP would fix responsibility for housing with general local government rather than with private developers or relatively autonomous special-purpose agency officials. It would ensure comprehensive rational planning for housing that was simultaneously responsive to diverse local conditions and to national goals of equity and dispersion. It would effectively link planning and implementation, guiding the distribution of housing subsidies. The HAP would merge housing with community-development planning to ensure mutually supportive activities. The HAP would ensure suburban participation in assisted housing programs. In sum, the HAP served as the pivot for a major reform of the housing-assistance system, integrating the fragments of the old system while instilling a new responsiveness to diverse conditions and needs.

Implementation of the New Structure

Reality falls short of the HAP's promise offered by the Housing and Community Development Act, yet remarkable changes in the delivery of subsidized housing have occurred since 1974. Distortions in implementation occurred not only from understandable variations in diverse applications throughout the country and from the initial trials and errors that attend any major reform, but also from predictable institutional forces. As a whole, however, the progress in overcoming the major structural obstacles of the past is testimony to the act's integrity of design. In the following discussion, we consider both the short-run implementation problems and the longer-term outcomes that are now becoming visible.

Delivery of Housing Resources: The Transition Period

In design, the HAP, supported by the Section 8 program's versatility, would ensure housing resources delivered in response to diverse local conditions and preferences. Although the HAP did help to fix responsibility for housing planning in local general-purpose government, in the critical first 2 years, it failed to guide resource delivery and therefore proved ineffective in tailoring housing to diverse local conditions and preferences. Findings from eight metropolitan areas showed no statistical correspondence whatsoever between communities' HAP goals and the assistance they received.

The incongruity resulted from powerful forces guiding HUD's delivery of housing assistance. First, substantial program resources were diverted from HAP response to more immediate HUD concerns. In the first 2 years, one-third of the total Section 8 resources were shifted to "loan management" to avert HUD-insured projects' financial failure rather than to respond to community needs. Although loan management no longer constitutes such a severe drain, new priorities—for example, Neighborhood Strategy Area programs—continue to receive special treatment and so undermine the HAP's function as locally determined distribution of housing assistance.[2]

Second, some presumed housing options were unworkable, notably Section 8 rehabilitation and, to a lesser extent, new construction for families. Of the 43,969 units of Section 8 delivered in the metropolitan areas studied, during the first 2 years of the program, only 5 percent were in rehabilitation projects.

Third, HUD was—and continues to be—under severe pressure from the Office of Management and Budget and, in a different way, from Congress to demonstrate high levels of production at lowest possible cost. This incentive biases program delivery toward the administrative convenience and relatively low unit costs of Section 8 existing housing (rental-subsidy) over new construction and rehabilitation.

Fourth, the system continued to rely on private developers who for various profit and management reasons strongly preferred elderly over family projects and new construction over rehabilitation projects. Communities received particular types of projects because developers proposed them, rather than because the communities had such goals.

Fifth, HUD's internal procedures for project approvals ignored the HAP; processing was governed by standards and procedures from the pre-1974 act era. Thus proposals were treated on a case-by-case basis with respect to developer credentials, financial feasibility, neighborhood and site standards, and other business-as-usual concerns for quality projects. Most important, the case-by-case review of proposals against customary criteria disregarded community preferences and interjurisdictional distribution. If a proposal ranked high acording to conventional standards, it was approved despite the locality's goals for a different kind of assistance to a different beneficiary in a different neighborhood. Since housing resources were scarce, communities were grateful for any assistance, even if it had no conformance with their HAPs, and rarely invoked their Section 213 power to reject a project. Where communities, under Section 213, or areawide planning organizations, under their A-95 review and comment authority, ranked proposals according to local or regional—as distinct from HUD—criteria, their priorities were ignored.

HUD's project-focused selection criteria neglected distributional concerns—including HUD's own fair-share distribution formula. While funds were, in fact, allocated by the objective factors of housing need mentioned earlier, so that funds were presumably earmarked equitably among jurisdictions, the focus during project selection on the proposal in isolation meant that in practice many projects might be selected in one jurisdiction, while none were selected in another equally needy community. The net effect of HUD's selection procedures reinforced developer preferences and, to a great extent, the old distribution pattern and inequities that the act was meant to remedy.

Housing Delivery: Adjustment and Response

For all these reasons, together with the skepticism born of local officials' experience, the HAP at the outset was largely perceived as a failure. For many observers, it seemed no more than a paper exercise, and indeed, many localities treated it as no more than a minor obstacle to be overcome in the struggle for federal funds. Yet we should be careful before writing off the HAP and the delivery structure of which it is a part, for there have been substantial changes in the housing system since 1974. In part, these may be attributed to the policies adopted in HUD by the Carter administration. But those policies were formulated and carried out within the 1974 act's framework, which has made it more difficult than formerly for localities to reject any responsibility for housing the poor. We look further at the form of local commitment later. Here we will discuss briefly some of the changes in HUD's procedures and HUD-local relations that have occurred and are still evolving.

Since 1974, HUD's Central Office has increasingly pressed Area Offices to enforce some elements of local HAPs. Localities, faced with legal commitments they may not have realized they were making, now find it harder to evade their responsibility. The pressure from the center has largely taken the form of pushing for local acceptance of housing and requiring that beneficiary (family and elderly) needs be addressed proportionately both at the housing-market level and community by community. Localities, faced with the problem of being held accountable for goals without control over the resources to meet them, had been able to avoid compliance. In some instances, compliance was not really expected by Area Offices. Moreover, the peculiar, original 3-year rolling targets created confusion as to which targets were supposed to be met when.[3] The latter problem was straightened out with the adoption of fixed 3-year HAP cycles. Local and Area Office laxity was shaken by a series of Central Office directives requiring preliminary allocation of subsidized housing resources in accordance with aggregate HAP proportions in the area and emphasizing the need for review and evaluation of local progress toward HAP goals. Although the changes in distribution of housing assistance that have occurred cannot be entirely attributed to these actions, the reactions of staff in field offices leaves us in no doubt that they were important. Moreover, in the absence of the HAP, with its clear, numerical goals, it seems unlikely that comparable leverage could be exerted through Area Offices to the local level.

Shifts in field office and local policy have not occurred simply from coercive efforts to press housing upon reluctant localities but also from changes in procedure that meet some of the problems described earlier. Some HUD field offices have modified their procedures to influence developers to submit proposals more consonant with HAP goals, for example, by advertising for only a particular kind of project beneficiary for target communities. At the same time, some jurisdictions and some areawide planning organizations have learned the entrepreneurial housing skills that formerly only large sophisticated housing authorities possessed. They have worked with developers and, in some cases, have underwritten land costs (thereby creating an intergovernmental piggy-back subsidy) to ensure feasible proposals reflecting their own goals. Innovations in signaling to developers can have surprising impacts. In a tight housing market, the Twin Cities Metropolitan Council in Minneapolis-St. Paul (using a special Section 8 bonus under the Areawide Housing Opportunity Program) advertised exclusively for large-family new construction in the suburbs and received a large number of quality proposals, a result HUD had considered virtually impossible.

Another sophisticated response has been the creation of new forms of consultation and planning in the allocation process, involving HUD field office staff, housing staff from areawide planning organizations, and representatives of local communities. Area Offices are beginning to keep track of the cumulative performance of local communities and work out subsidy allocations interactively rather than adhering to formulas.

The path of implementation suggests that the act's design for locally responsive housing was distorted by powerful institutional forces: diverting HUD priorities (for example, to bolster failing projects), inadequate developer incentives for rehabilitation and family new construction, pressures for least cost per unit and speedy production, reliance on developer preference, and maintenance of the old project selection procedures. All these forces are rooted in the complex system of interests: those of the bureaucracy, of the industry, and of both partisan and executive versus congressional politics. Then, too, most governmental changes develop in modest increments, in contrast with the near-radical reform the legislation offered. From this perspective, it is not surprising that implementation has taken time and that in the transition, procedures failed to keep pace with the act. Nevertheless, the overall patterns of response show surprising shifts, especially in the locations of assistance, after several years of operation.

Suburban Acceptance of Housing Responsibility

If implementation vitiated the HAP's operational function, it nonetheless exalted the HAP's symbolic function. Suburbs have irrevocably accepted responsibility for housing the poor.

Although HAP preparation incurred little political controversy (because it was remote and technical), it nonetheless committed suburban governments to accept housing assistance in accord with locally developed goals. Moreover, for a number of suburbs, the HAP served as a consciousness-raiser. Officials recognized, for the first time, that they had housing needs of their own, and needy constituents. Thus, both legally and symbolically, the HAP bound suburbs to housing assistance.

The extent of housing need in suburban areas has not received adequate study. Table 13-1 provides an estimate of the proportions of subsidy-eligible

Table 13-1
Intraregional Distribution of Very-Low-Income and Moderate-Income Households by Race in Selected Metropolitan Areas

	Suburban Share of All Low- and Moderate-Income Households in Region[a]		*Suburban Share of All Very Low-Income Households in Region*[b]	
Metropolitan Region	*Total Households (%)*	*Minority Households Only (%)*	*Total Households (%)*	*Minority Households Only (%)*
Boston	69.8	16.1	66.7	14.5
Los Angeles	48.7	28.1	47.1	25.7
Rochester	55.6	16.4	48.1	14.5
San Francisco	53.4	28.6	50.0	27.0
Seattle[c]	47.5	16.7	41.6	14.2
Washington, D.C.	61.4	27.8	53.6	22.7

Source: Annual Housing Survey Data provided by HUD's Economic Market Analysis Division.

[a]Defined as all households with incomes below 80 percent of the SMSA median income with income eligibility adjusted by family size.

[b]Defined as all households with incomes below 50 percent of the SMSA median income with income eligibility adjusted by family size.

[c]The Seattle data are based on the Seattle/Everett SMSA only, which comprises about one-half of the Puget Sound AHOP region.

households, both low-moderate and very-low income, living outside the central city in six metropolitan areas of varied size, location, and urban structure. In no instance do the suburbs contain less than 40 percent of very-low-income households. In the case of Boston, the proportion is as high as 67 percent. These figures are clearly influenced by the urban structure of the various areas—not all places outside the central city should properly be described as suburbs. However, within the limits of the data available from the Annual Housing Survey, non-central-city locations for assisted housing would evidently meet real need. However, it is also apparent from table 13-1 that the suburban poor are not minorities for the most part. The proportion of minority, very-low-income households outside the central cities is nowhere greater than 29 percent and generally much lower. Thus a shift to serving low-income need outside the central cities seems also to imply a shift away from serving minority populations.

The initial unintended program biases of Section 8 implementation functioned ideally to serve the suburbs. The emphasis on the Section 8 existing program gave suburbs their first, and most palatable, taste of housing assistance. Since the program is invisible and not politically threatening, it was an extremely popular means of introducing suburbs to their housing responsibilities. Then, too, new construction for the elderly served a growing and politically acceptable special interest. Thus the structural predispositions of the Section 8 program, which restrict response to HAP goals, had the unanticipated benefit of promoting housing dispersion without controversy.

The challenge, perceived by HUD and areawide organizations, was to induce suburbs to build new housing for families. The stereotype of visible, large, dense, crime-filled housing projects was understandably politically unattractive to suburbs. Beginning in 1976, HUD required that HAP goals be proportional to needs over a 3-year period. Thus, by 1978, *proportionality*, meaning that suburbs serve the relatively neglected families, became an issue. In response, HUD learned to target advertisements for developer proposals toward families, and localities learned to tailor family housing to community preferences. For example, some localities passed referenda limiting the number of units per project; others pursued scattered-site public housing; and others used Section 235 to replace eyesores with assisted housing compatible with the neighborhood. Montgomery County, Maryland passed an ordinance requiring that 15 percent of all units in developments of over fifty units be reserved for moderate-income housing, using county powers over scarce sewer allocations and zoning variations to create sufficient inducements for developer compliance. In short, a number of suburbs have found ways to make assisted housing for families conform, politically and physically, to community standards.

The record of suburban acceptance of assisted housing is impressive. Although there are no comprehensive data on the changing shares of housing assistance going to central cities and suburbs in metropolitan areas, the regions for which we have analyzed the HAP and the Areawide Housing Opportunity Program exhibited substantial shifts. Table 13-2 shows the cumulative share of all assisted housing located in suburbs for five metropolitan areas. In every one of these regions, the proportion of assisted housing outside the central city increased substantially in the 4 years between 1975 and 1979.[4] In most instances, the actual number of suburban assisted units more than doubled in those years. Whether these cases are representative of all metropolitan areas cannot be determined; they were all recipients of bonus-assisted housing under the AHOP program. However, in three other regions that were not part of that program, comparable absolute increases in suburban assisted housing did occur. Nationally, HUD data indicate that about 44 percent of Section 8 assistance has been going to suburbs, but there is no comparable aggregate information for the pre-1974 period. This pattern overcomes major social, political, and economic barriers, as well as HUD's programmatic concentration of housing assistance in central cities.

Our conclusion is that the HAP was instrumental in revealing the substantial housing needs of the suburbs, which in turn accepted their responsibility for assisting their own poor. The larger question of the suburbs' accepting responsibility for housing their fair share of their metropolitan area's poor, and of providing central-city residents access to their new housing resources, however, remains open. Except for the Twin Cities Metropolitan Area, there is little evidence that central-city poor are moving to assisted housing in the suburbs. In fact, many suburbs impose residency preferences to ensure that they serve only their own poor.

The shift toward the suburbs, although serving eligible populations, also may have shifted resources away from low-income minority households. It is hard to draw any other conclusion from tables 13-1 and 13-2

Table 13-2
Cumulative Deconcentration of Assisted Housing Over Two Time Periods

	Suburban Share of Total Assisted Units in Region			
	January 1975		*February 1979*	
Metropolitan Region	*Units in Suburbs*	*Suburban Share of Regional Total*	*Units in Suburbs*	*Suburban Share of Regional Total*
Washington, DC	16,620	42.8%	26,352	50.5%
Puget Sound	4,483	27.0	8,718	33.4
Los Angeles	32,816	51.2	69,025	57.5
Minneapolis-St. Paul	4,826	19.6	13,297	33.7
Miami Valley, Dayton	2,102	25.7	4,471	37.1
All Regions	60,847	39.3	121,863	48.8

Source: Berkeley Planning Associates' case studies of selected metropolitan areas.

considered jointly. However, since the suburban poor had evidently been underserved prior to the act, whether this shift constitutes an inequity remains open to question.

Dispersion without Equity

The 1974 act incorporated national goals for coherent housing planning, dispersion, and equitable distribution of housing resources in its essentially decentralized design. Its implementation skewed achievement of national, as well as local and regional, objectives.

Coherent housing planning was greatly inhibited by the initial gap between housing planning and delivery discussed earlier. Nonetheless, the HAPs, simply as paper documents, have identified complete housing needs for over 3,000 cities, the bulk of the nation's urbanized population. It is hardly clean data, and hardly comparable, for communities conducted their own surveys and developed their own criteria (for designating a unit substandard, for example). Nonetheless, in the aggregate, as well as individually, the HAPs constitute an important first step toward coherent housing planning. Moreover, some areawide planning organizations have developed high-quality regionally consistent data on housing needs.

The HAP also has served the goal of dispersion. The previous section has indicated the dispersion of housing resources away from impacted central cities and into suburbs. In addition, the HAP's requirement to identify nonimpacted neighborhoods for the location of new projects has evidently had some effect, even if project selection has tended to bypass HAP-specified sites and project types. In the first 2 years, although only half the new construction projects were located in HAP-specified tracts, at the same time only a fifth were located in impacted tracts, in contrast to the location of HUD-subsidized housing prior to the act.

The division of Section 8 resources by a needs-based formula was designed to treat all needs equally so that each community would receive its fair share, rather than disproportionate allocations resulting from grantsmanship skills or systemic vagaries. In the early phases of implementation, the HAP's minor role combined with program biases and developer preferences in such a way that even though funds were allocated by formula, their actual delivery had no connection with objective need indicators. As the implementation evolved, however, distribution came more into line with allocation. Aside from more refined advertising procedures, in some areas the HUD office or the areawide planning organization keeps a cumulative tally, checking which communities have a surplus or deficit with respect to their fair share. Thus the HAP/Section 8 system has made significant progress toward the national goal of equity.

Nonetheless, significant inequities may still characterize housing distribution. Section 8 existing housing is administratively simple, cheap, and politically palatable. It therefore tends to be overused, and although it serves low income people who pay excessive portions of their income for rent, it does not increase communities' stocks of standard housing, whether through rehabilitation or new construction assistance. Thus the program biases favor income-related needs to the disadvantage of cities with deteriorated stock, overcrowding, and an inadequate supply of housing. Similarly, the programmatic tendency toward new construction for the elderly, coupled with the strong current funding of the Section 202 program, treats the needs of families inequitably. Thus programmatic determinants have unequal effects on communities and their housing needs.

Another signficant systemic inequity results, in part at least, from pressure to spend all funds appropriated. Although national funds are subdivided among the regions according to fair-share formulas, they are recaptured and redistributed according to regions' capacities to spend expeditiously. For example, some state housing agencies, such as Massachusetts, may be able to deliver housing resources particularly efficiently. Whatever the additional causes (for example, bonus funding), the data show that in spite of fair share, metropolitan areas do not receive resources according to need and so do not have equal chances for addressing needs. For example, the 1976-1977 Berkeley Planning Associates (BPA) study showed funding levels in the metropolitan areas studied varied from $406 to $68 per needy household identified in HAPs. The 1979 study showed that these regional disparities persist. The different set of metropolitan areas studied in 1978-1979 showed funding levels varied from $16.59 to $6.48 per capita. Thus, while the act has remedied the most glaring distribution problems of the old housing system by replacing entrepreneurial responsiveness with a needs-based formula allocation, it nonetheless results in serious inequities.

Conclusions for the Future

The preceding sections have described the HAP's promise as the key link among program elements and levels of government in the housing and community-development system. In design, the 1974 act transformed the prior, fragmented, quasi-market housing-assistance complex into a rationally integrated system that could simultaneously address national goals of equity and dispersion and respond to diverse local conditions and preferences.

Despite difficulties in implementation during the transition period, the new structure has succeeded in inducing suburbs to take responsibility for housing the poor and, thereby, in dispersing subsidized housing. Although inequities among housing needs and regions still persist, the needs-based formula distribution of housing resources and the HAP's comprehensive assessments of housing needs have virtually reversed the former quasi-market distribution of resources and have gone a long way toward the national goal of equity. As localities, areawide planning organizations, and HUD's field offices learn to shape developer proposals, housing delivery can become increasingly responsive to communities.

In aggregate, the fair-share HAP and Section 8 innovations (particularly the existing housing program) have generated powerful trends toward dispersal of housing assistance and wider choice for the poor. Nevertheless, important and difficult issues remain. The new structure's success in dispersing assisted housing into the suburbs makes all the more evident the inadequacy of programs directed toward equal housing opportunity for minorities. As central-city governments realize the implications of the shifts in allocation of housing resources, this issue may well dominate conflicts over targeting of subsidies.

The institutional changes brought about by the act also have created tensions among the historic housing interest groups. The act—the peculiar product of a Nixonian Republican coalition with reformers—imposed truly major changes on a complex set of institutions (developers, special-purpose agencies, HUD field offices) that were quite comfortable in their old established relations. These institutions have distorted the act's implementation. The question for the future is: Will the trends generated by the act be overwhelmed by countertrends promoted by the older established interests? In the midst of the act's very real progress toward broad, equitable distribution of housing and integrated planning, new forms of specialized fragmentation intervene. For example, Urban Development Action Grants resurrected Urban Renewal and Neighborhood Strategy Areas created another special-purpose program outside the CDBG/HAP system. Shallow subsidies similarly truncate the integrity of the act's design for Section 8's versatile response to HAPs. The tension between fragmentation resulting from the demands of various interests for special-purpose efforts (which ensure inequities and create the opportunities for political, preferential treatment) and rational integration and equitable response embodied in the act is endemic to public policy.

In spite of fractionating tendencies, suburbanization of housing assistance seems to have taken hold. The act itself and the strong response of suburbs have created the conditions for the institutional recognition that *urban* does not mean merely the central city, but rather the metropolis.

Both spatially and institutionally the future seems to hold a more holistic view of housing and community development. Within HUD itself, the act has brought the housing and community-development sides one step closer to unification. This integrating evolution stems not only from the act's explicit program linkages, but also from the suburbanization of prevously exclusively central-city redevelopment concerns and the metropolitanwide involvement of insurance-type housing programs (previously concentrated in the suburbs). The merger is further reflected in the revision of housing distribution away from a nearly atomistic quasi-market approach to a more governmentally controlled, needs-based system. However, the institutional and bureaucratic divisions within HUD are old and deep. We cannot expect an attempt to impose a profoundly different structure upon a functioning intergovernmental system to succeed without interruptions and setbacks. That the 1974 act's structure has had the impact that can be seen so far in the planning and allocation of housing subsidy resources is remarkable enough.

Notes

1. Berkeley Planning Assocites, *Evaluation of Housing Assistance Plans*, vols. 1 through 5, 1977; and Berkeley Planning Associates, *Assessment of the Impact of the Housing Opportunity Plan (AHOP) Program*, vols. 1 and 2, 1979.
2. Loan management funds are now appropriated separately.
3. Originally, the HAP regulations called for new 3-year goals with each annual submission. The result was confusion about accountability. For example, in a given year, should a community be held responsible for the third-year goal of its HAP of 3 years previously, the second-year goal of its 2-year previous HAP, and the first-year goal of its prior-year HAP all at once?
4. To some degree, this shift had started with the Section 235 and 236 programs, as is evident from the Los Angeles data. However, suburban communities were relatively little involved and the subsidies were not directed toward very-low-income households.

14 The Salience of Housing Issues in Neighborhood Planning

John D. Hutcheson, Jr.

While housing costs for both homeowners and renters declined relative to incomes during the 1960s, major federal housing policies focused on attempts to alleviate substandard conditions and overcrowding among those at the bottom of the housing market—racial minorities, the poor, and the elderly. The housing-market process in urban areas, recently characterized as "a highly disjointed process in which the major decisions are made by thousands of individuals acting in their own interests," left many of those whose limited resources restricted their ability to protect their own interests without habitable housing.[1] Thus, "intervening at the margins" of the market process, federal policies in the late 1960s and early 1970s were directed toward ensuring decent housing for the disadvantaged.[2] Even though it would be misleading to suggest that federal policies were uniformly successful, by the mid-1970s, the numbers of households residing in substandard or overcrowded conditions had declined sharply.[3]

Yet in the 1970s, another trend, one that will undoubtedly continue into the 1980s, emerged. Sharp increases in the costs of housing have meant not only that economically disadvantaged households are expending larger proportions of their incomes on housing, but also that the range of housing opportunities available to middle-income families has contracted. Frieden and Solomon assert that "housing deprivation is changing from a problem of physically inadequate shelter to a problem of excessive cost."[4] To even the most casual of observers it would appear that housing issues in the 1980s will concern not only economically disadvantaged groups that traditionally have been the intended beneficiaries of federal housing programs, but also a broader spectrum of citizens, especially in urban areas where the upward spiral of housing costs has been most apparent.

Concurrently, federal efforts to increase public access to governmental planning and policymaking have broadened in the past 20 years. While programs such as the Community Action Program and Model Cities, which targeted deprived communities, popularized the notion of direct citizen participation in the 1960s and early 1970s, some form of citizen participation is now required in almost all federally sponsored programs, whatever the

The author wishes to acknowledge the assistance of Jim Prather, Rob Snow, Jill Auerbach, Loretta Lowrey, Maria Saporta, and Bob Thomas in the preparation of this chapter.

socioeconomic status of the citizens most directly affected.[5] Consequently, federally assisted housing programs now require broad-based participation in planning and policymaking. Local governments are directed to develop citizen participation plans and document the involvement of citizens likely to be affected by housing and community-development activities.[6] Yet Department of Housing and Urban Development (HUD) regulations do not prescribe specific procedures or criteria, since such "requirements would have imposed upon HUD the responsibility for specifying the manner in which local general purpose government related to its citizens."[7]

Numerous variations in approach and form have been developed and have proven acceptable under existing HUD regulations. In most large urban centers, general citizen participation mechanisms designed to include volunteer participants from the population at large and to address a full range of issues, including housing and community development, have evolved. In such situations, local governments faced with declining resources and increasing demands find it increasingly difficult to provide the information and technical assistance needed if citizens are to understand complex housing issues and programs and act effectively in the interests of their communities. Local governments, in order to facilitate effective citizen involvement in housing and community-development activities, must identify those communities in which housing-related issues are most salient and define the types of information and technical assistance that would be most beneficial to different types of communities.

The purpose of the analysis reported here is to define some of the conditions under which housing issues arise in neighborhood-based citizen-participation mechanisms and to suggest, on the basis of this analysis, how information about housing and socioeconomic conditions might be used in the allocation of resources devoted to the citizen-participation process. The allocation of such resources will become increasingly important as the accelerating cost of housing enlarges the proportion of citizens described as suffering from "housing deprivation."[8]

Context

In a recent survey of 1,473 cities, the International City Management Association found widespread use of citizen advisory committees among cities receiving Community Development Block Grants (CDBGs) and housing grants. Undoubtedly because of federal requirements, citizen participation was used more frequently in the development of CDBG and housing proposals than in all other types of proposals for federal funding. Over 65 percent of the cities receiving CDBGs and over 63 percent of the cities receiving housing funds utilized citizen advisory committees.[9] Typically, at least among cities of over 250,000 people, neighborhood-based organizations are involved in the planning process, and usually through intermediate organizational levels these neighborhood-based organizations contribute to the development of citywide plans. In many cases, neighborhood-based organizations participate in planning and policymaking processes unrelated to CDBGs and housing, and such organizations are usually provided some technical assistance by city government staff members.[10]

A review of approaches and mechanisms used in various cities across the country suggests that general citizen-participation mechanisms (those addressing a number of policy issues and including various types of communities) have evolved in numerous situations.[11] The neighborhood planning process employed in the city of Atlanta is one such mechanism. The Atlanta City Charter, which became effective in January of 1974, specifies that citizens be given the opportunity to participate in the city planning process, and the Neighborhood Planning Ordinance of 1974 specifies the structure and process through which citizens are to participate. About 200 neighborhoods, defined as areas with distinguishing characteristics or in which residents have a sense of identity or commonality of perceived interests, were grouped into twenty-four Neighborhood Planning Units (NPUs). NPUs were designed to be large enough to permit comprehensive approaches to problems and planning, but small enough to permit citizen identification.

Each NPU has a staff planner assigned to it, but citizens are free to write their own bylaws and the degree of formality of operations differs considerably from NPU to NPU. Similarly, the scope of NPU activities is broadly defined. In addition to participating in the development of NPU plans, which contribute to the development of the city's 1- , 5- , and 15-Year Comprehensive Development Plans, the Neighborhood Planning Committee:

> . . . may recommend an action, a policy or a comprehensive plan to the city and to any city agency on any matter affecting the livability of the neighborhood, including, but not limited to, land use, zoning, housing, community facilities, human resources, social and recreational programs, traffic and transportation, environmental quality, open space and parks; assist city agencies in determining priority needs for the neighborhood; and review items for inclusion in the city budget and make recommendations relating to budget items for neighborhood improvement.[12]

Thus the neighborhood planning process in Atlanta provides a mechanism through which neighborhood-based organizations may address a range of policy issues and a context for examining the conditions under which housing becomes a salient issue in neighborhood-based political activity. Atlanta seems to be representative of many other large cities in that it is becoming increasingly difficult to provide the resources required to meet the informational and technical assistance demands generated by citizens involved in neighborhood-based planning.

Data

The data used in this analysis were derived from several different sources. Data relative to perceptions of the importance of housing issues were obtained from two surveys conducted in late 1978, occurring after rapid increases in housing prices and occupancy rates in the city. Apartment occupancy increased from 94.5 to 98.6 percent from January 1977 to January 1979, and housing prices in some intown neighborhoods were estimated to have increased by as much as 25 percent during the same period. These two surveys were conducted in conjunction with an evaluation of the implementation of the Neighborhood Planning Ordinance by the Development Committee of the Atlanta City council. Four-hundred ninety-four participants in the neighborhood planning process returned questionnaires that had been distributed to approximately 900 randomly selected participants. Additionally, a telephone survey of 677 randomly selected residents of the city was conducted in order to assess the perceptions of the general public.[13]

Both sets of respondents were asked "How concerned do you think people in your neighborhood are about housing—very concerned, somewhat concerned, or not concerned?" Respondents in the mail survey (participants in the neighborhood planning process) were also asked "How much of your NPU's efforts have gone into working on problems related to housing—a lot, some, a little, or none?" The responses to these items are employed as indicators of the salience of housing issues.

The conditions under which housing becomes a salient issue in neighborhood-based political activity may range from idiosyncratic events occurring in a community to underlying political and social attitudes shared by community residents, and even to national economic conditions. These types of conditions are not specified in the following analysis. It is assumed that national economic conditions dictating increases in housing costs relative to income will continue. Because of the availability of current attitudinal data and the unpredictability of idiosyncratic events, specifying these sets of conditions as antecedents of the salience of housing as an issue in neighborhood-based political activity would be of little use to decision-makers responsible for the allocation of resources used for information and technical assistance.

However, aggregate-level socioeconomic and housing data are normally available to city governments. Thus the conditions specified in the following analysis were gleaned from two sources. Estimates of the mean income of residents of each NPU were derived from a survey of 5,503 randomly selected residents of the city conducted in 1976.[14] Population characteristics for each NPU (percentage population change for 1970-1974 and percentage Black) and housing characteristics for each NPU (percentage owner-occupancy, percentage deteriorated units, percentage new units for 1970-1975, and percentage public housing units) were obtained from *NPU Profiles* prepared by the Atlanta Bureau of Planning.[15]

Findings

As indicated earlier, the primary purpose of this chapter is to identify conditions under which housing issues are most likely to arise in neighborhood-based political activity. However, several related questions are addressed prior to the identification of antecedent conditions. It is possible, utilizing the data just described, to simply examine the characteristics of NPUs in which high proportions of participants in the neighborhood planning process indicate concern for housing issues. This, however, would ignore the possibility that participants neither accurately perceive the concerns of residents of their neighborhoods nor translate concern into action.

In order to address the question of whether participants in the neighborhood planning process reflect the concerns of the general public, participants' responses to the question "How concerned do you think people in your neighborhood are about housing?" were compared to responses of nonparticipants. Table 14-1 delineates this comparison and indicates that in only five of the twenty-four NPUs were the responses of participants significantly different from those of nonparticipants. In general, housing issues are more salient among participants than nonparticipants, and this is the case in four of the NPUs (*D,J,O,* and *W*) in which participants' responses differed significantly from those of nonparticipants.[16]

These data confirm that the general population's concern for housing is reflected by the perceptions of participants in the neighborhood planning process. As might be expected, participants perceive slightly more concern for housing than do nonparticipants. This concern appears to be translated into organizational efforts in the neighborhood planning process. Table 14-2 clearly indicates that perceived salience of housing as an issue is strongly related to participants' perceptions of the levels of effort expended by the NPUs in dealing with housing problems. Thus the general public's concern for housing is reflected by participants in the neighborhood planning process, and this concern appears to be translated into neighborhood-based political activity.

Table 14-1 clearly indicates that the majority of participants in most NPUs are very concerned with housing issues. However, there is still a great

Table 14-1
Salience of Housing Issues among Participants and Nonparticipants by NPU

	Participants				*Nonparticipants*				
NPU	*Very Concerned*	*Somewhat Concerned*	*Not Concerned*	*N*	*Very Concerned*	*Somewhat Concerned*	*Not Concerned*	*N*	χ^2 *(df = 2)*
A	37%	47%	16%	19	31%	19%	50%	16	5.39
B	50	38	13	24	40	41	19	63	.93
C	33	37	30	30	64	17	19	36	6.35*
D	43	57	0	14	26	35	39	23	7.24*
E	65	35	0	17	57	22	22	51	4.76
F	70	25	5	44	55	32	14	44	3.25
G	67	33	0	6	71	29	0	14	.47
H	77	23	0	13	59	24	18	17	2.66
I	72	17	11	18	63	20	18	40	.58
J	93	7	0	27	59	24	18	17	8.25*
K	64	27	9	11	69	19	13	16	.31
L	67	33	0	6	50	42	8	12	.77
M	74	17	9	23	76	21	3	29	.69
N	64	32	4	28	62	15	23	13	4.40
O	100	0	0	15	46	42	13	24	12.19*
P	60	30	10	10	65	29	6	17	.17
R	82	6	12	17	58	26	16	19	3.13
S	55	45	0	11	64	9	27	11	5.74
T	71	21	7	14	73	14	14	22	.64
V	90	5	5	20	60	20	20	15	4.38
W	93	7	0	15	52	44	4	27	7.49*
X	50	43	7	14	50	36	14	22	.42
Y	79	14	7	14	63	31	6	16	1.21
Z	57	29	14	7	44	38	19	16	.35
Total	67%	26%	7%	417	55%	28%	17%	580	22.48*

Sources: These data were obtained from two surveys (one of participants and one of nonparticipants in the neighborhood planning process) conducted in late 1978 by the staff of the Atlanta City Council. The author served as a consultant to the council and the council staff and assisted in the development of the sampling procedures and survey instruments employed.

$^*p < .05$

Table 14-2
Salience of Housing Issues by Amount of NPU's Effort Devoted to Housing (N = 323)

How Concerned Do You Think People in Your Neighborhood Are about Housing?	*How Much of Your NPU's Efforts Have Gone Into Working on Problems Related to Housing?*				
	A Lot	*Some*	*A Little*	*None*	*Totals*
Very concerned	61%	26%	6%	7%	71%
Somewhat concerned	15	51	22	12	24
Not concerned	13	25	19	44	5
Totals	48	32	11	10	100
$\chi^2 = 78.19$		$df = 6$	$p < .001$		

Source: These data are from the mail survey of participants in the neighborhood planning process conducted by the staff of the Atlanta City Council in 1978.

deal of variation from NPU to NPU in the salience of housing issues. In order to identify the conditions that are antecedent to variations in the levels of salience of housing issues, measures of various conditions within each NPU were used as contextual variables. These were defined as the contexts within which individual participants developed perceptions of the salience of housing as an issue in their neighborhoods. Housing (owner-occupied, deteriorated, new, and public housing units) and population (race and change in population) characteristics were defined in terms of rates within each NPU. Mean household income was employed as a measure of the socioeconomic environment of each NPU. These contextual variables were transformed into natural logarithms in order to decrease the effects of outlying values and heteroscedasticity of error variance in the multivariate discriminant analysis employed.[17]

Discriminant analysis permits an assessment of the degree to which each of the conditions (discriminating variables) distinguish the levels of salience (very concerned, somewhat concerned, and not concerned with housing issues).[18] Table 14-3 presents the results of the discriminant analysis. Part A represents a preliminary step in the analysis and includes the mean scores for each condition. The means for variables transformed into logarithms of rates (all conditions with the exception of mean income) are negative. Thus the closer the mean is to zero, the higher the rate of occurrence of the condition. Therefore, those participants responding that residents of their neighborhoods were very concerned about housing issues lived in NPUs with relatively low owner-occupancy, high proportions of deteriorated housing units, low percentages of new housing units, high percentages of blacks, and relatively low mean incomes. The univariate F's indicate the statistical significance of the differences among the levels of salience with reference to each condition.

Table 14-3
Conditions Affecting Salience of Housing Issues: Discriminant Analysis (N = 417

Part A

	Means			
Conditions	*Very Concerned*	*Somewhat Concerned*	*Not Concerned*	*Univariate F (df = 2,414*
Percentage owner-occupied housing units	−1.04	− .91	− .90	3.21*
Percentage deteriorated housing units	−1.45	−1.69	−1.97	6.40*
Percentage new housing units	−1.86	−1.77	−1.68	.23
Percentage public housing units	−2.66	−3.21	−3.12	4.91*
Percentage change in population	− .55	− .67	− .52	.31
Percentage black population	−1.54	−2.46	−2.61	12.31*
Mean income	9.46	9.68	9.86	13.50*

Part B

	Classification Function Coefficients			
Conditions	*Very Concerned*	*Somewhat Concerned*	*Not Concerned*	*Partial F (df = 1,408*
Percentage owner-occupied housing units	−84.28	−84.61	−84.53	1.61
Percentage deteriorated housing units	60.92	61.24	60.99	.97
Percentage new housing units	− .19	.02	.08	4.49*
Percentage public housing units	− 5.09	− 5.33	− 4.92	2.59
Percentage change in population	5.99	5.79	6.08	2.50
Percentage black population	16.91	16.64	16.81	4.32*
Mean income	200.22	200.78	202.39	3.51
Constant	−939.16	−945.41	−959.50	

Performance of discriminant functions in predicting salience of housing issues:
Multivariate (approximate) $F = 3.76$ $df = 14,816$ $p < .001$

Part C

	Univariate F Matrix (df = 7,408)	
	Very Concerned	*Somewhat Concerned*
Somewhat concerned	4.53*	—
Not concerned	3.60*	1.41

Part D

	Prediction Results of Predicted Group			
Actual Group	*Very Concerned*	*Somewhat Concerned*	*Not Concerned*	*N*
Very concerned	53.9%	21.1%	25.0%	28[illegible]
Somewhat concerned	32.1	28.3	39.6	10[illegible]
Not concerned	29.0	12.9	58.1	3[illegible]

Percentage of "grouped" cases correctly classified: 47.72%

*$p < .05$

Sources: The groups (levels of salience) in this analysis were defined by responses to an item in the 197 survey of participants in the neighborhood planning process conducted by the staff of the Atlanta Ci Council. Mean income for each Neighborhood Planning Unit was derived from a 1976 survey conducte by the Center for Urban Research and Service in the College of Urban Life at Georgia State Universi (see note 14). Other Neighborhood Planning Unit characteristics were obtained from *NPU Profil* prepared by the Atlanta Bureau of Planning (see note 15).

In Part B, unstandardized classification function coefficients are reported. These coefficients' weights and signs may be compared across levels of salience in order to determine the direction of differences between levels of salience. However, they should not be compared within levels of salience; the relative importance of each condition in distinguishing among levels of salience, when all other conditions are controlled, is indicated by the partial *F*'s. Thus, when all other specified conditions are controlled, the proportions of new housing units and blacks in a community best distinguish between the levels of salience of housing issues that, as has been shown earlier, are associated with the intensity of neighborhood-based organizations' efforts to address housing problems.

The *F* matrix (Part C) indicates that the conditions specified in the discriminant analysis performed best, in terms of distinguishing between the levels of salience, in discriminating between the very concerned and the somewhat and not concerned levels. The differences between the somewhat concerned and not concerned levels were not as distinct. Part D, presenting the prediction results, reflects this inability to distinguish between the somewhat concerned and not concerned levels, but demonstrates that the very concerned and not concerned levels of salience are quite distinct and predictable on the basis of the conditions used in the analysis.

Conclusions and Implications

The perceptual data used in the analyses just described were obtained during a period preceded by rapid increases in housing costs and occupancy rates. They also reflect the dynamics of a citizen-participation mechanism that is typical of those employed in large American cities. The analyses demonstrate that the level of salience of housing issues in a community may be predicted with moderate success on the basis of readily available housing and demographic data. In addition, the analyses suggest that participants reflect the housing-related concerns of the residents of the communities they represent and that these concerns are translated into neighborhood-based political activity focusing on the resolution of housing problems.

While concern for housing issues is widespread and is expressed in communities exhibiting differing socioeconomic characteristics, housing issues are most salient in lower-socioeconomic-status areas. Perhaps reflecting older housing stocks and the relatively limited opportunity for residential mobility of blacks, low proportions of new housing units and high proportions of black residents best distinguish those communities in which housing issues are most salient. Yet other conditions associated with lower-status areas also characterize communities in which housing issues are salient—low mean incomes, low owner-occupancy rates, high proportions of deteriorated units, and high proportions of public housing units.

If housing deprivation, in terms of excessive cost, continues to encompass residents of higher-status communities, concern for housing issues is likely to continue to increase the salience of housing issues in higher-status areas. But excessive cost is only one of the components of housing deprivation in lower-status communities. While excessive costs affect lower-status areas as well as higher-status communities, physically inadequate shelter is an additional source of deprivation in lower-status communities. Increasing costs relative to income may increase neighborhood-based organizations' efforts to address housing problems somewhat uniformly across levels of socioeconomic status, but housing issues will continue to be most salient in older, minority, lower-socioeconomic-status communities.

Faced with the probability of increasing demands for information and technical assistance with regard to housing problems, it is likely that city governments will be required to allocate resources among different types of neighborhoods. The types of communities in which housing issues are most salient are also those in which local government policies have the most potential for constructive change. Few local government policies have dramatic impacts on housing costs, which, to a large extent, reflect national economic conditions. The availability of habitable shelter, however, may be influenced by housing-code enforcement, local allocation of resources made available through federally sponsored programs, and a number of other locally controlled practices. Thus there appear to be compelling reasons to suggest that communities exhibiting high levels of concern for housing issues be given priority in the allocation of resources devoted to information and technical assistance related to housing. These communities are likely to be lower-socioeconomic-status communities best characterized by low proportions of new housing units and high proportions of minority residents, and indicators of these characteristics are readily available to local officials.

Notes

1. Robert E. Mendelson and Michael A. Quinn (eds.), *The Politics of Housing in Older Urban Areas* (New York: Praeger, 1976), p. xvi.

2. Ibid., p. xv.

3. Bernard J. Frieden and Arthur P. Solomon, *The Nation's Housing: 1975 to 1985* (Cambridge, Mass.: M.I.T.-Harvard Joint Center for Urban Studies, 1977), p. 87.

4. Ibid., p. 87.

5. John D. Hutcheson, Jr. and Jann Shevin, *Citizen Groups in Local Politics: A Bibliographic Review* (Santa Barbara, California: Clio Books, 1976), pp. 1-2.

6. For discussions of Department of Housing and Urban Development regulations and guidelines, see Michael Fagence, *Citizen Participation in Planning* (New York: Pergamon, 1977), pp. 229-233; and Patricia Marshall (ed.), *Citizen Participation Certification for Community Development: A Reader on The Citizen Participation Process* (Washington: National Association of Housing and Redevelopment Officials, 1977), pp. 1-16.

7. *Federal Register*, November 13, 1974, quoted in Marshall, *Citizen Participation Certification*, p. 5.

8. Frieden and Solomon, *The Nation's Housing*, pp. 99-130.

9. John Rehfuss, "Citizen Participation in Urban Fiscal Decisions," *Urban Data Service Reports* 10, 8, (August 1978):7-8.

10. Lawrence Johnson and Associates, Inc., *Citizen Participation in Community Development: A Catalog of Local Approaches* (Washington: U.S. Government Printing Office, 1978), pp. 3-54.

11. Ibid., pp. 5-10.

12. Neighborhood Planning Ordinance, City of Atlanta, Code of Ordinances, 1974.

13. Descriptions of the sampling procedures used in both 1978 surveys, including estimates of nonresponse bias, may be obtained from the author.

14. Initial analyses also included the mean perceived retail value of owner-occupied housing for each NPU. This variable, however, was found to be statistically inseparable from mean income and was therefore deleted. A full description of the 1976 survey may be found in *The 1976 Fulton County Survey: A User's Guide and Codebook* (Atlanta: Center for Urban Research and Service, Georgia State University, 1977).

15. Initial analyses determined that percentage of units with minor deterioration, percentage of units with major deterioration, and percentage of dilapidated units were not separable statistically. These measures were combined to derive percentage deteriorated units for each NPU. A profile of each NPU was prepared by the city of Atlanta, Bureau of Planning in 1976. The housing data are derived from the city of Atlanta PLAN File and reported in the *NPU Profiles*.

16. In all the analyses reported herein, cases with missing data or problem responses, such as "don't knows," were deleted. This results in variations in the numbers of cases included in analyses reported in different tables.

17. See Edward R. Tufte, *Data Analysis for Politics and Policy* (Englewood Cliffs, Prentice-Hall, 1974), pp. 108-131.

18. For a comprehensive discussion of discriminant analysis, see R. Gnanadesikan, *Methods for Statistical Analysis of Multivariate Observations* (New York: Wiley, 1977), pp. 82-120.

15 American Policy for Housing and Community Development: A Comparative Examination

Susan S. Fainstein

The United States has throughout the postwar period witnessed a general improvement in the aggregate quality of its housing stock. A similar trend has prevailed in the advanced industrial countries of northern Europe as well. In both America and northern Europe the public sector has constituted an important component of housing activity and urban development and is in varying degrees responsible for the price, quality, and distribution of shelter. This chapter examines the principal aims of government in housing and community development, compares American interventionist strategies with those of some comparably wealthy northern European nations, and discusses some political factors that have caused the United States to demonstrate a smaller and less consistent public effort toward providing a decent home for low-income citizens than the European countries under consideration.[1]

Patterns of Public Intervention

Major involvement by the American national government in housing and community development began, as did most of the large federal social programs, during the 1930s. At that time, leaders of the public housing movement like Edith Elmer Wood and Catherine Bauer were strongly influenced by European programs for housing development, which preceded American efforts by several decades.[2] Public-housing advocates pressed for construction and government ownership of dwellings for working-class renters corresponding to the model of British council housing. More influential, however, in shaping the ultimate character of American communities were the contemporaneous efforts to stabilize mortgage markets and maintain homeownership for the middle class. The legacy of the New Deal's urban programs is a relatively minor public-housing program by European standards, but a long history of major federal efforts to stimulate and make more secure the private market in property development.

The author would like to thank Roger Montgomery, Jerome Rose, and George Sternlieb for their helpful comments on an earlier draft of this chapter.

During the Depression and the immediate postwar period, governments both here and in Europe concentrated on strategies for increasing housing supply. In recent years, however, new realities have produced a more complex series of responses. Common contemporary trends include decline in the birthrate, causing population stabilization; increasing rates of new household formation among small family units or single individuals, resulting in a demand for smaller units; lack of suitable housing for specific population groups, especially nonwhite minorities in the United States and guest workers in Europe; active public resistance to large-scale slum-clearance programs; continued strong consumer demand for homeownership; and a decline in the private rental market. The United States resembles Great Britain, Sweden, Germany, and the Netherlands in using a mix of strategies directed toward housing and neighborhood improvement, reflecting the variety of different problems to which they are addressed. These include rent subsidies, rehabilitation grants and loans, demolition and clearance, below-market-interest-rate (BMIR) subsidized mortgages, tax incentives to homeownership, and construction and management of housing by public authorities.

The most important common shift in programs of publicly assisted housing has been from supply-side to demand-side subsidies. Reflecting a diminished concern over absolute suppply, these programs seek to make existing housing available to low-income persons. Howenstine estimates that consumer subsidies (housing allowances, rent rebates, and differential rents) had by 1970 risen to roughly 21 percent of the total housing subsidies of eleven West European governments.[3] The lessened preoccupation in Europe with new construction was in response to the same considerations that prompted the development of Section 8 of the Housing and Community Development Act of 1974 in the United States: tailoring subsidy to household need, dispersing low-income families, equalizing assistance for families with the same income so that rent is tied to family need rather than the dwelling unit.

Widespread criticism of major demolition and construction programs has prompted American and European governments to focus on improving the quality of the existing housing stock, with clearance usually restricted to small areas. Neighborhood conservation and housing rehabilitation programs have replaced Urban Renewal as the main thrust in improving the quality of deteriorated communities.[4] Continued priority to owner-occupancy has led all the major capitalist democracies to encourage homeownership and absorb substantial losses of government revenue through tax subsidies. While the United States still exceeds other countries in level of homeownership (see table 15-1), Great Britain is not too far behind, and other countries also have substantial homeowner populations.

Similarities in the content of programs offered by northern European

Table 15-1
Household Units by Tenure, Selected Countries

Country	Tenure of Households (Percentage) Owners	Renters
Germany, Fed. Rep. (1975)	37.0	63.0
Netherlands (1975)	38.0	62.0
Sweden (1975)	40.0	60.0
United Kingdom (1977)	53.6	46.4
United States (1977)	64.8	35.2

Sources: Press and Information Office of the Federal Government of Germany, "Housing and Town Planning" (Bonn); Netherlands Ministry of Foreign Affairs, *The Kingdom of the Netherlands, 1973/75: Welfare Policy* (The Hague, 1975); Swedish Institute, "Housing and Housing Policy in Sweden," *Fact Sheets on Sweden* (Stockholm, 1976); United Kingdom, Central Statistical Office, *Annual Abstract of Statistics, 1978* (London: HMSO, 1979); U.S. Bureau of the Census, *Statistical Abstract of the United States, 1978* (Washington: USGPO, 1979).

and American governments, however, obscure important variations. These can be summed up under three categories: extent of public subsidy, institutional structure of the housing sector, and consistency of policy. These differences are of particular importance to low-income and central-city populations.

Extent of Public Subsidy

Housing assistance in Europe is more universal than in the United States in that extensive assistance goes to renters as well as owners. Far larger numbers of people are eligible for aid, receipt of aid is not limited by the size of the appropriation, and landlords cannot refuse assisted tenants. In the United States, many families meet the income qualifications for Section 8 yet receive no aid, either because of budgetary restrictions or the unwillingness of landlords to accept Section 8 tenants. Furthermore, government-assisted rehabilitation loans are widely available in European countries regardless of the income of the applicant. These differences in the availability of subsidy are reflected in the size of the governmental budget devoted to housing and community-development assistance. Table 15-2 shows that the total public expenditure of the United States on housing and urban development is only 0.5 percent of gross national product (GNP) as compared with 4.1 percent

Table 15-2
Direct Public Expenditures on Housing and Community Development as Percentage of Gross National Product, Selected Countries

Country	*GNP*[a]	*Outlay*[b]	*Percentage of GNP*
United Kingdom (central government, local authorities, public corporations), 1976	£ 128.2 billion	£ 5.2 billion	4.1
Netherlands (central government), 1975	hfl 207.7 billion	hfl 5.2 billion	2.5
Sweden (central government), 1976	kr 323.3 billion	kr 7.4 billion	2.3
Germany, Fed. Rep. (all governments), 1975	DM 1030.3 billion	DM 19.2 billion	1.9
United States (all governments) 1976	$1706.5 billion	$8.3 billion	0.5

Sources: United Kingdom, Central Statistical Office, *Annual Abstract of Statistics, 1978* (London: HMSO, 1979); Netherlands Central Bureau of Statistics, *Statistical Yearbook of the Netherlands*, 1977 (The Hague: Staatsuitgeverij, 1978); Swedish Public Utility Housing Enterprises, *1977 Swedish Housing* (Stockholm: SABO, 1977); Federal Republic of Germany, *Statistisches Jahrbuch, 1978* (Wiesbaden: Statistisches Bundesamt, 1978); U.S. Bureau of the Census, *Statistical Abstract of the United States, 1978* (Washington: USGPO, 1979).

[a]Based on fiscal year where appropriate.

[b]Outlay figures are aggregates produced by the various national statistical services. They may not include expenditures of various off-budget loan funds and housing allowances dispersed by the public welfare system.

for the United Kingdom. Germany, which of the countries listed is closest to the United States in order of magnitude of outlay, still spends 3 times as much as a proportion of GNP. While different financing methods and accounting systems make the amounts attributed to governmental contributions for housing far less than perfectly comparable, the ranking of countries by proportion of GNP in table 15-2 seems intuitively valid.

Table 15-3 shows the proportion of new housing built by public, quasi-public, and private investors in various European countries as compared with the United States. Of the group, the United States has by far the largest private housing sector. In 1976 less than 1 percent of all units constructed were built by a public authority. In contrast, more than half the new housing in Great Britain was constructed under public auspices. In all the countries shown, government subsidy partially financed private-sector construction; thus differences in the amount of public property development are only partly explained by the larger subsidy of the European governments. They are also attributable to the American aversion to public ownership, so that a considerable proportion of direct governmental expenditure subsidizes private development in the United States. For example, whereas Section 8 subsidies here comprise part of the rent paid to private landlords, in

Table 15-3
Dwellings Completed in the United States and Selected European Countries by Type of Investor
(in percentages)

Country and Investor	*1970*	*1974*	*1976*
German Federal Republic			
Public authorities	2.3	3.5[b]	3.1
Housing associations and co-ops	18.4	15.2[b]	13.1
Private[a]	79.3	81.6[b]	83.8
Netherlands			
State, municipalities	16.3	4.2	3.1
Housing associations	31.6	37.4	33.9
Private[a]	52.1	58.4	63.0
Sweden			
State, local authorities	4.3	2.0	1.7
Semipublic bodies (public utilities)	38.3	30.3	19.8
Co-ops	15.6	8.8	6.9
Private[a]	41.8	58.5	71.6
United Kingdom			
Public sector	3.3	5.1	5.8
Local authorities, new town development corps.	48.6	42.2	45.8
Private[a]	48.1	52.7	48.4
United States			
Public authorities	2.3	0.9	0.7
Private[a]	97.7	99.1	99.3

Source: United Nations, Economic Commission for Europe, *Annual Bulletin of Housing and Building Statistics for Europe, 1977*, Vol. 21 (New York, 1979).
[a]Includes government-aided private construction.
[b]Figures are for 1975.

England rent supplements most often support tenants in publicly owned buildings.

Although the United States spends considerably less than the European countries for direct contributions to housing maintenance and development, it is roughly comparable in terms of indirect expenditures through tax concessions for interest deductions of the homeowner. The Organization for Economic Cooperation and Development (OECD) estimates the following revenue losses in the early 1970s as a proportion of gross domestic product (GDP) owing to homeowner deductions: Germany, 0.3 percent; the Netherlands, 0.9 percent; Sweden, 1.1 percent; the United Kingdom, 0.7 percent; and the United States, 0.6 percent.[5]

Institutional Structure of the Housing Sector

The institutional structure of the housing sector in northern Europe differs from that of the United States in several important aspects.[6] First, many more Europeans live in publicly owned housing, and while upper-class people in Europe as well as here tend to own their own homes, residence in housing projects by middle-class families is not stigmatizing. Because of a combination of rent control and the expansion of nonprofit ownership, the privately owned rental sector is rapidly shrinking. Most households seeking private rentals are poor families unable to qualify, because of residential or other requirements, for public housing. In Great Britain, for example, 70 percent of renter households are in government-owned units. Thus, while the proportion of homeowners among some European populations (see table 15-1) is approaching American levels, the remainder of the population tends to live in multifamily units owned either by governmental authorities or nonprofit associations of various kinds.

The existence of an important, nongovernmental, not-for-profit sector constitutes the second major institutional factor distinguishing the United States and Europe. Building societies, housing associations, and housing cooperatives have long histories in Europe, and governmental subsidies have encouraged their proliferation. Building societies and housing associations resemble American savings and loan institutions in using the savings of depositors for investments chosen by boards of directors. But whereas savings and loans only invest in mortgages, many of these European institutions act directly to develop housing and commercial property and may continue to own and manage the properties once they are constructed. Cooperatives differ from savings institutions in that they will raise money through bonds or equity sold to occupants rather than individual accounts.[7]

A third important factor in the development of some European urban areas (most notably Stockholm and Amsterdam) is public ownership of urban land. The purpose of such ownership is to ensure the availability of sites for future development and, in the case of built-up land, to cause the gains from locational advantage to revert to the public. Public ownership mitigates land speculation and its impact on the cost of real estate by preventing bidding for undeveloped land and by banking land for future public development. However, even when the land is publicly held, if it is available for private leasehold, the price of structures on it becomes extremely high. The large public presence in both land holding and real estate development means that property available to private actors is very scarce and very expensive. It also means, however, that housing costs of most renters are not affected by inflation in real estate.

Fourth, most European countries have sought to control and channel development through direct public construction of new towns. Although the number of new town inhabitants still constitutes only a small minority of total population, new towns have nevertheless reduced developmental pressures on the periphery of major metropolitan areas in England, Sweden, and the Netherlands. The substantial governmental role in their financing has meant that development has been sustained throughout the long period between site preparation and generation of income, the presence of industrial and commercial enterprises can be ensured, and housing is made available within them for low-income families.[8]

Fifth, the role of government in controlling all aspects of land use and development sharply differentiates the northern European countries from the United States. Central policy coordination is enhanced by lack of dependence on locally raised taxes and resulting fiscal mercantilist competition among localities. European national and regional planning involves restrictions on investment in developed regions, incentives to growth in designated development areas, direct governmental investment in housing and industry, and subsidization of labor costs. Many countries require planning permission for any new construction, and such permission accrues to land only when it conforms to national and regional master plans, which set development priorities and seek to contain urban sprawl.

Policy Consistency

While support of homeownership has been an unswerving element of U.S. policy, direct governmental involvement in housing production and community development has been erratic in terms of both level of appropriation and program direction since the origin of large-scale federal assistance in the 1930s. Department of Housing and Urban Development (HUD) expenditures as a percent of GNP have varied between 0.04 and 0.50 percent within a 16-year period.[9] The rapidity of change has meant that localities dependent on federal subsidy have either refrained from long-term planning or found themselves committed to projects that could no longer be funded.

Fluctuations in funding levels correspond to sharp changes in policies. Contrary to clichés concerning the difficulty of terminating government programs, the recent past has seen the rise and fall of Urban Renewal, the large BMIR programs (Section 235 and 236), Model Cities, and new construction of public housing. The introduction of Community Development Block Grants (CDBG) and Section 8 in the 1974 Housing Act promises more program stability, but does not insulate funding levels from annual changes in congressional sentiment toward federal expenditures. Section 8 is particularly vulnerable to fluctuation, both because it lacks popularity in Congress and because its full utilization depends on the initiative of local housing authorities and the willingness of private landlords to accept Section 8 tenants. Moreover, given a fixed total appropriation, rises in local fair-market rents mean a reduction in the number of recipients.

By contrast, European expenditures on housing and community development remain far more stable. This results from the large public-ownership component and the mandatory nature of housing assistance—rent subsidies, like Social Security benefits here, go to all eligible households. Although policy emphases change, the major program components that direct assistance to low- and moderate-income people continue. Localities cannot refuse to build and operate low-income housing, and rent supplements do not depend on individual initiatives and private landlord acquiesence.

Comparative Outcomes

Overall, the majority of Americans are probably as well or better housed than their counterparts abroad. As measured by dwelling units per 1,000 inhabitants (table 15-4), there is rough equivalence. The number of people living in units without running water and toilets is negligible in all the countries under consideration.[10] Other aspects of the quality of housing can only be compared subjectively. Americans have larger rooms and yards but lack the convenient public open spaces of European cities. Owner-occupied houses in the United States usually are detached and surrounded by a private yard; in Europe they are frequently semidetached or row houses. Within European metropolitan areas, the American-style free-standing house is restricted to the wealthy. Only in the United States and Great Britain do a majority of families own their own houses, but homeownership can be more of a burden than a joy for many people. A relatively inexpensive American home may have fewer amenities than an apartment in a British council estate; even if an American worker prefers free maintenance and a low rent bill to the privacy of owning his or her own dwelling unit, that option is not available.

Given the aggregate comparability in quality and quantity of housing between the United States and northern Europe, the important differences derive from shelter costs to households and measures of neighborhood

Table 15-4
Housing Stock, Selected Countries, 1975

Country	*Dwellings per 1,000 Inhabitants*
Germany, Fed. Rep.	383
Netherlands	320
Sweden	427
United Kingdom	364
United States	349

Source: United Nations, Economic Commission for Europe, *Annual Bulletin of Housing and Building Statistics for Europe, 1975*, Vol. 21 (New York, 1978).

quality. Universal systems of rent allowances, combined with subsidized supply, mean that European rents rarely constitute the proportion of income typical of the United States. International comparisons of the amounts that different income groups pay for rent are precluded by lack of uniform data, but there seems to be a consensus among housing officials in the northern European countries that shortages for people in certain statuses (for example, young couples, single people) and inconvenient locations are greater problems than rent levels for low-income people.

No European country has needed to assimilate racial minorities of the size that exist in the United States. Thus international comparisons on this dimension cannot be made fairly. The extent to which the private market exacts costs from these groups, however, can be evaluated through internal comparisons of the price and quality of housing for blacks. Only 40 percent of blacks owned their own homes in 1975 as compared with 67 percent of whites. Thirty-seven percent of blacks lived in housing rated as fair or poor as opposed to 15 percent of whites.[11] An extensive analysis of racial discrimination in housing led John Kain and John Quigley to conclude that "most types of housing are more expensive inside the ghetto, and that a premium is required to shift bundles to the ghetto submarket."[12] The absence of a large publicly owned sector means that governmental policy affects discrimination primarily through regulation. The American government lacks the direct control over supply that would permit it to give the housing needs of racial minorities immediate priority; indeed, as is discussed later, the connection between racial status and housing subsidy is an important explanation of the American reluctance to increase public sponsorship of housing.

Cross-national comparisons of neighborhood quality are even more difficult than those of housing quality. Bernard Frieden and Arthur Solomon estimated that in 1973 over 10 percent of all households and 15 percent of low-income households wanted to move because of neighborhood conditions. "Objectionable street conditions" were named as by far the single most important cause of dissatisfaction.[13] While comparable data are not available elsewhere, the major causes of neighborhood dissatisfaction mentioned by informants abroad are inconvenient access to shopping or public transportation and sterility of surroundings rather than social malaise.

The impact of housing and development policies in the United States overall has been to provide an ample supply of high-quality housing for a majority of the population. The spatial distribution of this housing, however, has not been subjected to national or regional priorities. As a result, all income groups have sacrificed the amenities associated with green-space preservation and compact development. The countervailing benefit for the middle and upper classes has been the private ownership of extensive space in yards and houses and control over enclave political jurisdictions. Lower-class households have benefited far less from federal policies either relative to the American upper classes or to corresponding groups abroad. Housing-market segmentation, produced by home rule, racial discrimination, and minimal federal intervention, has isolated the poor in residential areas remote from employment, lacking adequate tax bases, expensive relative to their income, and characterized by physical and social blight. Limitation of public housing to the poor, and an insufficient supply even for them, has meant that most low-income people must seek rental housing in a private market where there is a little profit to be made in providing them with a decent home. By the time previously sound dwelling units trickle down to the poor, they are often either themselves deteriorated or surrounded by a rapidly decaying neighborhood.

The Political Context

After World War II, the governments of the United States and northern Europe faced similar problems of housing shortages. In addition, they feared that demobilization would result in unemployment and insufficient aggregate demand. Their approaches to increasing the supply of housing while simultaneously priming the economy, however, differed sharply and have largely shaped the directions of today. Whereas northern Europe relied on national planning and development, the U.S. government sought to increase consumer demand in the private market. Within the United States, suburbanization and its multiplier effects on the market for consumer durables formed the basis for postwar economic expansion. In northern Europe, the large governmental sector provided the foundation for economic security and predictability. Both approaches operated within capitalist systems, but in the United States growth was fueled more directly by demand, while in Europe government assumption of many of the costs of reproducing the labor force (the "social wage") meant a lowering of labor costs for employers and consequent price competitiveness.

The 1949 and 1954 Housing Acts settled certain of the main parameters of American national policy toward housing and community development. Primary emphasis remained on private market subsidy, local autonomy, and new development or large-scale redevelopment. Despite a public-housing component, the main thrust of housing and urban-redevelopment efforts emerged primarily as distributive rather than redistributive or regulatory.[14] Their aim has been to serve all regions and types of cities without the establishment of development priorities.

The political forces that shape housing and development policy have created this distributive character and in turn been reinforced by it.[15] The dominant American ideology of liberal individualism was reinforced by the lobbying and propaganda campaigns of such private groups as the National

Association of Real Estate Boards (NAREB), the National Associations of Home Builders (NAHB), and the United States Savings and Loan League, which worked consistently to restrict the public-housing program: "It was, they declared, a threat by government to the well being and integrity of the private industry they represented."[16] This argument is reflected in the influential 1968 Kaiser Committee report. While the committee asserted that low-income groups required a subsidy to obtain decent housing, they also declared that "there must be a larger reliance on private enterprise to build the houses. . . . Building decent, subsidized homes for the poor is not distinctly different from building housing for the vast majority who can afford to pay for its costs. Private enterprise can be relied upon to do both well."[17]

Racial antagonism has further inhibited governmental activity in housing. During the 1950s, the political weakness of minority groups made them an ineffective constituency in calling for public housing. The irony of the more recent period, in terms of housing policy, is that the success of blacks in obtaining the civil rights statutes of the sixties exacerbated opposition to the provision of publicly supported housing. Now that fair-housing requirements apply to all government-subsidized structures, white communities adamantly block construction within their boundaries while the federal government prohibits it within homogeneously black areas. The demise of major activity under Sections 235 and 236 can largely be attributed to fears that developers, supported by court decisions against exclusionary zoning, would use funding under these programs to build low-income projects within suburban jurisdictions.

Lack of a supportive ideology and racial animosity thus constitute two important reasons for the weakness of the public-housing constituency. In addition, the United States has lacked two of the most influential actors on the European housing scene—social democratic political parties and housing cooperatives. In Europe these have been the most active proponents of public ownership and subsidy to nonprofit groups. Moreover, European parties have acted as unifying elements, causing the lower levels of government to conform to national priorities. In contrast, the linkage between American municipal officials and national party organizations is extremely attenuated. Big city mayors have more in common with other mayors than they do with their national party's leadership. Nor, of course, does the majority party leadership formulate specific housing proposals for city governments to follow. The mayors are organized into their own pressure group, the United States Conference of Mayors (USCM), which lobbies for federal assistance to cities but has no ideological commitment to public ownership or income redistribution. During the 1960s, the USCM favored commercial over residential renewal and clearance projects over rehabilitation, and it resisted federal controls and planning requirements. In other words, its objectives were determined by its situation as an interest group of mayors rather than, as would be the case for the cadres of a working-class political party, by ideological support for social reform.

American lower-class groups have recently mobilized around housing as an issue.[18] They have opposed demolition for Urban Renewal and public facilities, mounted rent strikes, taken over buildings as squatters, and in conjunction with middle-class apartment dwellers demanded rent control. Rarely, however, have their interests been articulated in terms of demands for public housing.[19] Even sweat equity represents a kind of collective privatism. Except for rent-control groups the portion of the working class involved in housing movements has tended to be nonwhite and unintegrated into the trade-union structure. The mass of the electorate has had little reason to support either public housing or rent subsidies, which provide it with no benefits. Moreover, the linkage between publicly financed construction and racial integration has been a key factor in diverting popular support from government-sponsored production except for the elderly.

The general character of American housing policy is thus grounded in political interests and institutions. Although the United States shares with the northern European countries a capitalist economy, it differs markedly in the way economic interests are represented politically and articulated ideologically. The lack of a coherent left pressing for a larger social wage and the institutional and ideological obstacles to central direction of urban development results in the fragmented and privatistic nature of its policy for housing and community development. The economic crisis of the 1930s and the threat to political stability that it posed caused American policymakers to look seriously at the European example of state intervention. In the present epoch, programs of the magnitude undertaken by the northern European governments, despite their relative success in addressing problems of housing and community development, are not imitated because there is no political force pressing for them. American urban problems persist in their acute form not for lack of examples in the world of successful strategies, but because of political immobilism.

Notes

1. Comparisons are restricted to the German Federal Republic, the Netherlands, Sweden, and the United Kingdom. These are the countries meant throughout the chapter, even when there are generic references, for the sake of brevity, to northern Europe or European. See Susan S. Fainstein and Norman I. Fainstein, "National Policy and Urban Development," *Social Problems* 26 (December 1978):125-146, for a more general comparative analysis of the American welfare state and its impact on metropolitan areas.

2. See Eugenie Ladner Birch, "Woman-Made America: The Case of Early Public Housing Policy," *Journal of the American Institute of Planners* 44 (April 1978):139-141. State subsidies to building societies and municipalities for construction of low-income housing began in the Netherlands with passage of the Housing Act of 1901, which also required municipalities to establish and enforce housing standards. In England, government subsidies for public (council) housing first became available in 1919. Sweden established both rent-control and housing-subsidy programs by 1917; in Germany, a special property tax was imposed in 1924 to subsidize new housing construction. See Amsterdam, Town Planning Section, Public Works Department, *Amsterdam Planning and Development* (Amsterdam, the Netherlands, 1975), p. 36; Daniel Mandelker, *Housing Subsidies in the United States and England* (Indianapolis: Bobbs-Merrill, 1973), p. 120; Paul F. Wendt, *Housing Policy—The Search for Solutions: A Comparison of the United Kingdom, Sweden, West Germany and the United States since World War II* (Berkeley: Univ. of California Press, 1962).

3. E. Jay Howenstine, "The Changing Roles of Housing Production Subsidies and Consumer Housing Subsidies in European National Housing Policy," *Land Economics* 51 (February 1975):86-94.

4. See J. Robert Dumouchel, *European Housing Rehabilitation Experience* (Washington: National Association of Housing and Redevelopment Officials, 1978).

5. OECD, "Public Expenditure Trends," *Studies in Resource Allocation* (June 1978):1978.

6. The most important references upon which this chapter is based are Wendt, *Housing Policy*; Mandelker, *Housing Subsidies*; Arnold J. Heidenheimer, Hugh Heclo, and Carolyn T. Adams, *Comparative Public Policy: The Politics of Social Choice in Europe and America* (New York: St. Martin's, 1975), chaps. 3,4; James L. Sundquist, *Dispersing Population: What America Can Learn from Europe* (Washington: Brookings Institution, 1975); Morris L. Sweet and S. George Walters, *Mandatory Housing Finance Programs: A Comparative International Analysis* (New York: Praeger, 1976); Coralie Bryant and Louise G. White, "Housing Policies and Comparative Urban Politics: Britain and the United States," in John Walton and Louis H. Masotti (eds.), *The City in Comparative Perspective* (New York: Wiley, 1976); Marion Clawson and Peter Hall, *Planning and Urban Growth: An Anglo-American Comparison* (Baltimore: Johns Hopkins Univ. Press, 1973); J.S. Fuerst (ed.), *Public Housing in Europe and America* (New York: Wiley, 1974); George W. Carey, "Land Tenure, Speculation, and the State of the Aging Metropolis," *The Geographical Review* 66 (July 1976):253-265. Further information derives from interviews of scholars and government officials done by the author in London and Amsterdam during 1977.

7. In 1971, 200,000 families lived in cooperatives in the United States. A large proportion of these were upper-income buildings in New York City and Co-op City in the Bronx. See U.S. Department of Housing and Urban Development (HUD), Office of International Affairs, "Cooperative Housing in the U.S.A.," *HUD International Brief* (February 13, 1972):9.

8. See HUD, Office of International Affairs, *Financing New Communities: Government and Private Experience in Europe and the United States* (Washington, 1973).

9. Fainstein and Fainstein, "National Policy and Urban Development," p. 135, presents a time series of outlays.

10. UN Department of Economic and Social Affairs, *World Housing Survey, 1974*, Document ST/ESA/30 (New York, 1976), Table 49. The United Nations sets three or more persons per room as its standard for crowding; all the advanced capitalist countries have more than 95 percent of their population living in conditions less crowded than this standard.

11. U.S. Bureau of the Census, *Annual Housing Survey: 1975*, Part E: *Urban and Rural Housing Characteristics*, Table A-1; Part B: *Indicators of Housing and Neighborhood Quality*, Tables A-2, A-6 (Washington, 1977).

12. John Kain and John Quigley, *Housing Markets and Racial Discrimination* (New York: National Bureau of Economic Research, 1975), p. 68.

13. Bernard Frieden and Arthur P. Solomon, *The Nation's Housing: 1975 to 1985* (Cambridge, Mass.: M.I.T.-Harvard Joint Center for Urban Studies, 1977), pp. 91-98.

14. See Theodore Lowi, "Four Systems of Policy, Politics and Choice," *Public Administration Review* (July-August 1972), for an explication of these terms; and Bryant and White, "Housing Policies and Comparative Urban Politics," for their application to housing.

15. See Suzanne Farkas, *Urban Lobbying* (New York: New York Univ. Press, 1971); Howard Wolman, *Politics of Federal Housing* (New York: Dodd, Mead, 1971); Mark Gelfand, *A Nation of Cities* (New York: Oxford Univ. Press, 1975); Frederic N. Cleveland (ed.), *Congress and Urban Problems* (Washington: Brookings Institution, 1969).

16. Leonard Freedman, *Public Housing: The Politics of Poverty* (New York: Holt, Rinehart and Winston, 1969), p. 61.

17. President's Committee on Urban Housing (Kaiser Committee), *A Decent Home* (Washington, 1969), p. 47.

18. See Manuel Castells, *The Urban Question* (Cambridge, Mass.: M.I.T. Press, 1977); Michael Lipsky, *Protest in City Politics* (Skokie: Rand McNally, 1970); Monica Lett, *Rent Control: Concepts, Realities and Mechanisms* (New Brunswick, N.J.: Center for Urban Policy Research, Rutgers University, 1976); Norman I. Fainstein and Susan S. Fainstein,

Urban Political Movements (Englewood Cliffs, N.J.: Prentice-Hall, 1974).

19. An exception was New York's West Side Urban Renewal Area; See James Clarence Davies III, *Neighborhood Groups and Urban Renewal* (New York: Columbia Univ. Press, 1966).

Indexes

Index of Names

Index of Subjects

About the Contributors

William C. Baer is director of the School of Urban and Regional Planning and acting dean of the Center for Public Affairs at the University of Southern California. Prior to receiving a master's degree in planning from the University of California, Berkeley, and the Ph.D. in political science from UCLA, he worked in local government on urban renewal and planning projects. His major areas in teaching and research include housing policy and neighborhood planning.

Karen Stromme Christensen is finishing her doctoral dissertation on intergovernmental constraints to planning in the Department of City and Regional Planning at the University of California, Berkeley. She was special assistant to the Department of Housing and Urban Development's regional administrator in San Francisco, where she concentrated on interagency and intergovernmental relations. She also has done program evaluation research both in and out of government.

David E. Dowall is an assistant professor in the Department of City and Regional Planning at the University of California, Berkeley. His teaching and research interests are in land-use planning and land economics. Currently he is completing a study of the effects of land-use and environmental controls on housing and land markets in the San Francisco Bay Area.

Susan S. Fainstein is professor of urban planning and policy development at Livingston College, Rutgers University. She is also a member of the senior research staff of the Community Development Strategies Evaluation Project, conducted under the sponsorship of the U.S. Department of Housing and Urban Development by the School of Public and Urban Policy of the University of Pennsylvania.

James W. Hughes is professor of urban planning and policy development at Livingston College, Rutgers University, and a research associate of the Center for Urban Policy Research.

John D. Hutcheson, Jr., is associate professor and director of the Center for Urban Research and Service in the college of Urban Life at Georgia State University. He is author of *Organized Citizen Participation in Urban Areas* (1970), *Racial Attitudes in Atlanta* (1973), and *Citizen Groups in Local Politics: A Bibliographic Review* (1976), and he has published articles in the *American Journal of Political Science*, the *Urban Affairs Quarterly*, the *Atlanta Economic Review*, and *Teaching Political Science*.

Sharon Perlman Krefetz is an associate professor of government at Clark University. She is the author of *Welfare Policy-Making and City Politics* and several articles on citizen participation, metropolitan government merger attempts, and teaching political science. Her fields of interest are urban and suburban politics and policies, and her current research is on housing and zoning politics.

Nonno A. Noto is an economist in the Congressional Research Service of the Library of Congress, specializing in topics of governmental finance and regional economic development. She received the Ph.D. in economics from Stanford University. From 1974 until 1979 she was a research economist at the Federal Reserve Bank of Philadelphia, conducting studies on municipal finance, regional employment, and intrametropolitan industry location for the Philadelphia area.

Robert Ohsfeldt is a research associate at the Southwest Center for Urban Research. He received the M.A. in economics in 1979 from the University of Houston. Mr. Ohsfeldt's areas of specialty are urban economics and microeconomic theory. His previous research includes analysis of racial discrimination in housing, redlining in the Houston housing market, and the theory of locational choice.

John M. Quigley is professor of public policy at the University of California, Berkeley, and is a member of the Economics Department at Yale University.

Elizabeth A. Roistacher is associate professor of economics at Queens College. She began the research contained here during her year as a Brookings Fellow with the Department of Housing and Urban Development. Dr. Roistacher has written on housing demand, discrimination, and local housing policy.

Alden F. Shiers received the B.S. in economics from the University of Maine in 1967 and the Ph.D. in economics from the University of California, Santa Barbara, in 1977. His research has been in the area of housing economics. He is currently assistant professor of economics at California Polytechnic State University.

Barton A. Smith is an associate professor of economics at the University of Houston and director of the Division of Socio-Economic Analysis at the Southwest Center for Urban Research. Dr. Barton received the Ph.D. in economics in 1973 from the University of Chicago. His areas of specialty are urban economics and public finance, with particular concentration in housing economics, urban growth policy, and environmental economics.

George Sternlieb is director of the Center for Urban Policy Research at Rutgers University. He received the M.B.A. and D.B.A. degrees from the Harvard Business School.

Mahlon R. Straszheim is currently professor of economics and director of the Project in the Economics of Discrimination at the University of Maryland. Dr. Straszheim received the Ph.D. from Harvard University in 1965 and taught in the Department of Economics at Harvard University from 1965 to 1971 and at the University of Maryland from 1971 to the present. Some of Dr. Straszheim's works include *The International Airline Industry* (1969) and *An Econometric Analysis of the Urban Housing Market* (1971). He is also the editor of *Current Issues in Urban Economics* (1979).

Michael B. Teitz is professor of city and regional planning at the University of California, Berkeley, where he teaches courses in housing, program planning and evaluation, and urban economics. Over the past 15 years, he has been engaged in program and policy evaluation research in housing and social services for the U.S. Department of Housing and Urban Development and other federal, state, and local government agencies.

Robert S. Weiss is a professor of sociology at the University of Massachusetts, Boston, and a lecturer in sociology in the Department of Psychiatry, Harvard Medical School. As director of the Unit for the Study of Social Ties in Harvard Medical School's Laboratory of Community Psychiatry, he has, since 1963, conducted studies of issues associated with marital disruption. Among his publications are *Loneliness: The Experience of Emotional and Social Isolation* (1973), *Marital Separation* (1975), and the forthcoming *Going It Alone: The Family Life and Social Situation of Single Parents.*

Janet Spratlin Young is an economist with the Federal Reserve Bank of New York. She writes on topics pertaining to the regional economies of New York and New Jersey and specializes in the New York financial industry.

About the Editors

Robert Montgomery is professor of urban design in the Department of Architecture and the Department of City and Regional Planning at the University of California, Berkeley. He attended Harvard Graduate School of Design, practiced architecture and planning, and taught at Harvard and at Washington University in St. Louis. He has contributed to many books and journals on housing, community development, and planning, has coedited (with Daniel Mandelker) *Housing in America*, now in a second edition, and has coauthored (with Sally Woodbridge) several books and articles on West Coast architecture and development history.

Dale Rogers Marshall is a professor of political science at the University of California, Davis. She is the author of *The Politics of Participation in Poverty*, editor of *Urban Policy Making*, and coauthor of *A Guide to Participation: Field Work, Role Playing Cases and Other Forms*. She has also written a number of articles on urban politics and policy. She is currently coprincipal investigator on a National Science Foundation-funded study of city government responsiveness to minorities from 1960 to 1979. She has served as a field associate for the Brookings Institution study of the Community Development Block Grant since its inception, and she has been a member of the executive council of the American Political Science Association and the editorial board of the *American Political Science Review*.

